Conditions of work digest

Volume 10 Number 1 1991

Child labour: Law and practice

International Labour Office Geneva

ISBN 92-2-107751-9
ISSN 0257-3512

Annual subscription (1991) for two issues: 80 Swiss francs
Price for individual issues: 45 Swiss francs
Editor: Michele B. Jankanish

The International Programme for the Improvement of Working Conditions and Environment (PIACT) was launched by the International Labour Organisation in 1976 at the request of the International Labour Conference and after extensive consultations with member States.
PIACT is designed to promote or support action by member States to set and attain definite objectives aiming at "making work more human". The Programme is thus concerned with improving the quality of working life in all its aspects: for example, the prevention of occupational accidents and diseases, a wider application of the principles of ergonomics, the arrangement of working time, the improvement of the content and organisation of work and of conditions of work in general, a greater concern for the human element in the transfer of technology. To achieve these aims, PIACT makes use of and co-ordinates the traditional means of ILO action, including:

- the preparation and revision of international labour standards;
- operational activities, including the dispatch of multidisciplinary teams to assist member States on request;
- tripartite meetings between representatives of governments, employers and workers, including industrial committees to study the problems facing major industries, regional meetings and meetings of experts;
- action-oriented studies and research; and
- clearing-house activities, especially through the International Occupational Safety and Health Information Centre (CIS) and the Clearing-house for the Dissemination of Information on Conditions of Work.

Cover photograph: J. Maillard, ILO

ILO publications can be obtained through major booksellers or ILO local offices in many countries, or direct from ILO Publications, International Labour Office, CH-1211 Geneva 22, Switzerland. A catalogue or list of new publications will be sent free of charge from the above address.

Printed in Switzerland PUB

Child labour: Law and practice

Table of contents

Pages

About this publication

The Conditions of Work Digest is published twice a year by the International Labour Office. Prepared by the Conditions of Work and Welfare Facilities Branch, Working Conditions and Environment Department, it is a reference source for all who are interested in working conditions and the quality of working life. Each issue is devoted to a subject of topical interest. The Digest includes information drawn from laws, regulations, collective agreements and other important texts. Additional features are included as appropriate, such as annotated bibliographies, relevant international standards, special sources of information and specialised glossaries.

Topics on conditions of work and quality of working life, such as the following, are covered:

- working time issues, including hours of work, shift work, part-time work and flexible hours;
- work organisation and job content;
- the impact of new technology on quality of working life;
- working conditions of specific groups, such as women workers, older workers, working children, homeworkers and clandestine workers;
- work-related welfare facilities and services, such as provision of feeding facilities, supply schemes, transportation to and from work, child care, housing, health, education and recreational facilities;
- shop-floor participation in the improvement of working conditions.

Clearing-house on Conditions of Work

The network of institutions of the Clearing-house on Conditions of Work was set up in 1979. Over 350 institutions in all regions of the world - including government agencies, employers' organisations, trade unions, research institutions and university departments - participate in this network by forwarding information about their research projects and activities and other information for use in the Digest and other publications of the Clearing-house.

Through the Clearing-house, the ILO aims to provide readily accessible, up-to-date, and practically oriented information to member States and to facilitate the exchange of information among them.

The Clearing-house operates a data base which is updated continually. Information on research projects and activities of institutions is entered into the data base and used to produce published compilations of current research.

Information on the institutions themselves is published in Conditions of Work and Quality of Working Life: A Directory of Institutions [Geneva, 2nd (revised) edition, 1986, ISBN 92-2-105328-8]. Up-to-date information on staff, funding, activities, training programmes, current research projects, meetings and publications is provided.

Inquiries may be addressed to the Clearing-house on Conditions of Work, Conditions of Work and Welfare Facilities Branch, International Labour Office, CH-1211 Geneva 22, Switzerland.

Other ILO serial publications of interest to users of the Digest include:

- Safety and health at work: ILO/CIS bulletin. References and abstracts covering books, articles, laws and regulations on all aspects of occupational safety and health (produced by the International Occupational Safety and Health Information Centre of the ILO);

- International Labour Review. Articles on economic and social topics affecting labour, research notes and book reviews;

- Social and Labour Bulletin. Notes on current significant events in the social and labour field, brief descriptions of major labour legislation, collective agreements, experiments in improving the work environment and so forth.

- Labour Law Documents (from 1919-1989 called Legislative Series). Reprints and translations of selected labour and social security legislation recently adopted in countries throughout the world.

ILO publications can be ordered from ILO Publications, International Labour Office, CH-1211 Geneva 22, Switzerland.

This publication may be cited as follows:

ILO: Conditions of Work Digest (Geneva), Volume 10, Number 1, 1991, on Child labour: Law and practice.

Acknowledgements

This issue of the Conditions of Work Digest was prepared by Assefa Bequele, Ronald Berghuys, H.T. Dao, Jean-Maurice Derrien, Claude Dumont, Mark Johnson, Shengjie Li, Victoria Sinclair, Ingrid Sipi, Gabriele Trah and Linda Wirth. Special appreciation to Kristine Falciola for the processing of the manuscript and administrative assistance.

Introduction

Introduction

Legislation prohibiting the employment of children below a certain age and defining the conditions under which they may be legally allowed to work has been the major instrument of intervention by governments in their campaigns against child labour.

Although the fight against child labour will not be won solely through legislation, it certainly cannot be won without it. Child labour laws are essential to deal with the worst forms of child work where they exist and to provide minimum levels of protection where child labour is unavoidable. Such laws can play a catalytic and supportive role in efforts to establish a more humane order and in prodding society to give the child the best that it has to offer. That is why national governments and, indeed, the ILO attach so much importance to the setting and implementation of international and national standards on the work and employment of children. However, several questions arise in this connection.

What is the place of legislation in national policy? How can it be applied effectively to provide and extend protection to working children and to enable developing and especially poor countries to move towards the objective of the elimination of child labour?

What is the state of legislation in the various parts of the world, where are the gaps, and in what way does existing legislation fall short of international conventions on the subject?

To what extent is national legislation on child labour enforced, and what are the reasons for the wide gap between national law and practice?

What mechanisms or procedures are available to the International Labour Office to promote and ensure some kind of coherence between internationally accepted principles and national laws? Far more importantly, how does the ILO verify the extent to which member States fulfill and comply with their obligations under international labour law, and what practical effect does its action have at the national level?

These questions are important for the assessment of progress, the formulation of effective national policies, including of course legislation, and for the promotion of a common set of international standards and shared values against the exploitation of children through and at work. This issue of the Conditions of Work Digest attempts to answer, albeit partially, these questions by providing a factual and analytical review of law and practice on child labour throughout the world. It is divided into the following parts:

- Part I reviews and assesses the various conflicting perceptions and views on strategies for dealing with child labour, especially in poor countries where the problem is most serious and the scope for action is most limited.

- Part II provides a brief overview of national legislation based on information contained in the fact sheets that are found in Part V.

- Part III contains a paper which provides a fascinating glimpse of how the ILO's system of standards can put pressure on countries to improve the legal protection that they provide for children. The legal provisions on minimum age for admission to employment in almost all countries at all stages of development have one thing in common: they probably owe something to the standards set by the ILO in its international labour Conventions and Recommendations concerning the protection of children. This part therefore provides a factual account of the manner in which the ILO's supervisory machinery operates by giving specific examples of progress that has been made as well as a number of current cases of extreme abuse and exploitation in specific countries.

- Part IV looks at the role of labour inspection in the application of national legislation, and suggests approaches for a more effective enforcement of national laws to protect children from and at work.

- Part V contains fact sheets summarising the legal provisions in 143 countries on the basic minimum age for admission to employment; the minimum age for admission to light and hazardous work or employment; the definition of light and hazardous work; and the scope of national legislation.

- Part VI provides summaries and selected provisions of the major international labour standards and other instruments on children in general, and child labour in particular.

We hope that this special issue -- Child labour: Law and practice -- will be useful for national policy-makers as well as those, especially in non-governmental organisations, who are interested in exerting pressure on national governments to provide a better deal for the millions of child workers who are subjected to various forms of exploitation and abuse throughout the world.

Part I

Combating child labour: Contrasting views and strategies for very poor countries

Part I

Combating child labour: Contrasting views and strategies for very poor countries

by

Assefa Bequele[1]

Although there is general agreement that child labour has to be abolished, there is less unanimity on how this is to be achieved. Views differ as to whether the best way to eliminate child labour is outright and immediate abolition, or a gradual and progressive raising of the minimum age for admission to work or employment combined with protective measures for those children who continue to work. Many believe that little can be done in practice because children need to work for their own survival and that of their parents, and that the very poor countries will be incapable of taking action to eliminate the problem until they achieve an adequate level of development.

The ILO has a clear position on this question, as set out in a resolution adopted by the International Labour Conference in 1979, which called for social and legislative action to progressively eliminate child labour and, during the transitional period until the elimination of child labour, to regulate it.

In the following text, which is a lightly edited version of a speech delivered in Amsterdam in 1990[2], Assefa Bequele assesses the practical implications of the contrasting views on how to combat child labour and outlines a strategy for action in very poor countries.

I. Introduction

Child labour has been virtually abolished in the industrialised countries. Universal primary education has been fully achieved and secondary-level education nearly so in these countries. Although there is concern about the reappearance of traditional and new forms of child labour in these countries, the magnitude of the problem is certainly much less and the possibilities for effective action much greater than in other regions of the world.

---

[1] Conditions of Work and Welfare Facilities Branch, International Labour Office.

[2] Keynote address given at the International Child Labour Seminar organised by the International Seminar for the Prevention of Child Abuse and Neglect, 28-31 August 1990, Amsterdam.

There are also additional reasons why special attention should be devoted to the problem of child labour in very poor countries. They contain the largest concentration of child workers in the world. Asia and Africa alone account for well over 90 per cent of the total child labour population in the world. The problem is especially serious in Africa, where well over 50 per cent of the children in several countries are not enrolled in school and could be working. Within these developing regions, it is in the very poor countries that child labour is most widespread and the scope for action is most constrained.

There is also one other important reason why I am personally interested in addressing this subject, and it is this: the pessimism or scepticism among various groups, especially those on the right and the left of the ideological spectrum, who argue that attempts to deal with the child labour problem in developing countries are futile and doomed to failure. I say it is not so, and I will try to show why.

II. The critiques

The critiques against an active strategy of combating child labour could be divided into several schools. For my purpose here I will divide them into three schools: the Marxist radical school; those who advocate or insist on immediate abolition; and those who prefer an evolutionary approach to the problem. In so doing, I will inevitably provide a deliberately simplified and stylised version of their positions in order to sharpen the issues. I should also point out that the arguments or positions which I attribute to the different schools are not articulated to my knowledge in any particular article or publication, although they appear in a rather scattered way here and there in the literature on the subject. For this reason, I am relying more on the interactions I have been privileged to share as a result of my work in this area.

The Marxist radical critique

I shall first begin with what could be referred to as the radical critique. Although it now seems a long time ago, it was quite fashionable only a couple of years ago for Marxist-oriented intellectuals to belittle or dismiss all attempts to deal with child labour in non-socialist or non-revolutionary societies. Although it is out of fashion now, I shall still address the position held by this school because of its undoubtedly respectable intellectual tradition and also because of its still important influence in much of the Third World today.

The view of the radical school can be summarised simply as follows. Child labour is a manifestation and a result of the exploitation and inequality in incomes and wealth that are characteristic of capitalist systems, in which the exploitation of labour, including child labour, is essential for the survival and profitability of profit-maximising enterprises. According to this view, as long as these characteristics persist, legislative and other efforts by governments are unlikely to succeed.

Shorn of its ideological rhetoric, there is considerable truth in the initial premise of this critique: child workers are exploited and child labour is a corollary of inequality in incomes and wealth. Various studies sponsored by the ILO, such as Abdalla's study of child labour in Cairo's leather tanning industry, Maria Cristina Salazar's study of Bogota's quarries and brickyards, and Oosterhout's study of children in deep-sea fishing in the Philippines, to mention only a few, substantiate the very low wages which child labourers frequently receive[3]. Moreover, the enterprises employing children often operate without official permit, and are characterised by low levels of technology, low levels of capital investment and the intensive use of labour. They also pay very low wages. But that is not all.

Exploitation takes other forms as well. Children are subjected to excessively long hours and, far more importantly, to subtle and often illegal forms of control, such as child bondage. From an employer's point of view, child labour is perhaps the most stable form of labour; children do not strike or disrupt production. On the other hand, they are also the easiest to dislodge in times of economic difficulty. Children are the cheapest to hire and the easiest to fire. They do not resist. They are physically and emotionally vulnerable and are often physically and psychologically abused, or threatened with the possibility of such abuse.

The case of the leather tanning industry in Cairo is a good example. When employers there were asked what their reaction would be if there was an effective legal ban, 72 per cent asserted that they would continue to employ children anyway. Far more significantly, an even higher percentage (78 per cent) said that they would continue to hire children even if their wages were raised to adult levels. The explanation for this apparent anomaly lies, I think, in the fact that the docility of children is perhaps their most attractive quality as far as employers are concerned and correspondingly a fundamental source of child exploitation.

The radical critique is therefore quite right as regards the exploitative relationships within which children work. It is correct in anticipating that the work of children becomes redundant and unnecessary with technological progress, as is confirmed by the fact that child labour is concentrated in small enterprises and the unorganised sector and found much less frequently in large-scale enterprises, which use more advanced technology. It is also right in identifying the serious limitations on choice and options arising from structural constraints.

However, the last few years have demonstrated unambiguously what should have been fairly obvious a long time ago, namely that the radical critique failed to anticipate the possibility, and indeed the fact, that the capitalist and mixed economies were successful, albeit not completely, in dealing with income insecurity and the worst aspects of economic deprivation through a combination of rapid growth and the provision of social security and insurance coverage. This failure to anticipate the flexibility of the capitalist system was of course a serious intellectual and political error, as was the insistence on the superiority of the alternative revolutionary model. An equally problematic aspect of the radical critique, in my view, is its conspiratorial assumptions. These are of two kinds.

The first is about the behaviour of governments. Although they are influenced by economic lobbies, I have difficulty in accepting the assertion that governments serve only the interests of the powerful. Nor is it true that governments, or government officials, bureaucrats and politicians, are so sold out to powerful capitalists that it is impossible to work with them in the defence of social rights, the weak and vulnerable. The commitment to the rule of law is not the monopoly of a particular political persuasion, much less of revolutionary groups.

---

[3] See A. Abdalla: "Child labour in Egypt: Leather tanning in Cairo"; M.C. Salazar: "Child labour in Colombia: Bogotá's quarries and brickyards"; and H. von Oosterhout: "Child labour in the Philippines": The Muro-Ami deep-sea fishing operation", in Assefa Bequele and Jo Boyden (editors): Combating child labour (ILO, Geneva, 1988).

Even so, governments need to be given support in their programmes and, where necessary, to come under pressure to take action. It is therefore important to create coalitions with supporters of progressive change. This has been shown to be true not only by the historical record of the developed countries, but also by the ongoing and dynamic changes that are sweeping many countries in Africa, Latin America and Asia. These opportunities were exploited in the past, and should be exploited in the future, by all those who are engaged in the campaign for human rights and children's rights.

But to my mind, a more serious objection to the radical critique is what it implies in terms of policy and politics. The radical critique insists on a total restructuring of economic and political power as a necessary condition for change or social progress. Given that such restructuring may take a long time or require violent revolutionary action, the radical perspective amounts to a prescription for inaction for those who have not taken up the revolutionary cause. And this is neither correct nor justified. Change and social progress can be brought about even under non-radical conditions and without resorting to violent actions. I will develop aspects of this argument later in this talk.

The "abolish-it-now" school

A second group, somewhat impatient with the work of many non-governmental organisations (NGOs) and international organisations, comprises those who advocate the immediate abolition of child labour. This group is composed of people with divergent interests and consists of:

(a) those lawyers who insist on a strict interpretation of the law or the constitution, which in almost all cases guarantees the protection of children and prohibits their employment below a certain age;

(b) radical activists in NGOs;

(c) employers in large and medium-sized enterprises who might feel threatened by competition from enterprises operating in an unregulated labour market and employing child workers; and

(d) workers in industrialised countries who fear job losses as a result of the shift of industries to countries which supply cheap labour, including child labour.

It seems to me that this heterogeneous group, for various reasons, runs the risk of disregarding the realities obtaining in much of the Third World -- realities that I shall talk about later. Some in this group would even oppose the provision of protective measures, on the grounds that these are palliative measures and could perpetuate and legitimate child labour.

Ironically, this group sometimes finds an unlikely ally in a certain kind of government official, who wishes to deny the existence in practice of what is not supposed to exist in law, and who therefore refuses to admit the prevalence of child labour. Such officials would be happy not to adopt an activist strategy of extending protection, because protection cannot be provided against something that is legally prohibited.

To my mind, the disadvantage in practice of this point of view is that it has been instrumental in hindering many a practical programme from becoming operational, because government officials would not authorise it, or because well-meaning NGO activists condemned programmes aimed at providing some kind of protection and services to child workers.

The evolutionary approach

Counterpoised against these two schools is the reticent view prevalent among a wide group of people in government, in employers' circles and in society in general, which favours a rather non-interventionist approach to the problem. The starting point for this approach is the well-known premise that child labour is the result of mass poverty and underdevelopment, and, more specifically, that children work because their parents are poor. The child may be a secondary income-earner and contribute as much as 30 to 40 per cent of household income. In some cases the child may be the only income-earner in the family. Salazar[4] found in her study that about half of the households surveyed contained at least one unemployed adult. Moreover, very few adult workers had stable wage employment. The problem of household poverty is reinforced or aggravated by the lack of schooling opportunities or the poor quality of schooling. In practice, the early involvement of children in work is favoured by parents on the grounds that it could lead to skill acquisition and an early start in career development. In other words, child labour cannot be abolished so long as poverty persists. Legislation prohibiting child employment is likely to lead to clandestine employment and therefore to greater exploitation. The best that can be done is perhaps to legitimise child employment and to ensure that child workers are provided with legal protection.

This raises several questions. Is poverty a sufficient explanation for the employment of children? Alternatively, why is it that some poor families send their children to school, and others to work? Going beyond the household level, is the absence or inadequate provision of compulsory universal schooling simply a result of underdevelopment and poverty or the direct reflection of misplaced national priorities and policies? At what point is a country considered rich enough to initiate action against child labour and to prohibit the employment of children? Why is it that poverty and budgetary constraints are not invoked in respect of certain other items, such as military expenditure? In other words, is it not possible to provide basic protection in the form of compulsory education and income security even at low levels of economic development?

The fallacy of the poverty argument

All the above questions are, in my view, valid. Although it is undoubtedly true that the elimination of poverty requires sustained and rapid economic growth, and that the complete or effective abolition of child labour requires the elimination of poverty, what is not, however, so obvious is: how rapid does growth have to be, and what level of per capita income has to be reached, before anti-poverty objectives are seriously addressed and child labour abolished?

The question cannot be dealt with in the abstract and can be meaningfully answered only in specific national and historical contexts. Nevertheless, the evidence so far seems to lead to two different conclusions. In some countries, the onset of declining poverty levels was preceded by a long period of rapid and sustained increases in per capita output. In contrast, in other countries, rapid growth was accompanied by increased poverty over a long period. However, in other cases it has been possible to effect a reduction in absolute and relative poverty levels and to provide increased access to social services by the poor even at low levels of development and per capita income. This suggests that while growth is a necessary condition for poverty alleviation,

[4] ibid., pages 217 to 222.

an equally important determinant is the pattern of growth, namely, the extent to which growth objectives correspond to social goals and the extent to which production is synchronised with mass consumption needs.

In the specific context of child labour, while not denying the conflicting and competing demands on national resources, it is definitely possible, as can be seen from the experience of some developing countries, to bring about significant reductions in the incidence of child labour and extend protection to working children even at low levels of per capita income and development.

There is also a moral imperative. Resources are and will always be limited; poverty in its varied forms is widely prevalent and will unfortunately persist in many countries for some time to come. Yet, "there are absolutes arising from the inherent dignity of the human person and recognised in international convenants which nations, irrespective of their level of development, have accepted and should therefore adhere to. [The protection of] children at least from the worst forms of exploitation and dangerous working conditions....need not and should not await structural changes or significant improvements in general standards of living. ...[To] invoke the pretext of poverty and underdevelopment for the transgression of universally accepted values is to accept the perpetuation of universally condemned abuses"[5]. In the contemporary world of extensive interactions in information and knowledge, economics cannot take complete precedence over universally accepted basic human rights and values. To do otherwise could in the long run be most perilous for governments and society at large.

In the end, the degree to which basic social objectives are pursued in the process of economic development and hence the extent to which increased equality of opportunity and greater access to education and social services are attained is ultimately a political question. It very much depends on the foresight, commitment and will of governments and citizens to protect the weak and vulnerable, to balance social and economic objectives, and to establish a stable and democratic order. We will come back to this point in the next section.

III. What can be done

Priority areas of action

But what, then, are the priority areas and types of actions that governments in very poor developing countries can carry out to bring about a reduction in the incidence of child labour and to provide a greater measure of protection for working children.

First and foremost is the identification of and the prohibition of child work in hazardous and unsafe activities. Millions of children in various parts of the developing world work under extremely difficult, abusive and exploitative conditions: in pesticide-soaked farms and plantations; in sweatshops and in small industrial enterprises in tasks that involve handling microscopically fine wires which lead to the loss of eyesight; as domestic servants in private households, where they may be subject to arduous and heavy work, excessively long hours, physical

---

5 ILO: Child labour, Report of the Director-General to the International Labour Conference, 1983, page 20.

violence and sexual abuse; in cafés, restaurants and even bars and public entertainment places, where legitimate work and child prostitution overlap; on the streets, often under the threat of violence or even subject to systematic terror, beating and murder by street gangs, organised killing squads and sometimes the police under the guise of keeping the streets clean and safe, as recent reports from Brazil and Colombia have testified.

These children are seen and found almost anywhere in the developing world. The long-term consequences for society of having a generation of intellectually, emotionally, and physically crippled children is all too easily forgotten, or overshadowed by the immediate benefits of child earnings to individual families. The few fortunate ones may work within the context of household production, but many are separated from their families and therefore devoid of any kind of protection. And almost all child workers have little or no real possibility of schooling. The prohibition of work by children in hazardous occupations and activities should be an object of immediate policy intervention.

Second, large numbers of child labourers are at risk, mainly because of the very early age at which they commence work. A surprisingly large number of children start work even before they are 10 years old. And these are found working in such activities as brick-making, quarrying and match-making. According to labour standards in many countries, work in these kinds of activities is prohibited not simply to young children but even to those in their mid-teens. The involvement of children at a very early age in work which is considered dangerous even for older workers is also confirmed in ILO studies on Colombia, India, Peru and the Philippines[6]. Therefore a second area of priority action is the protection of the youngest and most vulnerable. Many countries have the capacity for, and some have demonstrated the feasibility of, banning child employment before the completion of compulsory primary education or before the age of 12 to 13 years. Such a measure would almost at a stroke significantly reduce the incidence of child labour and provide protection for the youngest and most vulnerable groups.

Major means of action

There are three major means of action which deserve special attention.

First is the provision of universal compulsory education. Education is both a means and an end. "All advanced industrial countries and those contemporary developing countries that have made education compulsory regard education not as a right but as a duty. When education is made a duty, parents, irrespective of their economic circumstances and beliefs, are required by law to send their children to school; it is also the legal obligation of the State to provide an adequate number of schools, appropriately situated, and to ensure that no child fails to attend school"[7]. Education is of special significance because it is undoubtedly the single most important instrument for absorbing children away from the labour market. But for it to perform this role, several conditions must be met:

---

6 See Bequele and Boyden, op. cit.

7 M. Weiner: The child and the State in India (Princeton University Press, Princeton, 1991), page 180.

(a) the existing disparities between and within sectors and among socio-economic groups must be narrowed through the increased availability of educational facilities and services in relatively deprived sectors and the provision of incentives for increased access by deprived socio-economic groups;

(b) the quality of education, which remains quite unsatisfactory in many countries as measured by qualitative and quantitative criteria such as school attendance, drop-out rates, access to employment, and the value attached to it by poor people, needs to be improved so as to increase the attractiveness of schooling and justify its cost;

(c) the real economic cost of schooling to the poor must to the extent possible be reduced. Education is a social right, and the poor must not be denied that right because of their disadvantageous economic position and the associated explicit and/or implicit costs of schooling: for the poor, these costs may consist of such direct expenses as school fees, the cost of uniforms and school materials, and other incidental expenses. These may appear to be small by the standards of the well-to-do, but can be a significant burden on families who barely eke out a living. But perhaps far more important is the cost of sending children to school in terms of foregone earnings, which can be substantial. Some studies show that the earnings of child workers can account for as much as 30 per cent or more of household incomes. In such situations, families send their children to school only at their own peril. The long-term solution lies obviously in promoting income- and employment-generating schemes. But could society not consider alternative schemes, such as school feeding programmes and other innovative measures, in order to lighten the burden on poor families and make it attractive for them to send their children to school rather than to work?

A second and major tool for ensuring the abolition of child labour in hazardous employment is effective enforcement. Enforcement in many countries has been ineffective for various reasons. In many cases, the problem is simply that there just are not enough inspectors. In one region in Egypt, for example, there are only four inspectors to cover approximately 20,000 establishments and to examine all aspects of working conditions. In the Philippines, there are fewer than 200 labour inspectors nationwide for almost 400,000 employers. Further, labour inspectors lack the incentive to carry out their work effectively. Their salaries are low, sometimes even lower than the wages of child labourers, and they are therefore subject to corrupt practices. All of this suggests that if governments are serious about prohibiting child labour in hazardous employment, they must strengthen their enforcement and inspection machinery.

A third area of action is public mobilisation and pressure. Governments are not always capable of making fundamental changes in major policies and programmes. For changes to be brought about and sustained, there must be continued pressure from outside the government. Vested interests in agriculture, industry, hotels and tourism have been known time and again to subvert change. Sustained campaigns by human rights groups and non-governmental organisations, combined with full and vigorous exposure of abuses and dereliction of duty, are absolutely essential if governments are to give teeth to the law and fulfil their obligations to ensure that the child receives the best that society can give.

It is also necessary to take action within the public sector to overcome the influence of vested interests and to ensure that substantial changes penetrate the bureaucracy and gain a consistency of their own so that they are able to survive the departure of the individuals who originated or supported them. Myers[8] describes an approach, which he calls creating a policy dissonance, through which it is possible to institute a counterweight within the public sector, by creating alternative programmes, often with the support of local and community action groups, that can challenge and change existing policies and programmes.

IV. Conclusion

In conclusion, I am of the view that poor countries should not and need not await the nirvana of a socialist revolution or the affluence of capitalist growth before they can address the exploitation and cruelty of child labour. They may not be able to bring about the immediate and effective abolition of child labour. But they can take specific measures in that direction with the aim of dealing with the worst aspects of child labour.

They can and should prohibit the employment of children in hazardous activities and occupations which are manifestly dangerous to the safety, health and physical, emotional and moral development of the child. They can and should prohibit the employment of the very young and vulnerable. They can and should ensure the provision of universal, compulsory and free education for all their children, especially those under 12 or 13 years of age.

The objectives I set out above are not unattainable. Indeed they are very modest and feasible even in very poor countries. The problem is not economic or administrative feasibility, but one of national and political commitment. And it is for us - those in international organisations, in the media and in non-governmental organisations - to mobilise national and community pressure so that governments live up to their national and international obligations to ensure that the child is protected at home, on the street and at the workplace.

---

[8] W. Myers: "Alternative services for street children: The Brazilian approach", in Bequele and Boyden, op. cit., pages 125-141.

Part II

Child labour: National legislation on the minimum age for admission to employment or work

Part II

Child labour: National legislation on the minimum age for admission to employment or work

by

Victoria Sinclair and Gabriele Trah[1]

Introduction

Historically, the adoption of legislation is the policy instrument most frequently used by governments to combat child labour. Almost all countries have enacted some legislation to prohibit the employment of children below a certain age and to specify the conditions under which minors may work, where they are legally permitted to do so.

This part reviews trends in national legislation on the minimum age for admission to employment or work. The attached annexes provide a summary of the legislative provisions in the 143 countries covered by this survey. In addition, Part V of the Digest presents fact sheets in which the main laws and regulations on child labour have been summarised on a country-by-country basis.

It should, however, be stressed that legislation alone is not sufficient to eliminate child labour and should not be considered an end in itself. It is only a means, among others, of attaining the larger objective of abolishing child labour and protecting working children where they are legally permitted to work. At least two other elements of public policy also play a leading role in the struggle against child labour, namely enforcement and education. Problems relating to the enforcement of existing child labour legislation are discussed at length in Parts III and IV of the Digest.

Problems relating to the availability and quality of education are a major impediment to the effectiveness of national legislation and its enforcement in many developing countries. Compulsory, universal and free primary education is undoubtedly the single most important policy instrument through which the State can effectively remove children from the labour force. Indeed, the fight against child labour has nearly always historically coincided to a large extent with the spread of mass education. Every industrialising country has introduced the principle of compulsory primary education during its industrialisation process, and in some cases compulsory universal education preceded industrialisation.

---

[1] Conditions of Work and Welfare Facilities Branch, International Labour Office.

Past and contemporary experience has also shown that it is possible, in spite of a low per capita income, to provide mass primary education, if policy-makers and society as a whole genuinely believe in education as a duty. The State can and should stand "as the ultimate guardian of children, protecting them against both parents and would-be employers"[2].

The adoption of adequate legislation to combat child labour and the establishment of effective labour inspection systems to enforce it is a long and difficult process, extending over several decades. Almost all industrialised countries progressively expanded the scope and coverage of their legislation over time, concentrating in the beginning on the protection of the youngest and most vulnerable children and preventing the employment or work of children in hazardous occupations or industries. Indeed, this process cannot be considered complete, and child labour has not been fully eliminated anywhere, even in the most industrialised countries.

International minimum age standards

National legislation on child labour has been strongly influenced by international labour standards. The approach adopted in ILO Conventions has been to set a minimum age for admission to employment or work, either for a given sector of the economy or for the whole of it, and to allow certain exceptions where circumstances warrant this. The Conventions adopted before 1973 set minimum ages for employment or work in industry, non-industrial employment, agriculture, underground work and at sea. This sectoral approach allowed countries to ratify Conventions which applied to their own particular circumstances. Many countries were not -- and still are not -- capable of setting and implementing a minimum age for employment or work in all sectors of the economy. By ratifying and implementing a Convention which applies only to a limited sector, it has already been possible to make a great deal of progress.

In 1973 the Conference decided to establish a general instrument on the subject, which would gradually replace those applicable to limited economic sectors. It therefore adopted the Minimum Age Convention (No. 138) and Recommendation (No. 146) in 1973. The full texts of the two instruments are reproduced in Part VI of the Digest. These instruments are general in scope, and in principle cover all economic sectors and all employment or work, whether or not it is performed under a contract of employment. However, this Convention is not a static instrument, and is aimed at encouraging the progressive improvement of standards and at promoting sustained action to attain its objectives. The obligations assumed by ratifying States are flexible and conditioned by national circumstances and the level of the standards already achieved in each country. Provision is therefore made for several kinds of exclusions or exceptions in coverage, scope and standards.

---

2 M. Weiner: The child and the State in India: Child labour and education policy in comparative perspective (Princeton University Press, Princeton, 1991), page 3.

Table 1: Minimum ages set out in Convention No. 138

	General	Exceptions
Basic minimum age	15	14
Hazardous work	18	16
Light work	13 to 15	12 to 14

The following pages take the provisions contained in Convention No. 138 as a guideline for reviewing national child labour legislation, whether the countries in question have ratified Convention No. 138 or not.

Review of national minimum age legislation

Basic minimum age for admission to employment or work

The basic provision of the Minimum Age Convention is contained in Article 2, which requires that every member ratifying the Convention shall specify a minimum age for admission to employment or work. The term "employment or work" was specifically chosen in order to cover all economic activity regardless of the formal employment status of the person concerned. The Convention also provides that this basic minimum age shall not be less than the age of completion of compulsory schooling, and in any case, not less than 15 years. However, in the case of a member State whose economy and educational facilities are insufficiently developed, the Convention allows the minimum age to be set initially at 14.

Most countries have accepted the principle of a basic minimum age for admission to employment or work, although there are often gaps and shortcomings in the respective national laws, which mean that the minimum age is far from general in scope. The legislative approaches that have been adopted vary widely between, and sometimes within countries, as do the age threshold, the scope, complexity and completeness of national legislation.

The most generally adopted pattern, and the one followed by Convention No. 138, is to set a single minimum age applicable to all forms of work or employment and all economic sectors. A variation of this approach is to prohibit work by children until they have completed their compulsory schooling. A different arrangement is to set a minimum age in specific occupations, processes or sectors, which varies according to the perceived hazards of the work, the economic development of the country and the national capacity for enforcing this type of legislation (see also Annex 1).

Of the countries surveyed, the largest number (one-third) have opted to set a minimum age of 14. Of this group, however, only a handful specify in their legislation that admission to work or employment is to be linked to the completion of compulsory schooling.

The next largest group, representing slightly under one-third of the countries surveyed, have fixed the minimum age at 15. Over one-third of these countries state clearly in their legislation that admission to employment or work should either follow the completion of compulsory schooling or should in no way prejudice the individual's completion of schooling or performance at school.

Around 20 of the countries surveyed have adopted legislation which goes a step further than the Convention's basic provision by setting 16 as the minimum age for admission to employment or work, although in several cases this minimum age only applies to certain economic sectors. In contrast, in a group of comparable size, the legislation sets a minimum age of 12 or 13 for admission to work and employment. Although this low age is found in particular in the few countries which have not established compulsory schooling, a number of countries which have set the basic minimum age at 12 or 13 years have nevertheless established compulsory education beyond that age. Only a few of the countries, for example Costa Rica, specify that work may only be performed on condition that compulsory schooling has been completed or if it does not prevent its completion.

These cases illustrate the importance of co-ordinating the age at which compulsory schooling is completed and the basic minimum age for admission to employment or work. If the basic minimum age is lower than the age for completing compulsory education, the children and their parents will be tempted by the possibility of finding legal employment. If the legal minimum age is set higher than the school-leaving age, the children may find themselves with nothing to do for a year or more, and will therefore be likely to drift towards illegal forms of employment.

Some countries, rather than setting a minimum age for admission to employment or work, have adopted the approach of prohibiting the employment of young persons during school hours. In some cases, this approach has been adopted by only a few states in a federal union (e.g. Australia, Canada) or only for some economic sectors, while other sectors are covered by minimum age provisions (New Zealand).

Several countries specifically restrict their minimum age provisions to formal employment relationships in which the young person works under contract to another person. Only a minority of countries explicitly cover both employment and work in the sense of the Convention. Limiting the scope of minimum legislation in this way to formal employment relationships fails to cover the kinds of work that child labourers most often perform, namely work in family undertakings, home work and work on their own account.

Another approach is for minimum age legislation only to cover specific economic sectors. This leaves other sectors without minimum age regulations. The sector-by-sector approach often has the effect of establishing differences between sectors: the regulations may cover only formal employment in one sector, and employment and work in another; the minimum age may vary from one sector to another, with a higher minimum age normally being set in sectors such as industry and shipping.

In many cases, in addition to establishing a minimum age for work or employment, countries have adopted further regulations concerning the employment of young persons.

The most common requirement is that employment or work should not have a negative effect on school attendance or performance. In some countries, a medical examination and certification of fitness for employment and the express authorisation of a parent or guardian are required for the employment of young persons. In Haiti, an employer must obtain a permit to employ a minor aged 12 years in domestic service and must undertake to provide the required care for the child. The consent of the local trade union committee is required in the USSR before young persons of 15 years of age may be employed in work that is not specified as "light" (the basic minimum age in the USSR is 16). In Nigeria, where the basic minimum age is 12, young persons from 12 to 14 years old may be employed only on a daily wage, on a day-to-day basis and on condition that the child is able to return each night to the residence of his/her family or guardian.

Exceptions to the basic minimum age

Most countries that have established a basic minimum age for admission to work and employment also provide for exceptions to their basic age requirements either by occupation, by entire economic sector or for training purposes. Exceptions of this kind are also set out in Articles 4, 5 and 6 of Convention No. 138. However, in many cases these are a result of limitations in the scope of minimum age laws, rather than of specific legal exemptions.

Work in family undertakings, or under the authority of a parent, guardian or close relative, domestic work, or work in technical and vocational schools which is essentially of an educational nature, are the areas most commonly excluded from the minimum age requirements specified in legislation. Homeworkers, the self-employed and workers in the commercial sector are other categories which, while rarely specifically excluded, are often not covered by minimum age provisions.

There are several cases in which only the sectors specifically mentioned in legislation are covered by minimum age standards and it therefore has to be assumed that all other sectors are excluded.

In some Latin American countries (Argentina, Ecuador, El Salvador, Guatemala and Honduras), the law provides that work may be authorised by the competent authority if it is deemed essential to the subsistence of the young person or his/her family and does not affect compulsory schooling.

The sector most commonly exempted from minimum age requirements is agriculture, although it is a sector in which many children work. Article 5 of Convention No. 138 specifies that the basic minimum age shall be applicable as a minimum to, among other areas, "plantations and other agricultural undertakings mainly producing for commercial purposes, but excluding family and small-scale holdings producing for local consumption and not regularly employing hired workers". In some national laws, the exemption of agriculture is qualified by the wording "unless dangerous work is involved", although no further definitions are given. In Peru, legislation exempts from minimum age requirements those agricultural activities in which mechanical devices are not used. In Lebanon, agricultural corporations having "no connection with commerce or industry" are exempted from minimum age requirements. On the other hand, a few countries, such as the United States and France, have included specific activities in the agricultural sector (such as the handling of agricultural chemicals) in the list of hazardous activities requiring a higher minimum age for admission to employment.

Although industry is normally covered by minimum age legislation, a few countries (Bangladesh, Pakistan, Myanmar, Syrian Arab Republic) exempt small enterprises with fewer than ten or 20 employees. In Myanmar, for example, a special provision exempts small industrial enterprises using motive power with fewer than ten workers, or those without motive power and employing fewer than 20 workers.

In a few countries (for example Belize, Costa Rica), exceptions are specifically made for work for cultural or charitable organisations. Two unusual exceptions to minimum age restrictions occur in Somalia, for the armed forces, and Turkey, for janitor services in dwellings.

Artistic performances are an area in which, according to Article 8 of Convention No. 138, the competent authority may grant exceptions to the prohibition of employment or work under certain conditions. However, the majority of countries and, in particular developing countries, do not appear to have adopted specific regulations covering this type of work, despite the fact that children are employed in artistic performances in most countries. While many countries specify an even higher minimum age for work in night clubs, bars, cabarets or circuses, performing in plays and films and other public performances are frequently omitted from the provisions in spite of the fact that they may also present serious risks to the well-being of children.

In a number of countries, the legislation contains a more general provision permitting the competent authorities to authorise exceptions. Sometimes the law contains no further guidelines or restrictions on the use of this power. The competent authority in some countries is empowered to exempt undertakings or sectors from minimum age laws or grant partial exemptions from the basic minimum age. While in many cases no guidelines or conditions are set out for the exclusion of whole undertakings and sectors, partial exemptions and the lowering of the basic minimum age is usually only allowed under specified conditions.

In summary, the content of much of the legislation surveyed would indicate that those sectors of the economy which are exempted from the minimum age requirements tend to be informal or areas where, because of the small size and yet extensive spread of individual operations, it would be extremely difficult to enforce legislation.

Reduced minimum age for light work

Article 7 of Convention No. 138 provides that national laws or regulations may permit the employment or work of children of 13 to 15 years of age on light work which is not likely to be harmful to their health or development; and not such as to prejudice their attendance or performance at school or any other training institution. Light work may be permitted between the ages of 12 and 14 if the country has specified a basic minimum age of 14. Article 7 also requires the competent authorities to determine the type of work that is considered to be "light", as well as the number of hours and the conditions in which such employment or work may be undertaken.

Light work can be divided into two categories in relation to its economic importance to the child and the child's family. The first category applies mainly -- but not only -- to developing countries, where the aid of children is important to the family economy. This implies the danger that children will be considered as economic assets and asked to perform work beyond their strength or for too many hours. The second category applies mainly to children in developed countries, where they engage in light work outside school hours to make some extra money or gain experience purely for their own personal benefit.

Of the countries surveyed which set a lower age for the employment of minors on light work (roughly 60 per cent of all countries), minimum ages varied between 8 and 15, although some countries specified no minimum age for light work. Almost half set a minimum age of 12 for light work. Roughly one-third set either 13 or 14 years, and two countries established 15 as the minimum age for light work. The youngest age is 10 years for light agricultural work (Denmark and Tanzania) and 8 years for light work of a non-industrial nature (Lebanon).

Definitions of what constitutes light work vary considerably, and the number of hours permitted is not always specified (see Annex 2).

About 30 countries do not define light work or do not restrict it to any particular sector. In a large number of cases, light work performed by minors under the basic minimum age is allowed in agriculture, on condition that the child works with his/her family, that the work is of limited duration, and that it presents no hazards to the child's health and safety. In other cases, the definition is somewhat broader, allowing for "light work other than in industry", or, as in the Congo, "light non-industrial work which can only be performed by children". A number of countries also make provision for light work in domestic service at a lower age.

A large percentage of countries specify in their legislation that the performance of light work must not interfere with school instruction. In Japan, a certificate is required from the child's teacher stating that the work performed by the child does not hinder his/her school performance. A significant number of countries require authorisation by the Minister of Labour or the relevant competent authority for the performance of light work. The consent of a parent or a legal guardian is also required in a number of countries.

The survey of national legislation produced a number of different provisions on the number of hours during which light work may be performed by minors. In some cases, such work may not exceed two hours a day. In other cases, when combined with school time, total hours of work shall not be more than seven. Rest periods of at least 12 or 14 hours between days of work are also provided for in a number of countries. In other cases, work shall not be carried out on statutory holidays or weekly rest days. In some countries, work may only be performed during school holidays and for only one-half or two-thirds of the total holiday period.

Higher minimum age for hazardous work

Convention No. 138 provides in Article 3 for a minimum age of 18, that is a higher age than the basic minimum age, for admission to work "which by its nature or the circumstances in which it is carried out is likely to jeopardise the health, safety and morals of young persons". This age limit may be reduced to 16 "on condition that the health, safety and morals of the young persons concerned are fully protected and that the young persons have received adequate specific instruction or vocational training in the relevant branch of activity". The Convention requires that the types of work to which this provision applies should be determined by national law or regulations after consultation with the appropriate employers' and workers' organisations.

Almost all countries have adopted some measures to prohibit or restrict dangerous work by young persons although, as for the other requirements of Convention No. 138, there is considerable variety in the provisions that have been adopted. In some cases, the definition of hazardous work is limited to a general statement concerning work that is "dangerous, dirty, unhealthy or detrimental to morals", and no further elaboration of activities is provided. In other cases, hazardous occupations are listed in some detail.

Austria is an illustration of a country that has established a detailed listing of hazardous work or employment. Under Austrian legislation there is a minimum age of 18 for work in variety shows, cabarets, bars, sexshops, dance halls, discotheques, cinemas, circuses or similar enterprises where work may prejudice the minor's health or morals; work involving exposure to various substances or composites which are harmful to the health, in particular noxious or corrosive substances or substances which may cause irritation to the skin or mucous membranes (in such cases, the minimum age can be reduced to 16 for young persons who have completed half their vocational training, and who work under supervision and after medical examination; stricter regulations apply to women workers); various types of work with substances or composites where there is a risk of explosion or which are inflammable; various types of work involving exposure to hazardous levels of vibration, lasers and ionising rays (can be reduced for young persons undergoing vocational training under certain conditions); work involving particular physical strain (the transport of heavy loads; work involving exposure to heat, cold, high or low air pressure; diving; etc.); the operation of various motor-driven and other machinery, if no appropriate measures have been taken to reduce the danger of accidents (can be reduced to 16 in connection with vocational training or to 17 in some cases); work with enterprise fire brigades and gas rescue services; underground work (17 for men undergoing training, altogether prohibited for women); work in brick kilns; construction work; work on roofs or at exposed heights; railway work; operating lifts; operating vehicles, cranes and excavators; work as a member of the crew of a ship (unless undergoing training); various types of metal work (unless undergoing training; may be reduced to 17 if medically certified fit); work involving exposure to risks of infection; and itinerant trades among others. Minimum age of 17 for scheduled work in quarries, certain work related to glass, spray and dip painting, among others. Minimum age of 16 for piece-rate work.

Some countries have no general rule prohibiting dangerous or unhealthy work for young persons, but have enacted a higher minimum age for a limited number of types of work. As can be seen in Annex 3, underground work, maritime work (especially trimmers and stokers), work with explosives or noxious substances, work with lead paint/metallurgy, and work with machinery that is in motion are the areas most commonly singled out for special consideration and an increased minimum age requirement.

With few exceptions, 18 is the minimum age specified by most countries for work in underground mines and quarries. The prevailing minimum age requirement for work as trimmers and stokers or loading and unloading ships in the maritime industry (except for family-owned or training ships) is also 18, although in a number of countries, provision is made for two 16-year-olds to fill a trimmer and stoker position if a suitable person over 18 cannot be found for the job. The minimum age for work with lead, lead paint, or lead and zinc alloys varies from 15 (Syrian Arab Republic), 16 (Bahrain, Greece, Honduras, Mexico, United Kingdom), to 18 (over 20 countries) and 21 (Uruguay). Similarly, for the maintenance of machinery that is in motion, minimum age requirements range from 15 (Italy, Syrian Arab Republic) to 21 (Uruguay), with 18 as the most commonly specified age. Eighteen is the usual minimum age requirement for work involving the handling or manufacture of explosives and work with noxious substances generating harmful dust, fumes or gases. Two other areas often singled out for special consideration are the smelting of metal or work with molten glass; once again, 18 is the most common minimum age.

Other industries or activities that are commonly covered by a higher minimum age for employment include:

- work with various acids;
- work involving exposure to deadly biological agents or radiation;
- underwater work;
- the use of compressed gas or liquids, or dispersed gases;
- leather processing;
- work with inflammable liquids and benzene;
- the operation of dangerous motor-driven machines, including lifting machinery;
- the butchering of animals;
- work with drainage or sewage;
- and work involving the lifting and carrying of loads over 20 kg (in a number of countries, tables specifying the maximum weights which may be handled by different age groups are included in the legislation).

A significant provision in Cuban and Finnish legislation is the specification of a minimum age of 17 and 18 respectively for "work in which the young person's safety or that of others depends on his/her responsibility".

In a number of countries, there is a legal requirement for medical certificates attesting to the fitness of the young person before hazardous work can be performed. In Lesotho and Sierra Leone, for example, medical certificates are required for persons aged 16 years and over seeking employment in mines and quarries.

There are also variations in minimum age requirements between men and women in work that is considered to be potentially hazardous. In Spain, the legislation provides a list of activities in which the minimum age is set at 18 for men and 21 for women. In Norway, men may enter service at sea at the age of 16 and women at the age of 18.

The possible impact of certain types of work on the morals of young persons is taken into consideration in the national legislation in many countries. The activities that are specified in the various legislations as being hazardous in this sense include work in establishments where alcohol is sold, cinemas, nightclubs, casinos, cabarets and dance halls or similar establishments. Reference is made in some laws to work involving the delivery or sale of written or printed matter or materials deemed prejudicial to morals. In Chile, the minimum age for work in cabarets or other establishments presenting live performances and selling alcoholic beverages is 21. The average minimum age specified for work in these areas in the legislation surveyed, however, is 18.

A sector that is remarkable because it is not included in legislation concerning hazards to the morals of young persons is domestic service. Apart from a limited number of provisions requiring that domestic workers be allowed to return home at night, only one country (Denmark) provides for a higher minimum age for work in domestic service in private households.

In general, the legislation in a great number of countries fails to comprehensively cover employment or work in hazardous or dangerous work by young persons.

Concluding remarks

In its general survey on minimum age, the Committee of Experts on the Application of Conventions and Recommendations noted that "only a few States have achieved anything approaching full compliance with all the detailed requirements of" Convention No. 138[3]. It also added that this was understandable, since the standards set in this instrument are more comprehensive than those set forth in previous international standards, which had provided the broad inspiration for minimum age legislation in a great number of countries. In particular, the scope of national provisions often falls short of providing complete coverage by either excluding or omitting persons working otherwise than under a contract of employment, excluding categories of work from the coverage of the legislation, and excluding branches of economic activity.

The manner in which countries set the ages below which children may not work also varies considerably from country to country. Some countries set a definite overall age, some countries only set ages for certain sectors, and others link admission to employment or work in some way or another to the completion of compulsory schooling. No matter which approach has been chosen, it is important that measures be taken to cover, wherever possible, all forms of work or employment.

[3] International Labour Office: General Survey by the Committee of Experts on the Application of Conventions and Recommendations, Report III (Part 4B) on Minimum age, International Labour Conference, 67th Session, 1981, page 162.

The relationship between schooling and admission to work is also of great importance. Various problems may arise if the minimum age for admission to employment or work is not linked with the age of completion of compulsory schooling. If schooling ends before young persons are allowed to work legally, there may be a period of enforced idleness or clandestine and consequently unprotected employment, especially where there are few opportunities for secondary schooling or vocational training. On the other hand, to set a minimum age for admission to work that is below the age of completion of compulsory schooling is an obvious contradiction. In addition, such situations may contribute to high school drop-out rates and lower educational achievement by those children who go to school and work at the same time. Thus every conceivable effort should be made to ensure that children are not prevented from completing their basic education by starting work too early.

The adoption of minimum age legislation, and particularly legislation that is sufficiently comprehensive to provide full protection against child labour, is of necessity a long process. The progress that has been achieved in very many countries in the adoption of minimum age legislation has undoubtedly given children greater protection. It is tempting to see a general trend in the development of these measures from the application of minimum age rules in certain occupations and sectors, to the establishment of a general minimum age for admission to all employment. This has certainly been the course of development in certain countries and many others are following this path. In countries where the minimum age legislation is less advanced, governments have often concentrated on prohibiting child labour in certain of the more hazardous forms of employment or work and on protecting the youngest and most vulnerable children. This is how measures to prevent child labour started in most countries. It is to be hoped that such interim measures in these countries form part of a longer term policy to gradually extend the scope of protection to cover child labour as a whole.

Annex 1: Compulsory education and miminimum age for admission to employment

Note: The information given in this table may not reflect completely and in detail the situation in each of these countries. It is intended only to give a general picture. For more specific information, the country fact sheets in Part V of the Digest should be consulted. Countries that have ratified Convention No. 138 are marked with an asterisk (*). The data on compulsory education were taken from the UNESCO Statistical Yearbook 1990.

Part II: National legislation on the minimum age for admission to employment or work

Annex 1: Africa

Country	Compulsory education required to age	Minimum age			Exceptions to coverage	
		Basic minimum age	Light work	Dangerous work	Categories of work excluded	Sectors of activity excluded
Algeria *	15	16	None; authorisation necessary <2>	16 to 18 <1>	Domestic service, homeworkers	None
Angola	15	14	—	18	Family undertakings	None
Benin	11	14	12	18	None	None
Botswana	—	15	14	15 to 18 <3>	Domestic service, family undertakings, other exclusions possible <2>	Commerce, non-commercial agriculture, etc.
Burkina Faso	14	14	12	16 to 18 <4>	Exclusions possible <2>	None
Burundi	13	16	12	18	Family undertakings, domestic work in family, other exclusions possible <2>	None
Cameroon	12	14	—	18	Exclusions possible <2>	None
Cape Verde	13	14 to 15 <5>	12	16 to 18	Family undertakings, self-employment, etc. <5>	None
Central African Republic	14	14	12	16 to 18	Family undertakings, other exclusions possible <2>	None
Chad	14	12 to 14 <6>	12	16 to 18	Family undertakings, other exclusions possible	None
Comoros	16	15	—	— <7>	— <8>	None
Congo	16	16	12	16 to 18	Family undertakings, other exclusions possible <2>	None
Côte d'Ivoire	13	14	12	16 to 18	Domestic service	None
Djibouti	15	14	—	16 to 18	None	None
Egypt	15	12	—	15 to 17	Domestic service, family undertakings	Agriculture

Annex 1: Africa (continued)

Country	Compulsory education required to age	Minimum age			Exceptions to coverage	
		Basic minimum age	Light work	Dangerous work	Categories of work excluded	Sectors of activity excluded
Equatorial Guinea *	14	14	12 to 13	16	None	None
Ethiopia	13	14	—	18	Self-employment	None
Gabon	16	16	—	18	Family undertakings, other exclusions possible	None
Ghana	16	15	No limit	18	Family undertakings	None
Guinea	13	16 <9>	—	—	Self-employment, etc. <9>	None
Guinea Bissau	13	14 <10>	—	18	None	None
Kenya *	—	16 <11>	—	16	Family undertakings (industry), various <11>	Agriculture, commerce, etc. <11>
Lesotho	13	15 <12>	—	16	Family undertakings, self-employment, domestic service, etc. <12>	Agriculture <12>
Liberia	16	14 to 16 (by sector) <13>	—	18	None	None
Libyan Arab Jamahiriya *	15	15	—	18	Family undertakings, domestic service	Agriculture, maritime
Madagascar	13	14 to 15 (by sector) <14>	—	16 to 18	Exclusions possible <2>	None
Malawi	14	14 to 15 (by sector) <15>	12	18	Family undertakings, domestic service, self-employed <15>	Agriculture, commerce, etc. <15>
Mali	15	14	12	16 to 18	Family undertakings, domestic service, other exclusions possible <2>	None
Mauritania	—	14 to 15 (by sector) <14>	—	18	Exclusions possible <2>	None

Annex 1: Africa (continued)

Country	Compulsory education required to age	Minimum age			Exceptions to coverage	
		Basic minimum age	Light work	Dangerous work	Categories of work excluded	Sectors of activity excluded
Mauritius *	—	15	—	18	None	None
Morocco	14	12	—	16	None	None
Mozambique	14	15	—	18	None	None
Namibia	16	14 <16>	—	16	Domestic service, self-employment, etc. <16>	Agriculture, commerce, etc. <16>
Niger *	15	14	12	16 to 18	Exclusions possible <2>	None
Nigeria	12	12 to 15 (by sector) <17>	12	16 to 18	None	None
Rwanda *	15	14	—	—	None	None
Sao Tome and Principe	14	14 to 15	12	16 to 18	Family undertakings	None
Senegal	13	14 to 15 (by sector) <14>	12	16 to 18	Exclusions possible <2>	None
Seychelles	15	15	12	18	None	None
Sierra Leone	—	12 to 16 (by sector) <18>	No limit <19>	16 to 18	Family undertakings	None
Somalia	14	15	12	16 to 18	Family undertakings, other exclusions possible	None
Sudan	—	12	—	18	Family undertakings	None
Swaziland	—	13 to 15 (by sector) <20>	—	18	Family undertakings, self-employment	Agriculture <20>

Annex 1: Africa (continued)

Country	Compulsory education required to age	Minimum age			Exceptions to coverage	
		Basic minimum age	Light work	Dangerous work	Categories of work excluded	Sectors of activity excluded
Tanzania	14	12 to 15 (by sector) <21>	10	18	Family undertakings (maritime), other exclusions possible <2>	None
Togo *	12	14	—	18	Exclusions possible <2>	None
Tunisia	—	13 to 15 (by sector) <22>	13	18	Family undertakings, domestic service, self-employment	Commerce, etc. <22>
Uganda	—	— <23>	12	16 to 18	—	—
Zaire	12	16	14	18	None	None
Zambia *	14	14 <11>	—	18	Family undertakings, domestic service, self-employment	Agriculture, commerce, etc. <11>

Annex 1: Africa (continued)

<1> 16 for work that is dangerous, unhealthy or detrimental to morals. 18 for work in the maritime industry.

<2> Determined by the competent authority.

<3> 15 for work involving lifting, carrying or moving anything heavy; 18 for underground work and dangerous or harmful work.

<4> General minimum age for hazardous work is 16 years; 18 for work exceeding strength and harmful to morality.

<5> Minimum age of 14 for contract as a permanent worker; 15 for work in industry.

<6> General minimum age is 14 years; 12 years for specified agricultural work.

<7> Age limits and nature of work prohibited to adolescents to be determined by ministerial decision.

<8> Applies only to enterprises.

<9> Applies only to industry and contractual employment.

<10> Or upon completion of compulsory schooling.

<11> Basic minimum age applies only to industry.

<12> Basic minimum age applies only to commerce and industry.

<13> General minimum age is 14 years; 15 for work on fishing vessels and on school ships; 16 for work in industry, agriculture and on ships.

<14> General minimum age is 14 years; 15 for work at sea.

<15> Minimum age of 14 for work in industry; 15 for work at sea.

<16> Minimum age applies only to work in factories and mines.

<17> General minimum age is 12 years; 15 for work in industry and shipping (except family undertakings).

<18> General minimum age is 12 years; 15 for work in industry and at sea; 16 for work in mines.

<19> Authorised only where the work is not harmful to the child. Authorisation for light work is subject to approval by the competent authority.

<20> Minimum age of 13 in commercial undertakings; 15 in industrial undertakings.

<21> General minimum age is 12 years; 15 for work in industry.

<22> 13 years for work in agriculture; 15 for work in industry, fishing and work at sea.

<23> A person under the apparent age of 18 shall not be employed other than as provided for by decree.

Annex 1: Americas

Country	Compulsory education required to age	Minimum age			Exceptions to coverage	
		Basic minimum age	Light work	Dangerous work	Categories of work excluded	Sectors of activity excluded
Antigua and Barbuda *	16	16 <1>	14	—	Family undertakings, domestic service	Commerce <1>
Argentina	14	14	—	18	Family undertakings <2>, domestic service, other exclusions possible <3>	None
Bahamas	14	14 <4>	—	16 to 18	Family undertakings, domestic service, self-employment	Agriculture, commerce, etc. <4>
Barbados	16	15 to 16 <5>	—	18	Family undertakings, domestic service, self-employment	Agriculture, commerce, etc. <5>
Belize	14	12 to 15 (by sector) <6>	—	18	None	None
Bolivia	13	14	—	18	None	None
Brazil	14	14 <7>	—	18 to 21 <8>	None	None
Canada: Federal	16	— <9>	—	17 <10>	—	— <9>
Provinces	—	Various <11>	—	16 to 18	Various (e.g. family undertakings in some provinces)	Agriculture (most provinces)
Chile	13	15	14	18 to 21 <12>	None	None
Colombia	14	14	12	18	None	Commerce, fishing
Costa Rica *	15	12 to 15 <13>	12	18	Domestic service	None
Cuba *	11	15	—	17 to 18	None	None
Dominica *	15	15 <14>	—	18	Family undertakings, domestic service, self-employment	Agriculture, commerce, etc. <14>

Annex 1: Americas (continued)

Country	Compulsory education required to age	Minimum age			Exceptions to coverage	
		Basic minimum age	Light work	Dangerous work	Categories of work excluded	Sectors of activity excluded
Dominican Republic	14	14	—	18	—	Agriculture (except dangerous work)
Ecuador	14	12 to 15 <15>	—	18	Domestic service	None
El Salvador	15	14	—	18	Exclusions possible <3>	None
Guatemala *	14	14	—	16	Exclusions possible <3>	None
Guyana	14	14	—	16 to 18	Family undertakings	None
Haiti	12	12 to 15	—	18	None	None
Honduras *	13	14	—	16	Exclusions possible <3>	Small agricultural undertakings <17>
Jamaica	12	12 to 15 (by sector) <18>	No limit	16 to 17 <18>	Family undertakings (maritime)	None
Mexico	14	14	—	16	None	None
Nicaragua *	12	14 <4>	—	18	Various <4>	Agriculture, commerce, etc. <4>
Panama	15	14 to 16 <20>	12	18	None	None
Paraguay	13	15	12	18	Family undertakings	None
Peru	12	14 to 16 (by sector) <21>	—	18	Family undertakings, domestic service	Small agricultural undertakings <22>
Saint Lucia	15	12 to 14 (by sector) <23>	No limit	14 to 16	Family undertakings	None

Annex 1: Americas (continued)

Country	Compulsory education required to age	Minimum age			Exceptions to coverage	
		Basic minimum age	Light work	Dangerous work	Categories of work excluded	Sectors of activity excluded
Suriname	12	14	—	18	Family undertakings (agriculture), other exclusions possible <24>	None
Trinidad and Tobago	11	12 to 16 (by sector) <25>	—	14 to 18	Family undertakings	None
United States (Federal)	16	16	—	16 to 18	Family undertakings, domestic service, other exclusions possible <24>	Agriculture
Uruguay *	14	15	12	18 to 21	None	None
Venezuela *	14	14	—	18	Domestic service	Agriculture

<1> Minimum age applies only to agriculture and industrial undertakings and for work on ships.

<2> On condition that the work is not harmful or dangerous and that the hours do not interfere with primary schooling.

<3> The competent authority may authorise exceptions if it is essential for the maintenance of the person concerned or that person's family and on condition that minimum education is completed, or work does not interfere with minimal education requirements.

<4> Minimum age applies only to industrial undertakings.

<5> Minimum age applies only to industrial undertakings or ships, including work in mines and quarries, construction, transportation. Minimum age of 15 only if compulsory schooling is finished.

<6> General minimum age is 12 years; 14 for work in industry, mines and quarries, construction, transportation, etc.; 15 for work at sea.

<7> Except apprentices above the age of 12.

<8> Minimum age of 21 for stevedoring and underground work.

Annex 1: Americas (continued)

<9> The Canada Labour Code does not set an absolute minimum age for employment. It provides that an employer may employ a person under 17 years in (a) occupations as may be specified by regulation, and (b) subject to the conditions and at a wage of not less than the minimum wage prescribed, and (c) provided that persons under 17 years are not required by provincial law to be in attendance at school (the youngest age for leaving school as provided by the provinces is 15). (Branches and undertakings governed by federal jurisdiction include communications, international and national transport, broadcasting, banking, uranium extraction and nuclear energy, and also certain branches declared by Parliament to be of interest to the nation. Federal legislation covers 10 per cent of the active population.)

<10> Persons under 17 years cannot be employed in specified jobs or at night.

<11> According to province, or territory, and sector. In certain provinces and territories, the employment of young persons is prohibited for various sectors only during school hours.

<12> Minimum age of 21 for work in cabarets, etc., presenting live performances and offering alcoholic beverages.

<13> Minimum age of 12 only if compulsory schooling has been completed or work does not prevent its completion, and not for more than five hours a day. Minimum age of 15 to 18 for work not exceeding seven hours a day.

<14> Minimum age applies only to industrial undertakings, including mining, manufacturing, shipbuilding, electrical utilities, construction and transportation.

<15> General minimum age is 14; 12 for minors who are obliged to work for their or their family's living; 15 for work on fishing vessels.

<16> General minimum age is 15 years; 12 for domestic service.

<17> Undertakings employing less than ten workers.

<18> General minimum age is 12 years; 15 for work in industry, mines and quarries, construction, transportation, and work at sea.

<19> 16 years for work in sugar factories and work with machinery in motion; 17 for mining.

<20> General minimum age is 14 years; 15 years where the child has not yet finished school. 16 for work on ships.

<21> 14 years for agriculture and non-industrial work; 15 for work in industry; 16 for industrial fishing. Regulations apply to all work.

<22> Which do not possess agricultural machinery.

<23> General minimum age is 12 years; 14 for work in industry and on ships. No work may be performed during school hours, if the child is still completing schooling.

<24> Determined by the competent authority.

<25> General minimum age is 12 years; 14 for work in industry; 16 for work on ships.

Annex 1: Asia

Country	Compulsory education required to age	Minimum age			Exceptions to coverage	
		Basic minimum age	Light work	Dangerous work	Categories of work excluded	Sectors of activity excluded
Afghanistan	15	15	—	18	Domestic service, etc. <1>	Agriculture, commerce, etc. <1>
Australia	16	Varies according to province and sector <2>	—	16 to 18	—	—
Bahrain	—	14	—	16	Family undertakings, domestic service	Agriculture, maritime
Bangladesh	10	12 to 15 (by sector) <3>	—	16 to 18 <4>	Family undertakings (maritime), domestic service, various <5>	Small factories <5>, agricultural undertakings other than tea plantations <3>
China	16	16	—	18	Family undertakings	—
Fiji	—	12 to 15 (by sector) <6>	No limit	16 to 18	Family undertakings, other exclusions possible <7>	Exclusion of ships allowed
India	14	14 <8>	—	18	Family undertakings, various <8>	Agriculture, commerce, etc. <8>
Indonesia	13	14 <9>	—	18	Various <9>	Various <9>
Iran	10	15	—	18	None	None
Iraq *	12	15	—	18	Family undertakings	None
Israel *	16	15	—	16 to 18	None	Agriculture, commerce
Japan	15	15	12	18	Family undertakings, domestic service	None
Jordan	15	13	—	15	Family undertakings, domestic service	Agriculture
Kuwait	14	14	—	18	Casual or temporary work, domestic service	None

Annex 1: Asia (continued)

Country	Compulsory education required to age	Minimum age			Exceptions to coverage	
		Basic minimum age	Light work	Dangerous work	Categories of work excluded	Sectors of activity excluded
Lao People's Democratic Republic	15	15	—	18	None	None
Lebanon	—	13	8	16	Family undertakings, domestic service	Non-commercial agriculture
Malaysia	14	14	No limit	16	None	None
Mongolia	16	16	—	18	None	Agriculture
Myanmar	10	13 <10>	—	15 to 18	Domestic service, self-employment	Agriculture, small factories <10>
Nepal	11	14 <11>	—	18	Various <11>	Agriculture, commerce, etc. <11>
New Zealand	15	15 <12>	—	15 to 21	None	Agriculture, commerce, etc. <13>
Pakistan	—	14 to 15 (by sector) <14>	—	16 to 21	Various <15>	Small factories, agriculture; other exceptions possible <15>
Papua New Guinea	—	14 to 16	—	16	Family undertakings <16>	None
Philippines	13	15	No limit	18	Family undertakings	None
Qatar	—	12	—	—	Family undertakings, domestic service	None
Saudi Arabia	—	13	—	18	Family undertakings, domestic service	Agriculture
Singapore	—	12 to 14 (by sector)	12	16 to 18	—	—
Solomon Islands	—	12 to 15 (by sector) <17>	No limit	16 to 18	Family undertakings	None

Annex 1: Asia (continued)

Country	Compulsory education required to age	Minimum age			Exceptions to coverage	
		Basic minimum age	Light work	Dangerous work	Categories of work excluded	Sectors of activity excluded
Sri Lanka	15	14 to 15 (by sector) <18>	No limit	16 to 18	Family undertakings	None
Syrian Arab Republic	11	12 to 13 (by sector) <19>	—	15	Family undertakings, domestic service	Small undertakings <19>
Thailand	15	12 <20>	12	15 to 18	Various <20>	Agriculture
United Arab Emirates	12	15 <21>	—	18	Family undertakings, domestic service	Agriculture, small undertakings <21>
Yemen	—	12	—	—	Domestic service, temporary work	Agriculture

<1> Applies only to industry, administrations and co-operatives.

<2> Regulations cover only work at sea (16 years). Certain states and territories impose a minimum age in certain sectors; others merely prohibit the employment of young persons during school hours.

<3> Minimum age of 12 for work in shops and on tea plantations; 14 for work in factories; and 15 for work at sea.

<4> 16 for work in factories with machinery in motion; 17 for mining; 18 for work at sea as trimmers and stokers.

<5> According to the size of the undertaking. The Factories Act governs all undertakings which employ or have employed at least ten workers during the previous 12 months. Regulations apply in particular to tea plantations with a surface area of more than 25 acres (ten hectares) which employ at least 30 workers.

<6> General minimum age is 12 years; 15 for work in industry.

<7> Determined by the competent authority.

<8> Minimum age applies only to designated occupations.

<9> Children below 14 may work with the permission of parents or guardians up to four hours a day.

<10> Applies only to certain factories (those where motive power is installed which employ less than ten workers, and those without motive power employing less than 20 workers are excluded), commerce, the merchant navy and mineworks.

Annex 1: Asia (continued)

<11> Minimum age applies only to factories. Exemptions of factories possible.

<12> Minimum age applies only to factories, work at sea, fishing and railways.

<13> No child may be eployed during school hours or where this hinders or prevents the child from attending school.

<14> Minimum age of 14 for work in factories, shops and commerce, and work at sea; 15 for work in mines and on railways.

<15> Legislation in factories applies only to those employing at least ten workers. The competent authority may authorise the exclusion of any region or establishment from the scope of legislation concerning commerce.

<16> Minimum age of 11 for family undertakings.

<17> General minimum age is 12 years; 15 for work in industry and at sea.

<18> General minimum age is 14 years; 15 for work at sea.

<19> General minimum age is 12 years; 13 for work in industry. Applies only to undertakings with more than ten employees.

<20> Minimum age applies only to employment relationships.

<21> Minimum age applies only to undertakings with more than five employees.

Annex 1: Europe

Country	Compulsory education required to age	Minimum age			Exceptions to coverage	
		Basic minimum age	Light work	Dangerous work	Categories of work excluded	Sectors of activity excluded
Albania	13	15	—	18	Domestic service, etc. <1>	Agriculture, commerce, etc. <1>
Austria	15	15	12 <2>	16 to 18	Domestic service	None
Belgium *	18	14 <3>	—	16 to 21	Domestic service	None
Bulgaria *	16	16	15	18	None	None
Cyprus	15	13 to 16 (by sector) <4>	No limit	16 to 18	Family undertakings, domestic service	Agriculture
Czechoslovakia	16	16	—	18	None	None
Denmark	15	15	10 to 13 (according to the work)	16 to 18	Self-employment	None
Finland *	16	15 <3>	14	16 to 18	Home work	None
France *	16	16 <3>	12 to 14	16 to 18	Family undertakings	None
Germany *	18	15 <5>	13	18	None	None
Greece *	15	15	—	16 to 18	Family undertakings (agriculture only)	None
Hungary	16	15 <3>	14	16 to 18	None	None
Iceland	15	15 <6>	14	18 to 19	Domestic work, home work, self-employment, etc. <6>	Agriculture, commerce, etc. <6>
Ireland *	15	15 <3>	14	18	Exclusions possible <7>	Agriculture
Italy *	13	14 or 15 (by sector) <8>	14	15 to 18	None	None
Luxembourg *	15	15 <3>	—	18	None	None

Annex 1: Europe (continued)

Country	Compulsory education required to age	Minimum age			Exceptions to coverage	
		Basic minimum age	Light work	Dangerous work	Categories of work excluded	Sectors of activity excluded
Malta *	16	15 to 16 (by sector) <9>	—	18	Family undertakings	None
Netherlands *	16	15	13 to 15	18	None	None
Norway *	15	15 to 16 (by sector) <10>	13	18	None	None
Poland *	14	15	15	18	None	None
Portugal	14	14	—	18	None	None
Romania *	16	16	—	16 to 18	None	None
Spain *	15	16	—	18	None	None
Sweden *	16	16	13	18	None	None
Switzerland	15	15	13	16 to 18	Family undertakings, domestic service	Agriculture
Turkey	14	15	13	18	Family undertakings, domestic service, home work and janitorial services	Agriculture
United Kingdom	16	13 to 16 (by sector) <11>	—	16 to 18	None	None
USSR *	17	16	—	18	None	None
Yugoslavia *	15	15	—	18	None	None

Annex 1: Europe (continued)

<1> Minimum age applies only to enterprises, institutions and handicraft co-operative societies.

<2> No minimum age in agriculture.

<3> Provided compulsory schooling has been completed.

<4> General minimum age is 13 years; 14 for work in industry; 16 for work at sea (except vessels where only members of a single family are employed).

<5> Child must have completed compulsory schooling. Minimum age applied not only to employment relationships, but to all work, including the self-employed.

<6> Minimum age applies only to factories and transport. The child must have also completed compulsory schooling.

<7> Determined by the competent authorities on condition that well-being, safety and health are not endangered.

<8> General minimum age is 15 years; 14 for work in agriculture or to assist the family.

<9> General minimum age is 16 years; 15 for work on ships.

<10> General minimum age is 15 years and the completion of compulsory schooling. 16 to work in merchant shipping.

<11> General minimum age is 13 years; 16 for work in industry. Children below the age of 16 may not work during school hours or for more than two hours a day.

Annex 2: Legislative provisions for light work by minors

Definition of light work	Minimum age	Country
General, i.e. not restricted to any particular sectors	15	Bulgaria <1, 9, 13, 14>
	14	Antigua and Barbuda, Botswana <1, 2, 10, 11, 12, 19>, Chile <1, 2, 9 or 15, 17>, Finland <8, 13, 14, 20>, France <20>, Hungary <20>, Iceland, Tunisia <1, 2, 5, 7>, Zaire <1, 2, 23>
	13	Cyprus <11, 15>, Equatorial Guinea <1, 2>, Germany <1, 8, 17, 21>, Norway <1, 2, 15>, Sweden <1, 2>, Thailand <15>, Turkey <1, 2>
	12	Brazil <1, 2>, Burundi <1, 2, 12, 15, 16>, Colombia <9, 15, 23>, Cyprus <6, 11, 15>, France <1, 2, 11>, Malawi <15>, Singapore <13>, Somalia <1, 22>, Uganda <15>
	None	Malaysia <7, 11, 12>, Philippines <1, 2>
Light work of a non-industrial nature	15	Netherlands <2>
	14	Ireland <2>, Italy <1, 2>
	13	Switzerland <1, 2, 6, 8>, Tunisia <1, 2>, United Kingdom <1, 2, 6, 8>
	12	Chad <9, 15>, Central African Republic <9, 13, 15>, Congo <9, 15>, Japan <2, 7, 9>, Mali <15, 23>, Niger <2, 6, 7, 15>, Thailand <16>, Uruguay <15, 17, 18>
	8	Lebanon
	None	Jamaica <11>, Solomon Islands <11, 15>
Non-agricultural work, occasional, light assistance, of short duration and not equivalent to that of an employee	12	Austria <1, 2, 5, 6, 7, 8, 9>, Seychelles
Light agricultural, horticultural or plantation work	13	Germany <2, 8, 9, 24, 25>, Netherlands <6>
	12	Benin, Burkina Faso, Burundi <1, 2, 9, 12, 16>, Cape Verde, Central African Republic <9, 13, 15>, Congo <1, 9, 15>, Côte d'Ivoire <9, 23>, Equatorial Guinea <15>, Fiji <4>, Guinea Bissau, Mali <15, 23>, Niger <2, 6, 7>, Nigeria <11, 15>, Panama <2, 15>, Paraguay <1, 2, 7, 9, 13, 15, 23>, Sao Tome and Principe
	10	Denmark, Tanzania <8, 11, 15, 23>
	None	Austria <1, 4>, Belize <4>, Ghana <11>, Jamaica <11>, Saint Lucia <4>, Sierra Leone <6, 8, 11, 15>, Sri Lanka <4, 11>, United Kingdom <1, 2, 6, 8>
Domestic service	14	Botswana <1, 12>, Italy <1, 2, 4>
	12	Benin, Belize, Burkina Faso, Burundi <1, 2, 9, 12>, Central African Republic <9, 13, 15>, Chad <9, 15>, Congo <9, 15>, Côte d'Ivoire, Haiti <15>, Jamaica <11>, Mali <15, 23>, Niger <2, 6, 7>, Nigeria <11, 15>, Panama <2, 15>
	None	Sierra Leone <6, 8, 11, 15>
	Not covered by legislation	Afghanistan, Albania, Algeria, Antigua and Barbuda, Austria, Bahamas, Bahrain, Bangladesh, Cape Verde, Comoros, Costa Rica, Dominica, Ecuador, Egypt, India, Japan, Jordan, Kenya, Kuwait, Lebanon, Lesotho, Libyan Arab Jamahiriya, Malawi, Myanmar, Namibia, Nepal, Nicaragua, Pakistan, Peru, Qatar, Sao Tome and Principe, Saudi Arabia, Swaziland, Turkey, United Arab Emirates, Venezuela, Zambia

Annex 2: Legislative provisions for light work by minors (continued)

Definition of light work	Minimum age	Country
Shop assistants, work in laundries, ticketing goods, kiosks, bakeries, green-grocers, packing and sorting light articles, newspaper sale and delivery	15	Netherlands <2, 5>
	13	Denmark <6, 14>
Seasonal and intermittent work	15	Poland <15>
	12	Senegal <9>

<1> Work must not expose the minor to risk of accident, endanger physical or mental health or development, or jeopardise morals.

<2> Work must not interfere with school instruction/not during school hours.

<3> Not in industry, commerce or commercial agriculture.

<4> Only on parents' or guardians' lands, gardens or plantation.

<5> No work on weekly rest day or religious or statutory holidays.

<6> Work must not exceed two hours a day.

<7> Combined school and work hours must not exceed seven in any day.

<8> No work between 20:00 and 08:00/19:00 and 06:00, or similar time periods.

<9> Consent of a parent or guardian is required.

<10> Domestic service only where suitable accommodation is provided.

<11> Work allowed if performed for a member of the family, in a family undertaking or under parental supervision.

<12> No more than six hours a day or 30 hours a week.

<13> Medical examination required, either before acceptance for employment or on a regular basis during employment.

<14> Must have an interruption of at least 12 or 14 hours between days of work.

<15> Work must be authorised by the labour inspector or appropriate authority.

<16> Weight limits imposed for loads which may be lifted by minors.

<17> Provided compulsory schooling has been completed.

<18> Work is essential to the existence of the family.

<19> Child must return each night to parents' or guardians' residence.

<20> Work to be done only during school holidays and for a restricted time during the holidays.

<21> Light work up to seven hours a day and 35 hours a week.

<22> Work must be essential to the learning of the trade/apprenticeship.

<23> Work must not exceed four or four-and-a-half hours a day.

<24> No work before school on school days.

<25> Work must not exceed three hours a day.

Annex 3: Hazardous occupations and industries

Note: The information given in this table may not reflect completely and in detail the situations in the countries listed below. It is intended only to give a general picture. Some countries that cover the listed hazardous occupations or industries in their minimum age legislation may not be mentioned here, in particular if coverage is provided by a general prohibition of all types of employment or work which jeopardises the health, safety or morals of young persons.

Occupation/ Industry	Hazards	Minimum age	Country
Abattoirs and meat rendering	Injuries from cuts, burns, falls, dangerous equipment; exposure to infectious disease; heat stress	18	Central African Republic, Congo, Finland, Gabon, Luxembourg <1>, Togo, United States, Zaire
		16	Bahrain, Lebanon <2>
Acids (work with)	Risk of burns, inhalation of toxic fumes, eye injuries	18	Angola <1>, Austria, Bolivia, Cameroon, Chad, Colombia <1>, Congo, Cyprus, Denmark <1>, France, Germany, Spain <7>, Sudan, Togo
		16	Bahrain, Honduras, Mexico
Agriculture	Unsafe machinery; hazardous substances; accidents; chemical poisoning; arduous work; dangerous animals, insects and reptiles	21	Uruguay
		18	Colombia <1, 4>, Costa Rica <4>, Spain <4, 7>
		17	Australia (Queensland) <3>
		16 or 18	France <4, 5>
		16	Denmark <4>, United Kingdom <4>, United States <3, 4>
Alcohol production and/or sale	Intoxication, addiction; environment may be prejudicial to morals; risk of violence	21	Chile
		18	Argentina, Australia (Victoria), Bolivia, Brazil, Burundi, Cameroon, Colombia, Costa Rica, Dominican Republic, Ecuador, Equatorial Guinea, Haiti, Italy, Luxembourg, Mexico, Panama, Peru, Portugal, Spain <7>, Swaziland, Venezuela, Zaire
		16	Guatemala, Honduras, Mexico
		15	Jamaica, Thailand
Carpet weaving	Dust inhalation, poor lighting, poor posture (squatting); respiratory and musculo-skeletal disease; eye strain; chemical poisoning	14	India
Cement	Harmful chemicals, exposure to harmful dust; arduous work; respiratory and musculo-skeletal disease	18	Angola <1>, Cameroon, Colombia <1>
		14	India

Annex 3: Hazardous occupations and industries (continued)

Occupation/ Industry	Hazards	Minimum age	Country
Circular saws and other dangerous machines	Accidents (loss of limb or life, danger from unprotected moving parts)	18	Argentina, Australia (Victoria), Austria, Bolivia, Cameroon <1>, Colombia <1>, Denmark <1>, Djijouti, Ecuador, France, Gabon, India, Luxembourg, Madagascar, Mauritius, Nepal, Peru, Saudi Arabia, Spain, Trinidad and Tobago, United States, Zaire
		17	Pakistan
		16	Burkina Faso, Chad, Central African Republic, Congo, Malaysia <1>, Senegal, United Kingdom
Construction and/or demolition	Exposure to heat, cold, dust; falling objects; sharp objects; accidents; musculo-skeletal diseases	18	Austria, Bolivia, Burundi, Colombia <1, 11>, El Salvador, France, Gabon, Luxembourg, Madagascar <11>, Netherlands, Peru <11>, Spain <7>, United States
		16	Bahrain, Barbados, Burkina Faso <11>, Cameroon <11>, Central African Republic, Chad, Congo, Côte d'Ivoire <11>, Djibouti <11>, France, Kenya, Morocco, Senegal <11>, Somalia, United Kingdom
		15	Dominica, Jamaica
		14	Belize, Cyprus, India
Cranes/hoists /lifting machinery	Accidents; falling objects; musculo-skeletal diseases; risk of injury to others	18	Argentina, Austria, Canada, Central African Republic, Chad, Colombia <1>, Congo, Gabon, Japan, Luxembourg, Madagascar, Mauritius, Netherlands, United States, Zaire
		16	Bahrain, Denmark, France, Israel
Crystal and/or glass manufacture	Molten glass; extreme heat; poor ventilation; cuts from broken glass; carrying hot glass; burns; respiratory disease; heat stress; toxic dust	18	Angola <1>, Argentina, Austria, Bolivia, Cameroon, Côte d'Ivoire, Colombia <1>, Cyprus (women), Denmark <1>, Djibouti, Ecuador, Ireland, Madagascar, Senegal
		17	Austria <4>
		16 to 18	France <4, 5>
		16	Bahrain
		15	Syrian Arab Republic
Domestic service	Long hours; physical, emotional, sexual abuse; malnutrition; insufficient rest; isolation	16	Denmark
Electricity	Dangerous work with high voltage; risk of falling; high level of responsibility for safety of others	18	Angola <1>, Cameroon, Colombia <1>, France, Panama, Sweden, Uruguay, Zaire
		16	Bahrain, Mexico
		15	Dominica, Jamaica
		14	Belize

Annex 3: Hazardous occupations and industries (continued)

Occupation/ Industry	Hazards	Minimum age	Country
Entertain-ment (night clubs, bars, casinos, circuses, gambling halls)	Long, late hours; sexual abuse; exploitation; prejudical to morals	21	Chile, Seychelles (casinos), Uruguay
		18	Angola, Austria, Bolivia, Brazil, Burundi, Cameroon, Colombia, Ecuador, El Salvador, Italy, Luxembourg, Panama, Peru, Philippines, Seychelles, Switzerland
		16	France, Honduras
		15	Thailand
Explosives (manufacture and handling)	Risk of explosion, fire, burns, mortal danger	18	Angola <1>, Austria, Bolivia, Belgium, Burundi, Cameroon, Chad, Colombia <1>, Congo, Costa Rica, Côte d'Ivoire, Cyprus, Denmark <1>, Djibouti, Ecuador, El Salvador, Equatorial Guinea, Finland, France, Japan, Lao People's Democratic Republic, Luxembourg, Madagascar, Netherlands, Panama, Peru, Philippines, Portugal, Senegal, Spain <7>, Sweden, Switzerland, Thailand, Togo, United States, Zaire
		17	Canada (Federal)
		16	Bahrain, Dominican Republic, Honduras, Mexico, Morocco
		14	India
Fumes, dust, gas and other noxious substances	Chemical poisoning; damage to eyes; damage to respiratory system; poisoning	18	Angola <1>, Austria <1>, Bolivia, Colombia <1>, Congo, Czechoslovakia <1>, Denmark <1>, Ecuador, El Salvador, France, Germany <1>, Japan, Lao Peoples' Democratic Republic, Luxembourg, Madagascar, Netherlands, Nicaragua, Peru, Portugal, Spain <7>, Sudan, Sweden, Switzerland, Thailand, Togo
		17	Cuba
		16	Bahrain, Honduras, Mexico, Morocco, United Kingdom
		14	India
Hospitals and work with risk of infection	Infectious diseases; responsibility for well-being of others	18	Austria, Bangladesh, Czechoslovakia <1>, Luxembourg, Madagascar, Netherlands, Spain, Switzerland
		17	Israel <12>

Annex 3: Hazardous occupations and industries (continued)

Occupation/ Industry	Hazards	Minimum age	Country
Lead/zinc metallurgy; white lead; lead in paint	Cumulative poisoning; neurological damage	21	Uruguay
		18	Australia (Queensland, Victoria), Austria, Barbados, Belgium, Bolivia, Cameroon, Colombia <1>, Cyprus, Czechoslovakia <1>, Denmark <1>, Djibouti, Ecuador, France, Gabon, Germany, Ireland, Madagascar, Malta, Norway, Sudan, Sweden, Syrian Arab Republic, Togo, Zaire
		16	Bahrain, Greece (lead accumulators), Honduras, Mexico, United Kingdom
		15	Syrian Arab Republic
Machinery in motion (operation, cleaning, repairs, etc.)	Danger from moving engine parts; accidents; cuts, burns, exposure to heat and noise; noise stress; eye and ear injuries	21	Uruguay
		18	Argentina, Austria <1>, Bolivia, Burundi, Cameroon, Central African Republic, Colombia, Chad, Congo, Côte d'Ivoire, Cyprus, Denmark <1>, Djibouti, Dominica, Domincan Republic, El Salvador, Equatorial Guinea, France, Gabon, Greece, India, Ireland, Japan, Luxembourg, Madagascar, Malawi, Malta, Mauritius, Myanmar, Netherlands, Peru, Saudi Arabia, Spain, Sweden, Switzerland, Thailand, Zaire, Zambia
		17	Pakistan
		16	Bahrain, Bangladesh, Djibouti, Guyana, Jamaica, Malaysia <1>, Morocco, Nigeria, Saint Lucia, Senegal, Singapore, United Kingdom
		15	Italy <14>, Syrian Arab Republic
Maritime work (trimmers and stokers, stevedoring)	Accidents; heat, burns; falls from heights; heavy lifting, arduous work, musculo-skeletal disease; respiratory diseases	21	Brazil <10>
		19	Denmark <1>, Iceland
		18	Algeria, Argentina, Australia, Bahamas, Bangladesh, Belgium, Belize <6>, Burundi, China, Congo, Côte d'Ivoire, Djibouti, Ecuador, El Salvador, Fiji, Gabon, Iraq, Ireland, Japan, Kenya, Liberia, Luxembourg, Malawi, Malta, Myanmar, Nigeria <6>, Pakistan <6>, Peru, Philippines, Romania, Sierra Leone <6>, Singapore, Solomon Islands, Somalia, Sri Lanka, Sudan, Tanzania, Trinidad and Tobago, Tunisia, Yugoslavia, Zaire
		17	Canada (Federal), Cuba <10>

Annex 3: Hazardous occupations and industries (continued)

Occupation/ Industry	Hazards	Minimum age	Country
Mining, quarries, underground work	Exposure to dusts, gases, fumes, dirty conditions; respiratory and musculo-skeletal diseases; accidents; falling objects; arduous work; heavy loads	21	Brazil
		18	Afghanistan, Albania, Angola <1>, Argentina, Australia (South and Western), Austria <1>, Belgium, Bolivia, Botswana, Burundi, Byelorussian SSR, Cameroon <1>, Cape Verde, Central African Republic, Chad, Chile, Colombia <1>, Congo, Cuba, Cyprus <13>, Czechoslovakia <1>, Denmark <1>, Djibouti, Dominican Republic, Ecuador, El Salvador, Equatorial Guinea, Fiji, France, Gabon, Germany <1>, Ghana, Greece, Guinea Bissau, India, Indonesia, Iraq, Ireland, Israel, Italy, Japan, Jordan, Lao People's Democratic Republic, Luxembourg, Nicaragua, Panama, Peru, Philippines, Portugal, Sao Tome and Principe, Saudi Arabia, Somalia, Sudan, Swaziland, Switzerland, Tanzania, Thailand, Tunisia, Turkey, United States, USSR, Venezuela, Yugoslavia, Zaire, Zambia
		17	Australia (Victoria), Bangladesh, Canada (Federal), Jamaica, Myanmar <15>, Pakistan
		16	Bahrain, Barbados, Burkina Faso, Côte d'Ivoire, Hungary, Kenya, Lesotho <2>, Mexico, Nicaragua, Nigeria, Sierra Leone <2>, Singapore, Solomon Islands <2>, United Kingdom
		15	Dominica, Syrian Arab Republic
		14	Belize, Cyprus <13>
Radioactive substances or ionising radiation (work with)	Radiation	18	Argentina, Austria <1>, Belgium, Colombia <1>, Czechoslovakia <1>, Denmark <1>, Finland, France, Germany, India, Lao People's Democratic Republic, Luxembourg, Malta, Netherlands, Panama, Philippines, Sudan, Thailand, United States
		17	Canada (Federal)
		16	Bahrain, Guyana, Honduras, United Kingdom
Rubber	Heat, burns, chemical poisoning	18	Angola <1>, Cyprus
		16	Mexico

Annex 3: Hazardous occupations and industries (continued)

Occupation/ Industry	Hazards	Minimum age	Country
Street trades	Exposure to drugs, violence, criminal activities; heavy loads; musculo-skeletal diseases; venereal diseases; accidents	18	Austria, Bolivia, Brazil, Peru <7>
		16	Burkina Faso, Cyprus, Djibouti (women), Dominican Republic, Italy, United Kingdom
		15	Costa Rica <14>
		14	Sri Lanka
Tanneries	Chemical poisoning; sharp instruments; respiratory diseases	18	Chad, France, Gabon, Zaire
		17	Austria
		16	Dominican Republic, Mexico
		15	Syrian Arab Republic
		14	India
Tar, asphalt, bitumen	Exposure to heat, burns; chemical poisoning; respiratory diseases	18	Angola <1>, Czechoslovakia <1>, Luxembourg
		15	Syrian Arab Republic
Transportation, operating vehicles	Accidents; danger to self and passengers	18	Austria, Burundi, Central African Republic, Chad, Congo, Denmark <1>, Equatorial Guinea, Gabon, Pakistan <9>, Panama, Peru, Philippines, Spain <7>, United States, Zaire
		16	Barbados, Dominican Republic, Israel, Kenya, United Kingdom
		15	Dominica, Jamaica
		14	Belize, Cyprus
Underwater	Decompression illness; dangerous fish; death or injury	18	Austria, Colombia <1>, El Salvador, Lao People's Democratic Republic, Sudan, Sweden, Thailand, Turkey
		16	Dominican Republic, Mexico
Weights and loads <8>	Physical stress and strain; musculo-skeletal diseases	14 to 18	Australia (Victoria), Belgium, Belize, Bolivia, Botswana, Burkina Faso, Burundi, Cameroon, Central African Republic, Chad, Congo, Côte d'Ivoire, Cuba, Cyprus, Czechoslovakia, Djibouti, Ecuador, Gabon, India, Israel, Italy, Niger, Spain, Switzerland, Ukrainian SSR, Uruguay, USSR, Zaire
Welding and smelting of metals, metalworking	Exposure to extreme heat; flying sparks and hot metal objects; accidents; eye injuries; heat stress	18	Argentina, Austria <1>, Bolivia, Cameroon, Colombia <1>, Ecuador, Luxembourg, Spain <7>, Sudan, Sweden, United States
		16	Bahrain

Annex 3: Hazardous occupations and industries (continued)

<1> Except for apprenticeships.

<2> Medical certificate required.

<3> Application of agricultural chemicals (minimum age of 17 in Queensland, Australia; 16 in the United States).

<4> For specified tasks only.

<5> Different minimum age depending on the type of work.

<6> Where a person over 18 is unavailable for a trimmer and stoker position, this position may be filled by two 16-year-olds.

<7> Minimum age of 18 for men, 21 for women.

<8> Provision is made in legislation for maximum loads per age grouping.

<9> Minimum age of 21 in road transport services requiring the driving of a vehicle.

<10> Applies only to stevedoring.

<11> Applies only to work on scaffolding.

<12> Applies only to work involving contact with tubercolosis, leprosy or mental patients.

<13> Minimum age of 18 for underground work; 14 for other work in mines, quarries, etc.

<14> Minimum age of 15 for men, 18 for women (applies to street trades in Costa Rica for unmarried women only).

<15> Minimum age of 17 for underground work; 15 for other work in mines, quarries, etc.

Part III

International labour standards and their implementation

Part III

International labour standards and their implementation

by

H.T. Dao[1]

This part of the Digest is divided into three main sections. The first contains a review of the standards that have been adopted by the ILO for the protection of children (see also Part VI which reproduceds the most basic ILO standards); the second outlines the unique and effective procedures and machinery that have been set up within the ILO to supervise the implementation of these standards.

The third and longest section examines cases in which violations of the minimum age and forced labour Conventions have been noted. A description is given of cases in which the Committee of Experts for the Application of Conventions and Recommendations has noted with satisfaction changes in national legislation or enforcement that have made it possible to overcome problems in the application of ratified Conventions.

The final section also includes a more detailed description of a number of current cases of violations of minimum age standards in industry and agriculture and, in particular, situations in which children are the victims of bonded labour and other forms of forced labour. These examples, in which action has not yet been taken to give full effect to the Conventions in question, offer a fascinating glimpse of one way in which the ILO's system of standards instigates change at the national level.

*

*   *

1 Former Chief of the Application of Standards Branch and Co-ordinator for Human Rights Questions, International Labour Office.

Introduction

The struggle against child labour cannot be won only through legislative action, but it certainly cannot be fought without it.

The legal provisions on minimum age for admission to employment in countries of all regions and at all stages of development have one thing in common: they probably owe something to the standards set by the ILO in its international labour Conventions and Recommendations concerning the protection of children.

This is hardly surprising given the unique record of long-standing and intensive international legislative action undertaken by the ILO since its creation in 1919. The body of standards making up the International Labour Code currently comprises 172 Conventions and 179 Recommendations, of which over 40 instruments are concerned with, or include provisions for, the protection of children and young persons[2].

Furthermore, there are certain characteristics of the ILO system of standards, including various built-in procedures, which are conducive to its influence on national law and practice. In the first place, ILO Conventions and Recommendations as international instruments are not merely the brain-child of legal experts, but are the result of joint efforts through the various stages of preparation, discussion and finally adoption at the International Labour Conference by the ILO tripartite constituency made up of governments, employers' and workers' organisations. Member States are then required to submit Conventions and Recommendations, within a maximum of 18 months of their adoption by the Conference, to the national authorities competent to take implementing action, i.e. as a rule, the national Parliament. An ILO Convention, once ratified, takes on the binding force of an international treaty, and its application is the subject of periodic government reports and of ILO supervision. Member States are also required to report, when so requested by the ILO Governing Body, on the position of their national law and practice in respect of Conventions that they have not ratified and of Recommendations.

Another channel through which ILO standards can reach their national destinations is through technical co-operation projects, which must as a rule refer to relevant Conventions and Recommendations as guidelines, particularly, but not only, when they involve the drafting of legislation.

While there is a variety of ways in which ILO standards can exert influence, the ratification of Conventions and the record of their application as established by ILO supervision remain the most readily available and reliable gauges. The total of 5,541 ratifications of ILO Conventions registered as of 15 July 1991 -- including over 400 ratifications of Conventions concerning the protection of children -- and the findings of the ILO supervisory bodies as regards problems and progress in their application, provide objective information as to the law and practice of countries in the fields concerned.

The position as regards child labour will be reviewed below on the basis of such information.

---

2 See Classified guide to international labour standards, document APPL 10(1991), issued each year. See also Annex 1.

ILO standards for the protection of children

The protection of children was one of the priority tasks set for the new Organisation by the Preamble of the ILO Constitution of 1919. Accordingly, at its very first session in October 1919, the International Labour Conference adopted two Conventions, respectively on minimum age and night work of young persons in industry, and one Recommendation concerning the protection of women and young persons against lead poisoning.

A total of 18 Conventions and eight Recommendations now deal with minimum age, night work and the medical examination of young persons in various sectors of activity. Five Conventions and three Recommendations dealing with occupational safety and health contain provisions on minimum age and conditions of employment of children in hazardous work. Provisions on minimum age linked with schooling are also included in two Conventions on social policy and one Recommendation on unemployment of young persons. Annex 1 gives the complete list of these instruments.

In addition, other measures for the protection of children contained in ILO instruments include the limitation of hours of work and of overtime; compulsory minimum period of night rest, and longer weekly rest and holidays with pay; fair remuneration and protection of wages; and social security coverage. In the field of employment and training, special attention is given to the needs of young persons[3].

Children are also entitled, as dependent persons, to appropriate protection under ILO instruments on social security.

In addition to the ILO standards laying down measures of special protection, children and young persons are of course also entitled to the benefit without distinction from standards laid down in ILO instruments which are applicable to all workers in general.

---

[3] The relevant instruments and provisions are given below:

- Limitation of hours of work and of overtime: Reduction of Hours of Work Recommendation, 1962 (No. 116), Paragraphs 9 and 18; Minimum Age Recommendation, 1973 (No. 146), Paragraph 13(1)(b); Protection of Young Seafarers Recommendation, 1976 (No. 153), Part IV.

- Minimum night rest and weekly rest: Minimum Age Recommendation, 1973 (No. 146), Paragraph 13(1)(c); Wages, Hours of Work and Manning (Sea) Convention (Revised), 1958 (No. 109), Article 20; Protection of Young Seafarers Recommendation, 1976 (No. 153), Part IV.

- Longer weekly rest and holidays with pay: Holidays with Pay Recommendation, 1936 (No. 47), Paragraph 5; Conditions of Employment of Young Persons (Underground Work) Recommendation, 1965 (No. 125), Part II; Minimum Age Recommendation, 1973 (No. 146), Paragraph 13(1)(d).

- Fair remuneration, protection of wages and social security: Minimum Age Recommendation, 1973 (No. 146), Paragraph 13(1)(a) and (e); Protection of Young Seafarers Recommendation, 1976 (No. 153), Part IV.

- Employment and training: Unemployment (Young Persons) Recommendation, 1935 (No. 45); Employment Policy Recommendation, 1964 (No. 122), Paragraph 15; Special Youth Schemes Recommendation, 1970 (No. 136); Human Resources Development Recommendation, 1975 (No. 150), Paragraphs 7(1), 8(1)(a), 9(1)(a) and (b), 16(a), 18 and 41(b); Employment Policy (Supplementary Provisions) Recommendation, 1984 (No. 169), Part III.

Under the ILO standards dealing specifically with children, the basic protection, which conditions all other measures, is no doubt the requirement of a suitable minimum age for admission to employment.

Among ILO standards of general application, the prohibition of forced or compulsory labour, under the terms of the Forced Labour Convention, 1930 (No. 29), and the Abolition of Forced Labour Convention, 1957 (No. 105), constitutes a basic human right, although the infringement of this right is unfortunately not infrequent even where children are concerned. As will be seen, it is under Convention No. 29 (which, with 129 ratifications, is the most ratified ILO Convention, followed closely by Convention No. 105, which is in fifth position with 109 ratifications) that the most serious problems of exploitation of children, through debt bondage and other "contemporary forms of slavery", are examined by the ILO supervisory bodies, in close co-operation with the United Nations and other bodies concerned.

This review of the situation as regards child labour will accordingly focus on the two aspects of minimum age and forced labour.

Situation as to ratification

The ratification figures for Conventions dealing specifically with the protection of children and young persons are given in Annex 2, with more detailed indications concerning the minimum age Conventions (particularly Convention No. 138 which consolidates and revises all ten earlier instruments on minimum age). Annex 3 provides additional information on the levels of minimum age set in the relevant Conventions.

The ratification figures given in Table 2 show a cumulative total of 108 ratifications for the ILO standards on minimum age in industry (taking into account denunciations of earlier Conventions on the same subject, following the ratification of revising Conventions). This impressive number puts the relevant standards in the bracket of 100 plus ratifications reached by fundamental instruments such as the Conventions on forced labour, freedom of association, discrimination and labour inspection. These are closely followed by the standards on minimum age for general employment at sea, with 101 ratifications in force (taking into account the fact that a number of countries have no or negligible maritime activities). This large degree of acceptance for these two groups of standards reflects the fact that the "organised" sectors, such as industry and maritime activity, are more amenable to labour regulation and supervision in respect of minimum age than the "informal" sectors.

The reasonable figure of 71 ratifications has been achieved for the standards on minimum age in agriculture. The flexibility of Convention No. 10, which excludes family undertakings and work outside school hours, has no doubt facilitated its ratification. Convention No. 138 also provides for the exemption of such undertakings, as well as light work, under certain conditions.

There are only 60 ratifications, however, of minimum age standards for non-industrial employment. One reason may be that the non-industrial sector comprises most "informal" activities which are often left outside the scope of national measures for labour protection because of difficulties of both a regulatory and a supervisory nature.

ILO procedures and machinery for supervising the implementation of standards

The ILO system of standards is cohesive and comprehensive because it not only provides for the adoption of Conventions and Recommendations, but also lays down specific standards-related obligations and, more important still, procedures for supervising their compliance. These include both regular procedures based on periodic reporting by member States and contentious procedures based on the submission of complaints. The supervisory machinery developed by the ILO over the years is considered to be among the most advanced and effective of its kind.

The bulk of the supervisory work consists of monitoring the application of ratified Conventions through the regular procedures, which are based on government reports. This work is carried out by the standing supervisory machinery, which is comprised of two bodies that have both been functioning since 1927.

Technical evaluation by the Committee of Experts

The Committee of Experts on the Application of Conventions and Recommendations is entrusted with the technical evaluation of reports supplied by governments. This independent examination by a body of 20 experts serving in a personal capacity and predominantly composed of distinguished academics and high-level members of the judiciary, is designed to obtain an impartial, objective assessment of compliance with obligations.

In making its evaluation, the Committee takes into account legislation and other official documents, as well as information from ILO missions and technical co-operation projects. Observations from employers and workers' organisations are given careful consideration. There is also close co-operation with other bodies of the UN system and, as regards child labour, more particularly with the Working Group on Contemporary Forms of Slavery of the UN Sub-Commission on Prevention of Discrimination and Protection of Minorities.

The Committee of Experts meets in March each year and addresses its findings to governments, either in the form of "direct requests" or, in the more serious and persistent cases, in the form of "observations", which are published in the Committee's annual report[4].

Tripartite review by Conference Committee

The technical findings of the Committee of Experts contained in its report then form the basis of a tripartite review by the Committee on the Application of Standards, which is set up each year by, and reports to, the International Labour Conference. The "Conference Committee" selects from the Committee of Expert's report individual country cases which are deemed to require discussion, with the participation of representatives of the governments concerned. Employers' and workers' members of the Committee take full part in the proceedings on an equal footing with representatives

---

4 See Report III (Part 4A) to each session of the International Labour Conference: Report of the Committee of Experts on the Application of Conventions and Recommendations.

of governments. In making its conclusions, according to a practice which commenced in 1957, the Committee may decide to mention certain cases in special paragraphs and under special headings of its report, in order to draw attention to serious problems. The record of discussion of the cases, including the conclusions of the Committee, are published in its report[5].

The two standing supervisory committees referred to above also follow up decisions resulting from complaint procedures involving the application of ratified Conventions.

Some pointers concerning wording and procedures

Certain wording and procedures are used in the work of the Committee of Experts and of the Conference Committee to indicate cases which call for special attention.

Footnotes to observations by the Committee of Experts. The government may be asked to "report in detail" in the same year and/or "to supply full particulars to the Conference" at its coming session (the latter request is an indication to the Conference Committee to consider such a case for discussion).

Direct contacts. Under this procedure, which was initiated in 1969, a representative of the Director-General of the ILO visits a country at the request of the government concerned, to establish "direct contacts" with the competent bodies and services with a view to finding solutions to serious problems of application. (The Committee of Experts reviewed the first ten years of this procedure in its 1979 report. Subsequent reports of the Committee of Experts include indications on any further developments.)

Special listing and special paragraphs by the Conference Committee. According to a practice that commenced in 1957, the Conference Committee may decide after discussion of a case to draw attention to it in a special paragraph of its general report, or to list it under the heading "continued failure to implement".

Cases of progress. Since 1964, the Committee of Experts has also listed in its reports cases where the Committee, in the relevant observations, "notes with satisfaction" measures taken by the governments concerned following the Committee's previous comments to ensure better compliance with ratified Conventions. A total of 1,898 such cases has been listed since 1964.

The Conference Committee may also decide to note with satisfaction cases of progress and to list certain selected cases under the relevant heading of its report.

---

5 See for each session of the International Labour Conference: Record of Proceedings: Report of the Committee on the Application of Standards.

The work of the Committee of Experts and the Conference Committee, 1964-1991

The following facts and figures highlight the work of the Committee of Experts and the Conference Committee. The years 1964-1991 have been chosen as a period of reference because the listing of cases of progress by the Committee of Experts, which commenced in 1964, makes it easier to illustrate the impact of ILO standards and the effectiveness of the supervisory procedures.

Pending Committee of Expert comments concerning current child labour issues. Minimum age Conventions: 41 observations and direct requests; medical examination Conventions: 24 observations and direct requests; night work Conventions: 9 observations and direct requests; occupational safety and health Conventions: 9 observations and direct requests; forced labour Conventions: 13 observations and direct requests; total: 96 comments addressed to 68 countries.

Cases of progress concerning child labour noted by the Committee of Experts, 1964-1991: 170 cases, out of the total of 1,890 cases of progress in all areas which have been listed.

Cases concerning child labour discussed by the Conference Committee, 1964-1991: 79. Cases of progress listed by the Committee of Experts (as regards Conventions dealing specifically with children or young persons): 30.

Problems and progress in the application of standards
(an overview 1964-1991)

The examples given below, which are selected from cases examined by the Committee of Experts and the Conference Committee over the reference period 1964-1991, are intended to illustrate (i) the types of problems respecting child labour encountered under the relevant Conventions, the progress noted over the years and the serious difficulties that are still outstanding; and (ii) the working of the Committee of Experts and the Conference Committee through its special formulations and procedures (footnotes to observations, direct contacts, and the special list and paragraphs).

The cases will be reviewed under the following headings:

A. Cases of progress following discussion by the Conference Committee

B. Other cases of progress (by type of problem): coverage of minimum age and other provisions; unhealthy and hazardous work; light work; night work; annual medical examination; keeping of records

C. Outstanding difficulties still under examination: child labour in general; child labour under the forced labour Conventions (Nos. 29 and 105)

A. Cases of progress following discussion by the Conference Committee

1. Italy: Conventions Nos. 77, 78, 79 and 90

In 1964, the Committee of Experts, in its observations under the relevant Conventions, urged the Government to adopt legislation to ensure the application of the Conventions. The observations carried a footnote asking the Government to "supply full particulars to the Conference" at its coming session and "to report in detail for the period ending 30 June 1964".

In its 1964 discussion of these cases, the Conference Committee expressed the hope that national legislation would be brought into line with the Conventions in the near future.

In 1968, the Committee of Experts noted with satisfaction the adoption of legal provisions giving effect to various requirements of Convention No. 77 (medical examination before employment and renewal thereof up to 21 years of age in hazardous work; application of the Convention to homeworkers); Convention No. 78 (application of the Convention to domestic servants); Conventions Nos. 79 and 90 (prohibition of work by young persons under 18 years of age during the night period prescribed by the Convention).

2. Argentina: Conventions Nos. 77 and 78

In its 1966 observation, the Committee of Experts referred to the need for provisions to prescribe medical examinations in certain high-risk occupations and for them to be repeated at least until the age of 21 years.

The Conference Committee noted with interest in the same year the Government's announcement of the imminent adoption of the required legislation. The adopted legislation was noted with satisfaction by the Committee of Experts in 1967.

3. Central African Republic: Convention No. 33

In 1980, the Government informed the Conference Committee that, following direct contacts with a representative of the Director-General in 1978 and 1980, draft legislation had been prepared to lay down conditions for the employment of children between 12 to 14 years of age in light work, taking into account the comments of the Committee of Experts.

The adoption of the relevant legislation was noted with satisfaction by the Committee of Experts in 1989.

4. Guinea: Convention No. 16

In its 1978 observation, the Committee of Experts referred to draft legislation that was still to be adopted to give effect to the Convention.

The Conference Committee noted the difficulties of implementation and decided to mention this case in a special paragraph of its report.

The adoption of the relevant legislation was noted with satisfaction by the Committee of Experts in 1981.

5. Philippines: Convention No. 90

In its 1970 observation, the Committee of Experts recalled the repeated assurances given by the Government concerning its intention to adopt legislative amendments to prohibit night work of young persons of 16 to 18 years of age during a prescribed period of 12 consecutive hours and to restrict exceptions as required by the Convention.

The Conference Committee took note in 1971 and 1972 of the action envisaged by the Government.

In 1973, the Committee of Experts noted with satisfaction that the provisions had been adopted.

B. Other cases of progress

Coverage of minimum age and other provisions

1. Portugal: Convention No. 7

In its 1965 observation, the Committee of Experts noted with satisfaction that, following its requests of 1962 and 1963, the legislation on minimum age for maritime employment had been extended to the overseas provinces.

2. Chile: Convention No. 6

In its 1966 observation, the Committee of Experts noted with satisfaction the extension of the prohibition of night work provisions to all young persons employed in individual undertakings, whether or not they were engaged in manual work.

3. France: Conventions Nos. 77 and 78

In its 1966 observation concerning Convention No. 77, the Committee of Experts noted with satisfaction the extension to mines and quarries of provisions on the medical examination of young persons.

In 1968, the Committee of Experts noted with satisfaction, under Convention No. 78, the extension to domestic service of provisions on medical examinations.

4. Benin: Convention No. 6

In its 1979 observation, the Committee of Experts noted with satisfaction the measures adopted to limit exceptions to the prohibition of night work of young persons, in accordance with the Convention.

5. Hungary: Convention No. 6

In its 1980 observation, the Committee of Experts noted with satisfaction the limitation of exceptions to the prohibition of night work of young persons.

6. Finland: Convention No. 138

In its 1989 observation, the Committee of Experts noted with satisfaction that the provisions regulating the admission of young workers to dangerous work had been extended to agriculture, forestry and the transport of logs by water.

7. Norway: Convention No. 138

The Committee of Experts noted with satisfaction in 1989 the extension of the relevant provisions to agriculture and forestry.

Unhealthy and hazardous work

1. France: Convention No. 136

In its 1989 observation, the Committee of Experts noted with satisfaction the provisions to forbid exposure to benzene of workers under 18 years of age.

2. India: Convention No. 123

In its 1990 observation, the Committee of Experts noted with satisfaction the raising of minimum age for employment underground in mines from 16 to 18 years.

Light work

1. Congo: Convention No. 33

In its 1964 observation, the Committee of Experts noted with satisfaction the provisions regulating the duration of light work outside school hours for children over 12 years of age.

2. Italy: Convention No. 60

In its 1965 observation, the Committee of Experts noted with satisfaction provisions approving the list of light work permitted for children over 13 years of age.

Night work

The Committee of Experts noted with satisfaction the adoption of legal provisions in the countries listed below to prohibit the night work of young persons in accordance with the requirements of the relevant Conventions.

Convention No. 79. Spain: 1978; Peru: 1982; Bulgaria: 1988.

Convention No. 90. Spain: 1978; Peru: 1982; Guinea: 1983; Greece: 1990.

Medical examinations

The Committee of Experts noted with satisfaction the adoption of provisions requiring the annual repetition of medical examinations of young persons under 18 years of age employed at sea in the following cases:

Convention No. 16. Sierra Leone: 1964; Sweden: 1980.

The Committee of Experts noted with satisfaction that, following direct contacts between the government departments concerned and a representative of the Director-General of the ILO, legal provisions were adopted to prescribe medical examinations for young persons in accordance with the requirements of the Convention in the following countries:

Conventions Nos. 77 and 78. Guatemala: 1974; Peru: 1974.

The Committee of Experts noted with satisfaction the adoption of regulations providing for the medical examination of all workers engaged in underground work in mines in the following cases:

Convention No. 124. Byelorussian SSR, Ukrainian SSR, USSR: 1987.

Keeping of records

The Committee of Experts noted with satisfaction the adoption of provisions requiring the keeping of records and registers of young persons in employment, including their dates of birth and other particulars, in accordance with the requirements of the relevant Conventions in the following cases:

Convention No. 59. Mongolia, 1980.

Convention No. 79. Guatemala, 1974 (as a result of direct contacts).

Convention No. 90. Mexico, 1964.

Convention No. 123. France (New Caledonia), 1984; Australia and Malaysia: 1988.

C. Outstanding difficulties still under examination

The difficulties in the application of ILO standards concerning child labour which are outstanding in the current comments of the Committee of Experts in most cases reflect, and in some cases amplify, the type of difficulty that occurred in the cases given as examples under A and B above and for which progress was eventually achieved and noted.

A breakdown of the types of difficulties involved will give an overview of the situation, which will then be amplified by a more detailed analysis of the most important cases currently under examination by the Committee of Experts and the Conference Committee.

Child labour in general

1. Coverage

The scope of national provisions frequently falls short of the requirements of relevant ILO standards, especially in the following areas:

- Sector of activity. In one case concerning Convention No. 138, the minimum age provisions only cover industrial undertakings.

- Size of the undertakings and their activities. In one case related to Convention No. 138, family undertakings are exempted from the legal provisions on minimum age (the Convention explicitly allows such exemption only under certain criteria, and particularly as regards agriculture) and in two cases concerning Convention No. 77 (medical examination of young persons in industry). In a case relating to the application of Convention No. 77, it has been found that undertakings employing less than 20 workers are not covered in one country. In another case concerning Convention No. 58, the minimum age for employment at sea is not extended to vessels of less than 75 tons that are not engaged in foreign trade.

- Types of work. Industrial homeworkers and persons in domestic service are exempted from the relevant provisions in two cases concerning respectively Convention No. 138 (minimum age) and Convention No. 78 (medical examination in non-industrial occupations); the same applies to itinerant trades in one case under Convention No. 78.

- Types of employment. Relevant national provisions are frequently not applicable to persons who work outside an employment relationship in cases related to Convention No. 138 on minimum age (seven cases) and Convention No. 58 on minimum age for employment at sea (one case). In the application of Convention No. 78 (medical examination in non-industrial occupations), the Committee of Experts is raising the question of the exclusion of persons working on their own account in three cases and that of workers who are not wage-earners in one case. A frequent exclusion from minimum age provisions is made as regards apprentices (Convention No. 5: two cases; Convention No. 59: three cases; Convention No. 123 and Convention No. 138: one case each).

2. Levels of minimum age and other protective measures

The absence of a minimum age for admission to employment, or one which is set lower than that prescribed by ILO Conventions, may occur as regards general employment (one case under Convention No. 138), but more frequently as regards sectoral activities (one case each under Convention No. 10 concerning agriculture, Convention No. 58 concerning employment at sea and Convention No. 112 concerning fishermen).

Hazardous work. Shortcomings are particularly frequent in national provisions as regards the requirement of a higher minimum age as well as other protective conditions of work where hazardous work is concerned. This occurs both under the minimum age Conventions (Convention No. 59: two cases; Convention No. 138: ten cases, including one relating to work likely to prejudice the morals of young persons) and under the provisions aimed at the protection of children and young persons contained in the Conventions on occupational safety and health (Convention No. 13 concerning lead painting: three cases; Convention No. 127 on maximum weights: seven cases; Convention No. 136 on benzene: four cases; Convention No. 152 on dock work: six cases).

Light work. The conditions regulating the performance of light work by children and its authorisation are currently the subject of comments by the Committee of Experts in seven cases under Convention No. 138.

Night work. The most frequent difficulty concerns the definition of the night period during which the employment of children and young persons is prohibited (from 12 to 14 hours under the relevant Conventions). This question is raised by the Committee of Experts both under Convention No. 79 (two cases) and Convention No. 90 (five cases).

3. Medical examinations

In addition to shortcomings related to the scope of national provisions, two prevalent difficulties concern the annual repetition of medical examinations for young workers (five cases under Conventions Nos. 16, 77, 78 and 124) and the measures for the vocational guidance and physical and vocational rehabilitation of children and young persons who are found to be unsuited for work or to have physical disabilities or limitations (five cases under Convention No. 77; two cases under Convention No. 78).

4. Enforcement measures

Among the requirements of the relevant ILO Conventions, the keeping of records of the children and young persons employed, including particulars such as their date of birth, dates and types of employment, is a question that is frequently pursued in the comments of the Committee of Experts (Convention No. 123: four cases; Convention No. 124: one case; Convention No. 138: two cases). A related requirement, regarding the means of identification of children and young persons who are self-employed or are engaged in itinerant trading or in other occupations carried out on the streets or in places that are accessible to the public, is the subject of comments by the Committee of Experts under Convention No. 78 concerning medical examination in non-industrial occupations (three cases) and under Convention No. 79 concerning night work in non-industrial occupations (one case).

One important aspect of enforcement is the requirement for effective inspection. This point is stressed by the Committee of Experts under the relevant Conventions in all cases of deficiencies in the practical application of national provisions on minimum age and other measures for the protection of children. The question may also be pursued by the Committee of Experts as appropriate under the labour inspection Conventions No. 81 (industry and commerce) and No. 129 (agriculture).

5. Cases currently under examination by the Committee of Experts and the Conference Committee

(The text of the Committee of Expert's observations and the record of the discussions of the Conference Committee are published in the reports of the two Committees for the years in question.)

Minimum Age (Industry) Convention, 1919 (No. 5)

Bolivia (ratification: 1954). For a number of years, the Committee of Experts has been drawing the Government's attention to provisions of its national legislation which authorise the employment of children under 14 years of age as apprentices, in contradiction to Article 2 of the Convention.

The 1988 observation by the Committee of Experts carried a footnote asking the Government to provide full particulars to the Conference and to report in detail in the same year.

The Conference Committee, in discussing this case in 1988, noted with concern that there had been no change for many years and hoped that the Government would very soon take all the necessary measures, with the assistance of the ILO, to eliminate existing divergencies between the legislation and the Convention and serious problems in practice, so as to ensure full application of the Convention.

The Committee of Experts' observation of 1990 called for the adoption of the necessary provisions in the very near future.

Brazil (ratification. 1934). The application of this Convention by Brazil has been the subject of comments by the Committee of Experts for many years and, recently, of discussions by the Conference Committee each year since 1988.

The problems referred to by the Committee of Experts concern the employment of children under 14 years of age as apprentices and allegations that a large number of children between 6 and 14 years are employed in violation of the relevant legislation in various industries in Brazil, in particular in the State of Sao Paulo. The Committee of Experts' observation in 1988 stressed the importance of strengthening the inspection services and other supervisory measures, a concern which was also expressed by the National Confederation of Industrial Workers in its comments on the application of the Convention. The observation carried a footnote asking the Government to supply full particulars to the Conference and to report in detail in the same year.

During the discussion of the case by the Conference Committee in 1988, the Government communicated information on measures to strengthen the inspection services in view of the violations of the legislation concerning the work of minors under 14 years of age. The Conference Committee stressed the need to take all appropriate measures, such as labour inspection and tripartite consultation, for the effective application of national provisions on minimum age and to ensure full compliance with the Convention in law as well as in practice.

Among the salient points made during the detailed discussion at the Conference Committee in the following years, the Workers' member of Brazil expressed his concern in 1989 over the widely accepted position in Brazil that it was better to have minors working than hanging around in the streets without receiving any education, guidance, health services or food, and forming outcast gangs of juveniles. In 1990, the Government indicated in particular that the economic crisis had seriously aggravated the already chronic social problems of the country, that the number of abandoned minors and dispersed families was very high, and that there were a great many minors working in undertakings and industries who were not covered by the government assistance programmes for minors.

The Committee of Experts in its 1991 observation again called for the measures necessary to be taken to ensure conformity with the Convention, both in law and in practice.

At the Conference Committee in 1991, the Workers' members stressed the magnitude of the problems (half the population of Brazil is younger than 20 years of age). The Workers' member of Colombia stated that the problem was very important not only for Brazil but also for all Latin America and the unacceptable reality of the exploitation of child labour could not be ignored. The Conference Committee expressed its profound regret at the seriousness of the situation, and very firmly hoped that real and substantial progress could be achieved in law and practice in the very near future.

Minimum Age (Agriculture) Convention, 1921 (No. 10)

Dominican Republic (ratification: 1933). In its 1991 observation, the Committee of Experts raised the following points:

- the exclusion of young persons employed in agricultural work from the scope of Section 232 of the Labour Code prohibiting the employment of young persons under the age of 14 years -- the minimum age in agriculture is 10 years;

- information contained in the report of the direct contacts mission of January 1991 that the lack of labour has resulted in plantations resorting to child labour for cutting sugar cane (see also under Convention No. 105 below).

The Committee of Experts requested the Government to supply information on measures taken to give effect to the Convention as well as copies of reports of the inspection services, including data on the violations reported and the sanctions imposed in relation to the employment of young persons.

The Government indicated to the Conference Committee in 1991 that Section 232 of the Labour Code would be repealed, and as regards the work of children on sugar-cane plantations, that the individual contract of each worker (which was drafted as a result of Executive Decree No. 417/90) provides that "he cannot be accompanied by or use his children or relatives under 14 years of age to haul or cut sugar cane or in any other work".

Child labour under the forced labour Conventions Nos. 29 and 105

As noted earlier, the Forced Labour Convention, 1929 (No. 29) and the Abolition of Forced Labour Convention, 1957 (No. 105) hold the first and fifth positions for the number of ratifications (129 and 109 respectively) of ILO instruments, positions which reflect the fundamental importance of the right of the human person to be free from "any form of forced or compulsory labour"[6].

Practically all of the most serious and reprehensible instances of child labour unfortunately occur in violation of the right established by these Conventions.

The main provisions that apply in such cases are:

- as regards Convention No. 29, the undertaking "to suppress the use of forced or compulsory labour in all its forms", meaning "all work or service exacted from any person under the menace of any penalty and for which the said person has not offered himself voluntarily", but which does not include inter alia "compulsory military service for work of a purely military character" or "minor communal services ..... in the direct interest" of the community concerned;

---

[6] A review of the implementation of the forced labour Conventions Nos. 29 and 105 was last carried out in ILO: Abolition of Forced Labour, General Survey by the Committee of Experts on the Application of Conventions and Recommendations, International Labour Conference, 65th Session, 1979, Report III (Part 4B).

- as regards Convention No. 105, the undertaking to abolish any form of forced or compulsory labour, inter alia, "as a method of mobilising and using labour for purposes of economic development" and "as a means of labour discipline".

There are two principal kinds of situations involving child labour that fall within the terms of the above ILO standards.

Non-military compulsory service and other similar schemes

In violation of the relevant provisions of Convention No. 29, young persons may be required during their military service to perform work which is not of a purely military character, or to perform various forms of civic service and work under compulsory schemes for general development purposes or for the mobilisation of youth.

This question is being pursued by the Committee of Experts in comments addressed to 17 countries. The cases examined here are limited to those which appear to involve young persons below 18 years of age (the higher age level stipulated in relevant ILO standards and that laid down in the UN Convention on the Rights of the Child, 1989).

In one case, the 1991 direct request of the Committee of Experts raises the question of a scheme for national service and youth training in which school-leavers from Form III to Form IV at secondary schools as well as post-secondary school-leavers may be enrolled. The government has been requested to supply detailed information on the application of the scheme.

The second case is described below.

Bonded labour and other forms of forced or compulsory labour

In this type of situation children and young persons are victims of social malpractices which affect larger groups and segments of the population, such as bonded labour and traditional slavery, and are victims of other "contemporary forms of slavery", such as the sale and the sexual and other forms of exploitation of children. (As will be seen, in most of the cases examined by the ILO supervisory bodies, reference is made to the proceedings of the Working Group on Contemporary Forms of Slavery of the UN Sub-Commission on Prevention of Discrimination and Protection of Minorities.)

All cases involving children in such situations are under current examination by both the Committee of Experts and the Conference Committee and are described in greater detail below.

In another case, the Committee of Experts addressed a direct request in 1991 to the government concerned calling for full information on allegations that were contained in information submitted to the UN Working Group relating to child labour exploitation in domestic service, shops, private coaches, the tourist industry and fishing camps.

Cases currently under examination by the Committee of Experts and the Conference Committee

(The text of the Committee of Expert's observations and the record of discussions by the Conference Committee are published in the reports of the two Committees for the years in question.)

Forced Labour Convention, 1930 (No. 29)

Compulsory civic service

Cameroon (ratification: 1960). In its 1990 observation, the Committee of Experts recalled that legislation to set up the National Civic Service for Participation in Development is contrary to the Convention because it provides that work in the general interest can be imposed on citizens aged between 16 and 55 years for a period of 24 months, subject to penalities of imprisonment in case of refusal.

A Government representative indicated to the Conference Committee in 1990 that the penalty provisions of the legislation in question had been deleted in the draft amendment Bill and that in fact recruitment to the civic service was on a voluntary basis. It was also stated that the National Civic Service in question had been abolished. The Conference Committee took note of this information and hoped that there would be no further discrepancies between either legislation or practice and the Convention.

Bonded labour and other forms of forced labour

Bangladesh (ratification: 1972). In its 1990 observation, the Committee of Experts referred to information set out in the report of the 1989 South Asian Seminar on Child Servitude attended by representatives of NGOs from five countries, and submitted by the Anti-Slavery Society to the UN Working Group on Contemporary Forms of Slavery in 1989. This information relates to the situation in Bangladesh of children of underprivileged classes who, because of their parents' debt bondage to local landlords or money lenders, have to take up work as domestic workers in private homes, in shops, restaurants, in "bidi" and tobacco factories, etc., in conditions described as exploitation and slavery, in violation of national legislation on the employment of children and of legal and constitutional provisions on child servitude. The Committee of Experts recalled that under Convention No. 29, penalties against the exaction of forced labour need be adequate and strictly enforced.

A Government representative stated to the Conference Committee in 1990 that the information concerning child labour under debt bondage did not reflect reality.

In the Conference Committee discussion, emphasis was placed on the use of penal sanctions to effectively enforce legislation in practice.

Dominican Republic (ratification: 1956). See under Convention No. 105 below.

Haiti (ratification: 1958). In its 1990 observation, the Committee of Experts referred to a report on children's rights in Haiti, submitted to the UN Working Group on Contemporary Forms of Slavery, according to which many poor families in Haiti sell their children to urban families to work as domestic servants in conditions which are not unlike servitude (a practice known in Creole as "restavek" from the French "rester avec" or "to stay with"). The Committee of Experts requested the Government to supply information in answer to these allegations and asked the Government to supply full particulars to the Conference.

A Government representative stated to the Conference Committee in 1990 that in Haiti children were in fact employed as domestic servants, because peasant parents faced with insoluble financial problems had to entrust them to more or less better-off acquaintances in town. There was no question of slavery as such, although the children worked under conditions that left much to be desired. The new Government would take measures for the effective application of the provisions of the Labour Code on the protection of children employed as domestic servants.

The Conference Committee expressed the firm hope that the Government would be able to report that both national legislation and practice are in complete conformity with this extremely important Convention.

India (ratification: 1954). In its observations, the Committee of Experts has pursued over a number of years the question of the implementation of the Bonded Labour System (Abolition) Act, 1976 (the adoption of which it noted with satisfaction in 1976).

In its 1991 observation, the Committee of Experts devoted special attention to the question of child bonded labour and referred to the report of the 1989 South Asian Seminar on Child Servitude (see under Bangladesh above). According to this report, children in bondage are working in numerous occupations in India, under inhuman and hazardous conditions, in the most exploitative forms of child servitude which involve several million children, while existing constitutional and legislative provisions to protect children are not being applied and exploiters have no fear of being punished. The Committee of Experts recalled that the penalties imposed against forced labour should be adequate and strictly enforced and requested information in that respect, including copies of court decisions.

At the Conference Committee in 1991, the Workers' and Employers' members stressed that legislative provisions were not applied and exploiters of children not punished. The Government representative referred to the National Child Labour Policy of 1987 which proposed an integrated approach to curbing the problem, including education and vocational training, nutrition and health care programmes, stricter enforcement of the relevant legislation and a government awareness campaign with the help of voluntary organisations. An ILO technical co-operation programme was helping to strengthen the national policy.

The Conference Committee noted that, despite the efforts that had been made, a great deal still remained to be done to overcome the serious problems involved. The Committee trusted that the Government would spare no effort to achieve the effective elimination of debt bondage, including child bondage.

Pakistan (ratification: 1957). The Committee of Experts in its 1988 observation referred to the report to the Government of Pakistan submitted by the ILO's Sectoral Review Mission of 1986, in which a reference was made to the employment of bonded children in "Kharkar" camps who work at night in irrigation tunnels in remote rural areas.

In statements made to the Conference Committee in 1988 and 1989, the Government representative denied the existence of "Kharkar" camps and of bonded labour in the country. The Conference Committee decided in 1988 to mention this case in a special paragraph of its report and in 1989 again expressed its great concern regarding the points discussed. The Government subsequently indicated that, in order to dispel any apprehensions in this regard, it proposed to introduce a law to abolish and make punishable all exploitation of labour, including bonded labour.

In its 1990 and 1991 observations, the Committee of Experts noted these indications with interest and hoped that the Government would provide information on the action taken.

The Committee of Experts also referred to the report on the 1989 South Asian Seminar on Child Servitude (see under Bangladesh above). According to this report, large-scale exploitation of bonded labourers was to be found in Pakistan in the brick-making, carpet weaving, fish cleaning and packing, shoe-making, bidi-making, auto repair, agriculture, mining, quarrying and stone-crushing industries.

In a further report submitted to the Working Group by a representative of Anti-Slavery International (formerly the Anti-Slavery Society), reference was made to the brick-kiln labourers who were considered bonded labourers by an order of the Supreme Court of Pakistan of 18 September 1988. The representative, who was the President of the Bhatta Mazdoor Mahaz (Brick Kiln Labourers' Front) and of the Bonded Labour Liberation Front of Pakistan (BLLFP), estimated that about 20 million people, among then 7.5 million children, fell into the category of "bonded labourers", of which 2 million families alone were working in the brick kiln industry as virtual slaves. The BLLFP has established branches throughout the country and has approached the Government for legislation to abolish the bonded labour system and measures for the rehabilitation of bonded labourers.

At the Conference Committee in 1990, a Government representative stated that the Government had decided to abolish bonded labour through a law which had been approved by the Cabinet and was expected to be enacted soon. The Conference Committee noted the Government's good will but urged it to give the highest priority to the question.

The Government representative stated to the Conference Committee in 1991 that the draft law was on the agenda of the National Assembly when it was dissolved in 1990. It was hoped that the proposed Bill would be submitted to the new legislature soon. It was also stated that the illegal hiring of children is punishable under the Employment of Children Act, 1991.

The Conference Committee hoped that the draft law would be submitted and adopted rapidly and that forced or bonded labour would be subject to truly effective and strictly applied penal sanctions.

Sudan (ratification: 1957). In its 1989 observation, the Committee of Experts noted information received by the UN Sub-Commission on the Prevention of Discrimination and Protection of Minorities in 1988 from the Anti-Slavery Society concerning allegations of the capture and trade in slaves arising in the context of civil unrest in the country, and involving children and young persons.

The Government representative stated to the Conference Committee in 1989 that national legislation prohibited any form of exploitation and forced labour and that arrangements were made for a visit by the Anti-Slavery Society. The Conference Committee expressed the hope that the Government would be in a position to provide substantive information on measures taken to ensure that penalties for the exaction of forced labour would be truly effective and fully applied in practice.

The Committee of Experts in its 1990 observation asked the Government to supply full information on the application of the relevant provisions of the Penal Code, including details on the number of cases of prosecution and the sentences and penalties imposed.

Thailand (ratification: 1969). In its 1991 observation, the Committee of Experts recalled its previous comments concerning allegations brought before the UN Sub-Commission on Prevention of Discrimination and Protection of Minorities that children were bought and sold in Thailand for work in private houses, restaurants, factories and brothels; that shops had specialised in the sale of children and teenagers; and that child catchers and recruiters were operating in the country and, although laws for the protection of children existed, there was a lack of enforcement by the police.

The Committee of Experts requested the Government in particular to supply detailed information on the measures taken to curb the sale and purchase of children, and to remove children from nightclubs and brothels and from illegal employment elsewhere.

In its discussion of the case in 1990, the Conference Committee, while noting the information supplied by the Government on the measures that had been taken, expressed doubts as to whether they were sufficient to curtail the serious situation of child labour in the country.

The Conference Committee took note in 1991 of the information supplied by the Government on the additional measures that had been taken to ensure the protection of children. It expressed, however, deep concern at the lack of effectiveness of the practical implementation of these measures, in particular as regards the application of sanctions. The Conference Committee urged the Government to take all the necessary measures to remedy the serious situation and to eliminate child labour. It decided to include its conclusions in a special paragraph of the Committee's report.

Abolition of Forced Labour Convention, 1957 (No. 105)

Dominican Republic (ratification: 1958). The conditions of workers of Haitian origin on sugar-cane plantations in the Dominican Republic have been examined by the Committee of Experts and Conference Committee since 1984, following up the recommendations made by the Commission of Inquiry set up in 1983[7].

In January 1991, a direct contacts mission took place which referred in its report to the use of child labour in sugar-cane harvesting. The question is raised in the 1991 observation of the Committee of Experts concerning the application of Convention No. 10 in the Dominican Republic (see above).

In the discussion concerning Convention No. 105 at the Committee of Experts in 1991, attention was drawn to the recruitment of children for plantation work.

The Government representative stated, regarding the protection of minors, that a programme for the placement of youth labour had been set up in sugar-cane areas and that the repatriation of some of the persons concerned had taken place. A circular from the State Sugar Board (CEA), dated 9 May 1991, contained instructions for the control in practice of the employment of minors and strong disciplinary measures against offenders. The Government representative referred to the economic restrictions prevailing in the country and trusted that international collaboration and ILO co-operation would be of assistance in finding solutions.

[7] See "Report of the Commission of Inquiry appointed under article 26 of the Constitution of the International Labour Organisation to examine the observance of certain international labour Conventions by the Dominican Republic and Haiti with respect to the employment of Haitian workers on the sugar plantations of the Dominican Republic", in ILO Bulletin (Geneva), Volume 66, Series B, 1983.

Concluding remarks

This review of the application of the Conventions that are relevant to child labour bears out the opening remark that the struggle against child labour cannot be won only through legislative action, but cannot be fought without it.

Ratification of the relevant ILO Conventions -- and other international instruments -- formally commits the countries concerned to take action against child labour through their legislation and practice, and international supervision helps them to fulfill that commitment.

The review has shown that, over the years, difficulties in the application of Conventions have been brought to light by ILO supervisory procedures and progress has eventually been achieved as a result.

The ratification of Conventions remains therefore a priority objective. While relevant ILO standards, and particularly those on minimum age, have received a large degree of formal acceptance, there is room for further progress. Some 40 countries have yet to ratify any minimum age Convention, even in respect of industry, and the ratification scores of the minimum age Conventions concerning non-industrial occupations and also those concerning agriculture could certainly be improved. Further ratification of Convention No. 138, the comprehensive and up-to-date instrument on minimum age, is particularly desirable, bearing in mind not only the requirements, but also the flexibility of its provisions, especially as regards developing countries.

In the application of ratified Conventions, difficulties noted in current comments by the Committee of Experts show that, in many cases, national law still falls short of the requirements of the relevant ILO standards. Indeed, in some of the most serious cases, it is the uncovering of problems that has led to their being acknowledged by the authorities concerned, and to legislation being envisaged.

Legislation alone, however, cannot eliminate child labour. Adequate enforcement measures, including effective inspection and penalties, and the administrative and political will to apply such measures have been strongly stressed by the ILO supervisory bodies, particularly in cases involving grave problems, and accordingly in cases of children victims of bonded labour and other "contemporary forms of slavery".

This last remark brings out the true dimension of the issue. Child labour has its roots in economic and social conditions, and above all, in poverty. The elimination of child labour demands action on many fronts. Legislation -- ILO standards and the national laws derived from them -- set the principles and the objectives and also provide a conducive environment in which other action, including international technical co-operation, can be developed and assist in the elimination of this fundamental social problem.

Annex 1: ILO Conventions and Recommendations for the protection of children and young persons

Minimum age

Minimum Age (Industry) Convention, 1919 (No. 5)
Minimum Age (Industry) Convention (Revised), 1937 (No. 59)
Minimum Age (Sea) Convention, 1920 (No. 7)
Minimum Age (Trimmers and Stokers) Convention, 1921 (No. 15)
Minimum Age (Sea) Convention (Revised), 1936 (No. 58)
Minimum Age (Agriculture) Convention, 1921 (No. 10)
Minimum Age (Non-Industrial Employment) Convention, 1932 (No. 33)
Minimum Age (Non-Industrial Employment) Convention (Revised), 1937 (No. 60)
Minimum Age (Fishermen) Convention, 1959 (No. 112)
Minimum Age (Underground Work) Convention, 1965 (No. 123)
Minimum Age Convention, 1973 (No. 138)

Minimum Age (Non-Industrial Employment) Recommendation, 1932 (No. 41)
Minimum Age (Family Undertaking) Recommendation, 1937 (No. 52)
Minimum Age (Coal Mines) Recommendation, 1953 (No. 96)
Minimum Age (Underground Work) Recommendation, 1965 (No. 124)
Minimum Age Recommendation, 1973 (No. 146)

Night work

Night Work of Young Persons (Industry) Convention, 1919 (No. 6)
Night Work of Young Persons (Industry) Convention (Revised), 1948 (No. 90)
Night Work of Young Persons (Non-Industrial Occupations) Convention, 1946 (No. 79)

Night Work of Young Persons (Agriculture) Recommendation, 1921 (No. 14)
Night Work of Young Persons (Non-Industrial Occupations) Recommendation, 1946 (No. 80)

Medical examination

Medical Examination of Young Persons (Sea) Convention, 1921 (No. 16)
Medical Examination of Young Persons (Industry) Convention, 1946 (No. 77)
Medical Examination of Young Persons (Non-Industrial Occupations) Convention, 1946 (No. 78)
Medical Examination of Young Persons (Underground Work) Convention, 1965 (No. 124)

Medical Examination of Young Persons Recommendation, 1946 (No. 79)

Annex 1: ILO Conventions and Recommendations for the protection of children and young persons (continued)

Unhealthy and dangerous work

White Lead (Painting) Convention, 1921 (No. 13), Article 3, Paragraph 1
Radiation Protection Convention, 1960 (No. 115), Article 7
Maximum Weight Convention, 1967 (No. 127), Articles 1 and 7
Benzene Convention, 1971 (No. 136), Article 11, Paragraph 2
Occupational Safety and Health (Dock Work) Convention, 1979 (No. 152), Article 38, Paragraph 2

Lead Poisoning (Women and Children) Recommendation, 1919 (No. 4), Paragraphs 1 and 2
Conditions of Employment of Young Persons (Underground Work) Recommendation, 1965 (No. 125)
Maximum Weight Recommendation, 1967 (No. 128)
Benzene Recommendation, 1971 (No. 144), Paragraph 20

Other provisions*

Social Policy (Non-Metropolitan Territories) Convention, 1947 (No. 82), Article 19
Social Policy (Basic Aims and Standards) Convention, 1962 (No. 117), Article 15

Unemployment (Young Persons) Recommendation, 1935 (No. 45), Paragraph 1

* The relevant provisions of the above instruments call for a minimum age for employment linked to the school-leaving age and educational facilities.

Annex 2: Ratification of ILO Conventions on the protection of children*
(as at 15 July 1991)

Minimum age

Convention No.	Title of Convention	Total of ratifications (in brackets, total of denunciations following ratification of revising Conventions)
5	Minimum Age (Industry), 1979	69 [21]
59	Minimum Age (Industry) (Revised), 1937	35 [15]
7	Minimum Age (Sea), 1920	51 [21]
58	Minimum Age (Sea) (Revised), 1936	50 [19]
10	Minimum Age (Agriculture), 1921	51 [20]
15	Minimum Age (Trimmers and Stokers), 1921	67 [27]
33	Minimum Age (Non-Industrial Employment), 1932	25 [7]
60	Minimum Age (Non-Industrial Employment) (Revised), 1937	11 [9]
112	Minimum Age (Fishermen), 1959	30 [16]
123	Minimum Age (Underground Work), 1965	40 [8]

Convention No. 138: Minimum Age, 1973
(list of countries with specified minimum age in brackets)

Algeria [16], Antigua and Barbuda [16], Belgium [15], Bulgaria [16], Byelorussian SSR [16], Costa Rica [15], Cuba [15], Dominica [15], Equatorial Guinea [14], Finland [15], France [16], Germany [15], Greece [15], Guatemala [14], Honduras [14], Iraq [15], Ireland [15], Israel [15], Italy [15], Kenya [16], Libyan Arab Jamahiriya [15], Luxembourg [15], Malta [16], Mauritius [15], Netherlands [15], Nicaragua [14], Niger [14], Norway [15], Poland [15], Romania [16], Rwanda [14], Spain [15], Sweden [15], Togo [14], Ukrainian SSR [16], Union of Soviet Socialist Republics [16], Uruguay [15], Venezuela [14], Yugoslavia [15], Zambia [15].

Total number of ratifications of Convention No. 138, as at 15 July 1991: 40

* For list of countries and other particulars, see ILO Chart of Ratifications of International Labour Conventions, published 1 January and 30 June each year.

Annex 2: Ratification of ILO Conventions on the protection of children (continued)

Night work

Convention No.	Title of Convention	Total of ratifications
6	Night Work of Young Persons (Industry), 1919	57
10	Night Work of Young Persons (Industry) (Revised), 1948	41
79	Night Work of Young Persons (Non-Industrial Occupations), 1946	16

Medical examinations

Convention No.	Title of Convention	Total of ratifications
16	Medical Examination of Young Persons (Sea), 1921	69
77	Medical Examination of Young Persons (Industry), 1946	38
78	Medical Examination of Young Persons (Non-Industrial Occupations), 1946	34
124	Medical Examination of Young Persons (Underground Work), 1965	37

Annex 3: Levels of minimum age set in the relevant Conventions

Basic minimum age for admission to employment and work*

14 years	Conventions Nos. 5, 7, 10, 33 and Convention No. 138 (for countries "whose economy and educational facilities are insufficiently developed")
15 years	Conventions Nos. 58, 59, 60, 112 and 138

Reduced minimum age for light work

12-13 years	Two years lower than the basic minimum age set respectively under Conventions Nos. 33, 60 and 138

Higher minimum age for unhealthy and hazardous work

16 years	Convention No. 123
18 years	Conventions Nos. 15, 112, 138 and the Conventions dealing with night work and other hazardous work

---

* Under Convention No. 138, the basic minimum age "shall not be less than the age of completion of compulsory schooling". Conventions Nos. 33 and 60 (non-industrial employment) prohibit the employment of children who are over the minimum age but "who are still required .... to attend primary school".

Part IV

Labour inspection and child labour

Part IV

Labour inspection and child labour

by

Jean-Maurice Derrien[1]

Historical perspective

Labour inspection initially emerged as a by-product of the first measures to protect children from work. There is therefore an almost perfect parallel between the first laws to combat child labour and the basic texts on labour inspection.

These laws were adopted in the 19th century as a reaction to the shock of the first industrial revolution, when populations which were largely rural in origin were unprepared for the savage and almost completely unregulated industrialisation which took place at that time. The prospect of children working from the age of 5 years in the cotton and wool industries, the presence of women in coal mines, the occurrence of mining disasters, the serious accidents caused by new machines, the high percentage of sick and deformed persons among the original workers of industrial towns, and finally the fear of working class revolts, all persuaded some leading industrialists and certain governments to establish the first restraints on laissez-faire and to recognise that the State had the right and duty to find out what was happening behind the doors of industry. This was the origin of the right of access of labour inspectors.

First in England in 1802, then successively in Germany in 1837, Belgium in 1840 and France in 1841, legislation was adopted to set a minimum age for admission to work. This limited the working hours of children and created a supervisory body for the application of the first labour laws.

In France, the Act of 22 March 1841 prohibited work by children under 8 years; children between 8 and 12 years could only work eight hours a day with breaks, while children from 12 to 16 years could work for a maximum of 12 hours a day. The supervision of enterprises was entrusted to volunteers called "child labour inspectors". Certain of these took their function very much to heart. For example, in the North of France in 1852, a labour inspector visited 572 establishments in one year, or around two factories every day. He also visited the dormitories in which the children lived and the unhealthy workshops in which they worked in order to call for better hygiene[2]. However, in many regions, inspections were carried out by commissions of well-known persons who warned the employer before the visit and only very rarely imposed sanctions.

---

[1] Labour Administration Branch, International Labour Office.

[2] Jean Sandrin: Enfants trouvés, enfants ouvriers, 17ème et 19ème siècles (Aubier, Paris, 1982), page 199.

It was rapidly realised that commissions of volunteers were not very effective and that the only institution that was capable of combating the exploitation of children was a labour inspectorate composed of permanent officials, who were independent of the local authorities and of employers, and whose principal and only function would be to inspect the conditions of employment of children and of women and to monitor health and safety conditions at the workplace.

This fundamental step was taken in England in 1833, with the establishment of factory inspectors, and then in 1853 in Germany and 1874 in France. The rest of Europe and North America then followed during a period that also saw workers becoming organised into trade unions and claiming protective legislation and real supervision of their conditions of work.

These initial experiences helped establish the general principles for the organisation of labour inspection, which were to be discussed by the International Labour Organisation as soon as it was founded. It is significant that the same parallel between measures to combat child labour and the promotion of labour inspection occurred at both the national and international levels.

In 1919, the Treaty of Versailles, which brought an end to the First World War and created the ILO, laid down in Article 427 that "each State should make provision for a system of inspection ..... in order to ensure the enforcement of the laws and regulations for the protection of the employed". In the same year, at its first Session, the International Labour Conference adopted :

- the Labour Inspection (Health Services) Recommendation (No. 5), which recommended member States to establish, as soon as possible, "not only a system of efficient factory inspection, but also in addition thereto a government service especially charged with the duty of safeguarding the health of workers";

- the Minimum Age (Industry) Convention (No. 5), setting the minimum age for admission to industrial work at 14 years, and the Night Work of Young Persons (Industry) Convention (No. 6).

Conventions on child labour then followed one another to cover progressively all sectors of activity:

- maritime labour in 1920 and 1921 (Conventions Nos 7, 15 and 16);

- agriculture in 1921 (Convention No. 10);

- non-industrial employment in 1932 (Convention No. 33);

- underground work in 1937 and 1965 (Conventions Nos 59 and 123);

- fishing in 1959 (Convention No. 112).

In 1973, the International Labour Conference adopted the Minimum Age Convention (No. 138), which was to gradually replace existing instruments that applied to limited economic sectors, with a view to the total abolition of child labour.

At the same time, four new Recommendations were adopted on labour inspection:

- in 1923, the Labour Inspection Recommendation (No. 20), setting out the general principles for the organisation of labour inspection;

- in 1926, the Labour Inspection (Seamen) Recommendation (No. 28);

- in 1937, the Inspection (Building) Recommendation (No. 54);

- in 1939, the Labour Inspectorates (Indigenous Workers) Recommendation (No. 59).

A key year for labour inspection was 1947, when more than 30 years of effort were crowned by the adoption of:

- the Labour Inspection Convention (No. 81) and Recommendation (No. 81);

- the Labour Inspectorates (Non-Metropolitan Territories) Convention (No. 85);

- and the Labour Inspection (Mining and Transport) Recommendation (No. 82).

Finally, in 1969, the labour inspection instruments were completed with the adoption of the Labour Inspection (Agriculture) Convention (No. 129) and Recommendation (No. 133).

Henceforth, as for child labour, international labour standards on labour inspection covered all the major sectors of activity. Moreover, these basic standards explicitly laid down that the labour inspectorate was responsible for ensuring the application of legal provisions, and particularly those on the employment of children and young persons.

Furthermore, in addition to these specific texts, many Conventions and Recommendations contain clauses providing for the establishment of an inspection system to apply legal provisions in other areas, such as forced labour and health and safety in industry, plantations or ports (see Annex 1).

By the 1970s, it could be said that the international legal framework was more or less complete. The conditions of work and employment of children, and in particular the minimum age for their admission to employment or work, had been established and provision had also been made for institutions to implement these rules.

The harsh reality: Millions of working children

In his Report to the International Labour Conference in 1964, the Director-General stated that "labour legislation without inspection is an essay in ethics rather than a binding social discipline". The Committee of Experts on the Application of Conventions and Recommendations emphasised in its report that "the existence of an efficient labour inspectorate provides the surest guarantee that national and international labour standards are complied with not only in law but also in fact"[3]. In its latest General Survey on labour inspection (1985), the Committee

[3] International Labour Conference: Report of the Committee of Experts on the Application of Conventions and Recommendations, ILC, 48th Session, Geneva, 1964, Report III (Part IV), Part One: General Report, page 8.

also emphasised, in the following terms, that "However advanced it may be, a country's labour legislation is liable to remain a dead letter if there is no system of labour inspection to enforce it. This is particularly important in times of economic recession when the improvement of working conditions tends to be pushed into the background"[4].

With 107 ratifications, the Labour Inspection Convention (No. 81) holds seventh position among the most ratified Conventions. However, much remains to be done in terms of the ratification of the Conventions on child labour and labour inspection in agriculture, where the largest number of children work. The Labour Inspection (Agriculture) Convention, 1969 (No. 129), has only been ratified by 26 countries.

There is no doubt that international labour standards have acted as a stimulus. In nearly all countries, the labour inspectorate is responsible for ensuring the application of the legal measures that establish a minimum age for admission to employment and work and which lay down rules governing dangerous work, night work and the working hours of children. Yet, although many laws have been adopted and the bodies responsible for their application have been set up, millions of children work illegally.

In 1980, a book appeared in France with the following title: Cinquante deux millions d'enfants au travail (52 million working children)[5]. This title reflects ILO estimates of the number of child workers worldwide, although the ILO itself recognised in a work that appeared in 1980 that the "figure of 52 million may well be an underestimate, since in some countries young workers less than 15 years old are not included in the labour force statistics. In others, young people who both work and go to school are rarely considered to be part of the labour force. Again, the statutes cover only those youngsters who have a fixed job, and thus exclude the majority of those who work only occasionally. In short, it is impossible to make an accurate estimate of the numbers employed, for the simple reason that, since in most countries child labour is clandestine, it is in the interest of all the parties concerned to conceal it"[6].

Even if the figures are approximate, the message is clear: millions of children are working illegally, that is, at an age at which work is prohibited. They carry out dangerous types of prohibited work, such as work in mines, in quarries and on building sites; they carry excessively heavy loads, handle chemical products and are in contact with pesticides; they work nine, ten or 12 hours a day and do not benefit from daily rest periods; their remuneration is derisory in comparison to the work that they do, and is in any case much lower than the remuneration of adults

[4] International Labour Conference: Labour inspection, General Survey of the Committee of Experts on the Application of Conventions and Recommendations, ILC, 71st Session, Geneva, 1985, page 1.

[5] Christiane Rimbaud: Cinquante deux millions d'enfants au travail (Plon, Paris, 1980), 204 pages.

[6] E. Mendelievich (editor): Children at work (ILO, Geneva, 1980), pages 23 to 28.

employed in the same work. They are not registered with the social security authorities and have no channel of appeal in the event of accidents. All this is forbidden by national legislation[7]. How can this enormous discrepancy be explained between laws which prohibit or regulate child labour and the evidently illegal situations that exist and seriously prejudice the dignity and development of children?

Responsibility for this discrepancy does not lie exclusively with the labour inspectorate. Because children are prisoners of their environment, the gap between prescribed standards and reality can only be adequately understood by examining the issue of the exploitation of child workers in the context of the system for the protection of children. It is also necessary to identify those aspects of the problem for which responsibility can be attributed to the labour inspection system, and those aspects upon which the labour inspectorate cannot be expected to have any influence.

The system for the protection of children and their environment

In the first place, the system for the protection of children has to be defined: it consists of a set of actors, institutions and organisations which, with a semblance of coherence, in a particular environment, contribute to producing the conditions in which children live, work and develop, and which, in one capacity or another, contribute either directly or indirectly to encouraging or compromising the future of the children.

The participants in this system for the protection of children are the following:

- in the first place, the family;
- and then health-care establishments, such as establishments for the protection of mothers and children;
- teaching, training and leisure establishments;
- technical and vocational training establishments, and apprenticeship centres;
- institutions responsible for protecting working children: the labour inspectorate and labour laws, trade unions, occupational physicians, social security institutions, etc.;
- judicial and social protection institutions;
- and finally, associations, bodies, groups and co-operatives which, in some way, work for the protection of children.

---

[7] See for example, Smitu Kothari: "There's blood on those matchsticks: Child labour in Sivakasi", in Economic and Political Weekly, Volume 18, No. 27, 2 July 1984, and Roger Bernheim: "Child slavery in India", in Swiss Review of World Affairs, June 1990.

In theory, all these institutions have the function of preventing or correcting the harmful effects on children of their economic, cultural, social and ecological environment. If any of these institutions do not exist, or do not properly fulfill their function, the harmful effects of this environment are worsened.

An unfavourable economic and cultural environment

Labour inspectors in developing countries, who are responsible for the application of protective legislation, are aware that child labour is very often a question of survival for both the child and its family. They are also very well aware that it is a result of poverty and that poverty cannot be abolished by decree. Nor are they unaware of the fact that the illegal employment that they are combating is a product of two factors: the demand for employment by children who are seeking a subsistence income; and the availability of low-skilled, cheap work. For enterprises which serve an internal market with a low purchasing power, children are docile workers who are obliged to accept the working conditions, wages, precariousness and insecurity of the jobs which are on offer[8].

Labour inspectors also work in a cultural environment which, to say the least, does not encourage action to reduce the incidence of child labour.

In most cases, the parents of child workers also worked at a very early age and only in rare cases attended school. Because they see many educated adults affected by unemployment or underemployment, they believe that it is better for their children to learn a trade on-the-job rather than to go to school. Parents also think that the help provided by children in agricultural work, in commerce, in craft work or at home is not work: real work is done by adults in industrial enterprises[9].

Working gives children value in their own eyes and in those of their parents. It enables them to acquire financial and psychological independence and to help their families, even if this responsibility has to be won at the price of exploitation and very harsh working conditions.

Labour inspectors who try to apply laws to protect children from work encounter a wall of such incomprehension that many decide not to combat the economic and cultural resistance alone and prefer to devote themselves to other work, such as the settlement of individual and collective disputes which are submitted to them by the trade unions.

The origins of child labour described above, which are related to the economic and cultural environment, are compounded by factors which lie within the competence of the system for the protection of children.

---

[8] Assefa Bequele and Jo Boyden: Combating child labour (ILO, Geneva, 1988).

[9] William E. Myers: "Urban working children: A comparison of four surveys from South America", in International Labour Review, Vol. 128, No. 3, 1989, pages 321-335.

Factors that lie within the competence of the system for the protection of children

Labour inspectors are called upon to apply fairly advanced legislation on the minimum age for admission to employment and work in an environment in which schools are overcrowded and parents are unable to pay for school registration fees, school supplies and decent clothes for their children to wear to school. In some cases, limitations on the working hours of children are designed to enable them to attend school and to learn a trade; but is the standard of the technical and vocational training provided by teaching and training establishments sufficiently high for the children to want to make the (sometimes considerable) effort that is required to follow the courses that they provide? Certain national laws have established long lists of dangerous types of work which are prohibited for children, but do health-care establishments, doctors, parents or teachers inform labour inspectors when children are the victims work-related accidents or diseases?

The lack of relations between the institutions that are responsible for protecting children therefore results in incoherent and ineffective action. Because of the lack of co-ordination, responsibilities are neglected.

Better co-ordination between all these actors would undoubtedly make it possible to bring hidden problems to the surface. Labour inspectors only see the tip of the iceberg. Most child labour is hidden below the water line. Home work, work on the streets and unpaid family work, in the absence of an employment relationship between an employer and an employee, is not protected by the law. Unseen work in rural areas and in small workshops does not lie within the scope of the law and, as anything which is not prohibited is legal, this invisible work lies outside the competence of the labour inspectorate. This is one of the major contradictions of labour inspection: it is not possible to protect the most underprivileged and exposed children if labour inspectors do not have access to small workshops, farms and distant worksites, and all locations on which home work is carried out.

Failings of the labour inspection system

The most evident failing of the labour inspection system is certainly the lack of resources. Labour inspection is often described as the poor relative of labour administration. This poverty takes the form of a lack of vehicles to visit enterprises, a lack of legal and technical documentation and unsuitable premises. There are often insufficient numbers of labour inspectors to visit all the enterprises in the formal sector, quite apart from the small workshops and informal-sector enterprises in rural areas. The training of labour inspectors is not always appropriate for the tasks that are demanded of them, and they cannot easily call upon the assistance of experts such as engineers, physicians, psychologists, trainers and other specialists.

Labour Inspection Convention, 1947 (No. 81)

Article 10

The number of labour inspectors shall be sufficient to secure the effective discharge of the duties of the inspectorate and shall be determined with due regard for:

(a) the importance of the duties which inspectors have to perform, in particular -

(i) the number, nature, size and situation of the workplaces liable to inspection;

(ii) the number and classes of workers employed in such workplaces; and

(iii) the number and complexity of the legal provisions to be enforced;

(b) the material means placed at the disposal of the inspectors; and

(c) the practical conditions under which visits of inspection must be carried out in order to be effective.

Article 11

1. The competent authority shall make the necessary arrangements to furnish labour inspectors with -

(a) local offices, suitably equipped in accordance with the requirements of the service, and accessible to all persons concerned;

(b) the transport facilities necessary for the performance of their duties in cases where suitable public facilities do not exist.

2. The competent authority shall make the necessary arrangements to reimburse to labour inspectors any travelling and incidental expenses which may be necessary for the performance of their duties.

The weakness of the action taken by labour inspection services against the exploitation of child workers also has its origins in the multiplicity of tasks entrusted to labour inspectors.

Originally, the labour inspectorate was made responsible only for child labour. This responsibility was then extended very rapidly to the protection of women at work, to occupational safety and health, and to working time.

Inspection systems then became progressively more diversified. In certain countries a new labour inspection institution or body was set up each time a new right was enshrined in law or a branch of activity came to be considered dangerous. In some Latin American countries, labour inspection for child workers remained the responsibility of a specialised body, while other services covered occupational safety and health, industrial relations and wages, employment protection and vocational training. In one Latin American country, 16 different labour inspection services cover the various aspects of labour legislation.

However, in other countries the inspection of all the new rights obtained by workers has been entrusted to a single body. On site, the same labour inspector has to respond to issues ranging from wages and collective agreements, the right of association and the protection of workers' representatives, to employment promotion measures and technical questions related to occupational safety and health. In the developing countries that have adopted this general model, and where child labour is very widespread, the function of protecting children rapidly became submerged by other urgent tasks.

For example, in several Latin American, African and European countries, labour inspectors very frequently intervene in individual and collective labour disputes. Their intervention is sometimes compulsory and they may be called upon to chair conciliation and arbitration tribunals. In many cases, these functions take up most of the inspectors' time so that they are no longer available to inspect enterprises and supervise the application of the law on the spot, particularly as regards child labour.

Another hypothesis that needs to be taken into account is that the ineffectiveness of the action that is taken by the labour inspectorate in the field of child labour has its origins in the lack of co-ordination between the various labour inspection bodies or between the central and outlying inspection services.

In some countries, labour inspection comes under the responsibility of the Ministry of Labour and the labour inspectorate is the only body that is responsible for inspecting all workplaces in all branches of economic activity. This unified system of inspection, which comes under a central authority, is capable of pursuing an overall and coherent policy to control child labour.

In other countries, where specialised services have been established for industry, agriculture, transport, mining and home work, these services generally come under the authority of various ministries and in most cases are not in contact with each other. Horizontal co-ordination on issues such as child labour is therefore very difficult to implement.

Finally, irrespective of the system of labour inspection and the type of administration that have been adopted in the various countries, it is always difficult to design means of action that are appropriate to the complexity of the problem of child labour.

If labour inspectorates take little action in relation to child labour, this is perhaps largely due to the fact that means of action have not yet been found which simultaneously take into account:

- the right of extremely poor children and their families to survive, and their need to earn some money;

- and the right of children, as set out in the law, to be protected against the exploitation of their labour.

The attempts that have been made to resolve this contradiction provide a basis upon which it is possible to outline an approach that could be adopted by labour inspectorates as their contribution to the formulation of a national policy for the protection of child workers and for the abolition of child labour. This approach has three aspects: observation, evaluation and action.

Labour inspection: Towards a coherent policy to combat child labour

Taking the initiative of observing working situations

From the information gathered in a number of countries, labour inspectors seem more likely to take action in their various fields of competence as a result of complaints rather than at their own initiative. It is very rare for children to come forward and complain themselves. The same applies to parents and trade union organisations, especially since children are not unionised (in certain countries, such as Comoros, Niger and Senegal, only minors aged over 16 years can join a trade union). Few children have the status of employees in a regular employment relationship and children who work illegally are too afraid to complain. Similarly, if labour inspectors wait for employment accidents before they intervene and inspect an enterprise, they will miss many dangerous situations to which children are exposed, particularly since accidents that occur to workers who are in an irregular employment situation are almost never reported.

If labour inspectors do not take the initiative of going to the workplace to inspect enterprises and to all the places where children work, they deny themselves the possibility of taking any effective action for the protection of children, or indeed for other workers. Inspecting the workplace is the very basis of their activities and a necessary precondition for labour inspection. For this reason, the first right granted to labour inspectors by Convention No. 81 and by national laws is to enter enterprises at any hour of the day or night without prior notification. In many countries, labour inspectors have once again to find the will and the means to get out of their offices and seek out the workers in factories, on building sites, on plantations and on the street.

Labour Inspection Convention, 1947 (No. 81)

Article 12

1. Labour inspectors provided with proper credentials shall be empowered:

(a) to enter freely and without previous notice at any hour of the day or night any workplace liable to inspection;

(b) to enter by day any premises which they may have reasonable cause to believe to be liable to inspection; and

(c) to carry out any examination, test or enquiry which they may consider necessary in order to satisfy themselves that the legal provisions are being strictly observed, and in particular -

(i) to interrogate, alone or in the presence of witnesses, the employer or the staff of the undertaking on any matters concerning the application of the legal provisions;

(ii) to require the production of any books, registers or other documents the keeping of which is prescribed by national laws or regulations relating to conditions of work, in order to see that they are in conformity with the legal provisions, and to copy such documents or make extracts from them;

(iii) to enforce the posting of notices required by the legal provisions;

(iv) to take or remove for purposes of analysis samples of materials and substances used or handled, subject to the employer or his representative being notified of any samples or substances taken or removed for such purpose.

2. On the occasion of an inspection visit, inspectors shall notify the employer or his representative of their presence, unless they consider that such a notification may be prejudicial to the performance of their duties.

However, labour inspectors need a reliable basis of information in order to target their inspection activities. If they try to visit all enterprises in all branches of activity, there is a high risk of missing the target and not finding the child workers they are seeking.

The inspectorate therefore needs a reliable information system. In which branches of activity and types of enterprises are children working? Are they in agriculture or stock-raising, in mines or quarries, in commerce or craftwork, in industry or services? Are they in the formal or informal sector? Are they concentrated in towns or rural areas? Are they homeworkers or domestic workers?

A preliminary study is needed in order to gather information from all the available sources. There are many such sources; labour inspectors can request information from official and non-governmental institutions, from teaching establishments, health-care centres, the judicial services and other associations. The information exists, but it is dispersed. The labour inspectorate therefore has to take the initiative of going out and finding the information.

Various surveys show that children work in a limited number of branches of activity and trades. The labour inspectorate can therefore concentrate its attention on these sectors so that, with statistical support, it can assess the scope of the problem of child labour.

The approach adopted by inspectors during their visits to the workplace is clearly of great importance. They can take the option of limiting themselves to noting the age of children who work there. Alternatively, they can broaden their investigation to cover all the conditions of work of child labourers.

Under most national laws, the employer has to make permanently available to the inspector a register containing the names and age of the workers who are employed at the establishment from the moment of their recruitment. If labour inspectors suspect anything, they can demand to see the identity documents of the workers. In certain countries, children who are authorised to work have to be able to present a work permit or workbook issued by the labour inspectorate. Although all these supervisory methods can easily be circumvented, they should always be designed to achieve two objectives: in the short term, to protect children who are compelled by their poverty to work; and, in the long term, to eliminate child labour. Moreover, there is also a danger that the strict application of the law, which in most cases of the violation of minimum age laws would result in the dismissal of the child worker, may simply result in the replacement of one child labourer by another under the same exploitative conditions.

It is worthwhile to take the time to observe all the factors which go to make up the physical and mental burden of child workers. These include the age of the children, their apparent physical condition, their strength and, where appropriate, their disabilities, as well as the work that they are performing, the materials and machines they are using, the products they are handling and their physical and human environment, their working hours, remuneration and status. Labour inspectors, in accordance with international conventions, are empowered to intervene in all these areas. In order to do so they need a table for the observation of work situations. It is therefore the responsibility of each labour inspection system to prepare inspection forms that enable the inspectors to gather the maximum information at the workplace on the real conditions of child labourers.

Moreover, labour inspectors cannot observe on their own without talking to each other. Nor should they use the cold eye of the detached observer. Labour inspectors have the right to question child workers, but they should also listen to them and take an interest in what they are doing and why they are working. They have to listen to their pride in contributing to the survival of their families, but also to their fatigue, their fear of accidents and disease, their desire to learn and to escape from poverty. This method, which respects the child, was adopted as early as 1840 by Dr. Villermé in order to investigate poverty without humiliating the poor, and to obtain a description of the physical and moral state of the workers employed in the production of cotton, wool and silk in the North of France[10].

Evaluating the risks of child labour

A rigorous and methodical observation of the conditions in which children have to work can provide the labour inspectorate with a mass of information, which has to be processed in order to obtain a reasonably true picture of the situation of the children and select the correct course of action.

In order to assess the seriousness of the risks to which child labourers are exposed, labour inspectors cannot merely add together the various factors as if they were all of equivalent weight. The concept of the accumulation of handicaps and constraints also has to be taken into account.

The physical and mental burden borne by young newspaper distributors or shoeshiners is not the same as that of children who work long hours in gold or diamond mines, squashed into narrow unprotected galleries in the humidity and heat, and with the constant fear of cave-ins. Even if the number of children working in mines, building sites or waste dumps is smaller than the number employed in domestic work, it may be necessary to begin by combating child labour in the most hazardous sectors, in which the unsafe nature of the work is compounded by the long hours, the lack of safety equipment and rest periods, malnutrition and the climate.

It would be valuable at this stage for the labour inspectorate to possess a table for the evaluation of the occupational risks of children, which it could use to assess risk factors and their accumulation. This table should contain the following sections:

- individual and family characteristics: age and physical condition of the children; level of general and vocational education; family environment;

- the work performed: is it monotonous or varied, light or arduous, complex, dangerous or such as to require sustained concentration[11]?

---

10 L.R. Villermé: Tableau de l'état physique et moral des ouvriers employés dans les manufactures de coton, de laine et de soie (Description of the physical and moral state of the workers employed in the production of cotton, wool and silk) (Edition 10-18, Paris, 1971).

11 In France, labour inspectors may authorise employment, for half of the school holidays, of young persons aged from 14 to 16 years "in work which does not involve, taking into account the sex and age of the child, any abnormal fatigue, either due to the nature of the work or the specific conditions in which it is performed. In particular, any employment by children is prohibited in work that is repetitive or performed in surroundings or at a pace which gives it an arduous nature" (Section D.211-3 of the Labour Code).

- the working environment:
  - the physical environment, including climate, extreme weather conditions, and the unhealthy state of the premises, street or house;
  - the equipment and products used;
  - the human environment: are the children in contact with the public or clients, or are they exposed to violence or the insecurity of the area or the street?
- work organisation and working hours:
  - a distinction should be made between full-time work with a fairly heavy timetable and part-time, intermittent or occasional work;
  - greatest emphasis should be placed on sectors in which children work at night and where they do not benefit from daily rest periods, weekly rest days or annual leave;
  - account should be taken of time devoted to school work and household tasks;
- remuneration and status:
  - a distinction should be made between work that is performed free-of-charge; irregular and occasional wages; and piece-work, task work and fixed wages;
  - finally, the precarious status of the child worker should be taken into account; is the child employed on a permanent, seasonal, daily or occasional basis?

Should this evaluation be undertaken solely by the labour inspectorate[12]? Experience suggests that it should not. It is not sufficient to apply the criteria laid down by law, because these criteria never take into account the accumulation of handicaps and constraints and they disregard the concept of the overall burden of work.

For this reason, both in observation and evaluation, the labour inspectorate should be able to consult experts, physicians, teachers and parents' associations. It should endeavour to reach agreement with them on how to evaluate the risks to which child workers are subjected. The choice of priority options depends on this evaluation and support.

Long-term action

Before taking action, the labour inspectorate needs to ensure that it has a clear vision of its short-, medium- and long-term objectives. It must be capable of using different methods in order to achieve these different objectives.

In the short term, the use of sanctions and the threat of sanctions cannot be totally ruled out. It is necessary to show firmness in manifestly hazardous situations, such as in enterprises in the formal sector which use children for dangerous or unhealthy work and employ them by night or for excessive hours. Labour inspectors have at their disposal a broad range of legal measures for this purpose.

---

12 See, for example, Niger, Section 138 of CAP Decree No. 67/126 of 7 September 1967: "The employment of children is prohibited in any work that endangers their life or health. The labour inspector shall decide upon the hazardous nature of the work".

In the medium term, the objective is to improve the working conditions of children. It is not possible to dismiss all child workers tomorrow, because that would reduce them to an even worse situation. However, it is possible to try to act upon several factors which can diminish the overall burden and constraints that are felt by children in areas such as:

- working hours. It is necessary to achieve a progressive reduction in the working hours of children and, in exchange, to obtain time for them to attend school and receive vocational training. Labour inspectors can also make use of the legal provisions which, in most countries, prohibit night work for children, and which lay down that rest periods for children must consist of 11 or 12 consecutive hours, that children may not be employed in work for over six or eight hours per day or in excess of a working week that is set out by law (30 hours in Ecuador and 33 hours in Peru for children aged 13 to 14 years). Other laws provide that no uninterrupted effective period of work for children may exceed three hours (Ecuador, Mexico and Peru) or four-and-a-half hours (France).

- the work performed. It is possible to suggest a change in the organisation of work so that adults perform heavy maintenance work and the most arduous work is mechanised in order to save human strength and energy. In case of doubt, labour inspectors can request a physician to examine the young workers in order to ascertain that the work does not exceed their strength, as set out in various national laws. The advice of an expert can make it possible to convince the employer to change the way in which the work is organised, without resorting to the solution of replacing the children when they can no longer keep up the required pace.

- the working environment. Action to improve the ventilation of the workplace, its cleanliness, its equipment and products, as well as to increase the safety of equipment and vehicles, benefits both children and adults. This type of action is durable and its benefits are felt throughout the workplace.

- facilities. Wash basins and the provision of drinks and hot meals are not a luxury, but simply a means of lightening the burden of work. By insisting on these minimum conditions, which are generally set out in law, labour inspectors can contribute to improving the welfare of both children and adults.

In the long term, the objective is the abolition of child labour. This is a long process to which the labour inspectorate must contribute with the specific means at its disposal.

By improving the effectiveness of its usual means of action for all workers, the labour inspectorate can have an indirect effect on certain of the causes of child labour. Children are often obliged to work because their parents' wages are insufficiently high or are paid very late. In other cases, the father may have died in an employment accident or the mother can no longer work in an unhealthy environment, such as a pesticide factory. In the event of sickness, the parents may not be covered by social security. The parents may have been dismissed and may not have received the indemnities that are due to them. In all these cases, the child has to work for the survival of the family. The labour inspectorate can reduce the incidence of child labour by ensuring that the rights of workers are respected.

For many years, emphasis has been placed on developing labour legislation and on supervision by the labour inspectorate. This is justified, because shortcomings in the application of labour legislation are still enormous. However, to take long-term action, the labour inspectorate will have to find a new balance between its supervisory function and its advisory role. It will have to develop its educational function, diversify its means of action and participate with other institutions in the dissemination of information and in the provision of training. For example, labour inspectors could train teachers to provide children with information about their minimum rights and about simple protective measures at work. In the same way as they are taught to repair a car or use a tool, why not teach children the minimum standards relating to working hours, safety, wages and labour contracts? The labour inspectorate cannot be everywhere. It therefore has to select target groups and teachers can help it give its activities a greater multiplier effect.

*

* *

The implementation of a coherent labour inspection policy for the conditions of employment and work of children will certainly involve modifications in the organisation of the inspection services in most labour inspection systems. It will also require an important effort to train labour inspectors in new methods of work. This may involve a redistribution of functions in the inspection system, grouping together certain services, making others more specialised and certainly improving co-ordination within the labour administration and with other institutions.

In particular, it will be necessary to provide labour inspectors who are responsible for child labour with a good technical training so that they are capable of observing work situations, evaluating risks and taking choices. It is particularly urgent for labour inspectors to learn how to communicate with the child labourers whom they are responsible for protecting, with their employers, with workers' representatives and with the other institutions concerned.

The political will to provide the labour inspectorate with the resources to carry out its mission to protect workers, and particularly children, is a prerequisite for a coherent and concerted national policy for the elimination of child labour.

Annex 1

Standard-setting activities of the ILO in the field of labour inspection

Brief historical overview

I. Specific texts

1919: In the Treaty of Versailles, which created the ILO, it is laid down (Part 13, Article 427, Point 9) that: "Each State should make provision for a system of inspection in which women should take part, in order to ensure the enforcement of the laws and regulations for the protection of the employed".

1919: At its first session, the Conference adopted the Labour Inspection (Health Services) Recommendation (No. 5), which recommended the establishment of an inspection system to safeguard the health of the workers.

1923: The Labour Inspection Recommendation (No. 20) (general principles for the organisation of the labour inspection service).

1926: The Labour Inspection (Seamen) Recommendation (No. 28);

1937: The Inspection (Building) Recommendation (No. 54).

1939: The Labour Inspectorates (Indigenous Workers) Recommendation (No. 59).

1940: Labour inspection was included in the agenda of the 26th Session of the Conference, but was only taken up after the war.

1947: The Labour Inspection Convention (No. 81) and Recommendation (No. 81); the Labour Inspectorates (Non-Metropolitan Territories) Convention (No. 85); and the Labour Inspection (Mining and Transport) Recommendation (No. 82).

1969: The Labour Inspection (Agriculture) Convention (No. 129) and Recommendation (No. 133).

II. Other ILO texts

Reference may be made, among the Conventions and Recommendations providing for the establishment of a system of inspection to apply national and international standards, to the following instruments:

1929: The Prevention of Industrial Accidents Recommendation (No. 31).

1930: The Forced Labour Convention (No. 29).

1958: The Plantations Convention (No. 110).

1963: The Guarding of Machinery Convention (No. 119).

1964: The Hygiene (Commerce and Offices) Recommendation (No. 120).

1974: The Occupational Cancer Convention (No. 139).

1977: The Working Environment (Air Pollution, Noise and Vibration) Convention (No. 148).

1979: The Occupational Safety and Health (Dock Work) Convention (No. 152).

1981: The Occupational Safety and Health Convention (No. 155).

1985: The Occupational Health Services Convention (No. 161).

1986: The Asbestos Convention (No. 162).

Part V

National legal provisions on the minimum age for admission to employment

Part V

National legal provisions on the minimum age for admission to employment

The following fact sheets summarise national legislative provisions on minimum age for admission to employment or work from 143 countries on a country-by-country basis. The available information has been subdivided into three categories:

- Basic minimum age. This section contains the minimum age laid down for admission to employment or work; this age may apply either to all occupations and economic sectors, or only to specific activities and sectors. Exclusions from the application of these minimum age provisions, either by category of work or by sector, as well as the conditions under which young persons may work when they are legally permitted to do so, are also contained in this category.

- Light work. Under many national legislations, children are allowed to undertake certain kinds of light, non-hazardous activities at a lower age than the generally applicable minimum age, or upon completion of compulsory schooling. This section includes the absolute minimum age at which children may engage in such light activities, definitions of light work if they exist, as well as any conditions related to the granting of permission for children to undertake light work.

- Hazardous work. Much legislation contains provisions setting out a higher minimum age for admission to work which is likely to jeopardise the health, safety or morals of young persons. This section contains the minimum ages set either in general for all types of hazardous work or for specific occupations or industries which are defined as being dangerous, according to the approach adopted by the country concerned.

The entries are brief and cover only basic provisions. Their main purpose is to illustrate the progress, or lack of progress, as the case may be, in the adoption of legislative provisions to protect children and young persons from work that is considered unsuitable to their well-being and development.

A word of caution may be necessary as regards the accuracy and completeness of the information provided. In many countries, provisions on employment or work of children are found in a great variety of legislative provisions, ranging from education acts over specific acts on certain sectors (e.g. agriculture, shipping) to safety and health regulations. In particular, in countries where legislative provisions on child or youth employment differ by occupations or areas of economic activity, some of the relevant laws or regulations may have been missed. Thus, the information provided may occasionally be incomplete or even give a wrong impression.

Since all the relevant details may not have been included, and since terminology has been translated or adapted with a view to comprehensibility rather than strict adherence to the original wording, the original source should be consulted for authoritative information on the content of the legislation. A list of sources is given at the end of the fact sheets for all countries. Where a basic text has been reprinted and/or translated in the Labour Law Documents [formerly Legislative Series], an ILO publication containing selected labour and social security legislation, the citation to the publication is also given.

A descriptive summary of national legislation on child labour as well as tables providing an overview of national legislative provisions can be found in Part II of this Digest.

Minimum age for admission to employment: Legal provisions

AFGHANISTAN	Basic minimum age. 15 for employment in all state and mixed enterprises, administrations and institutes, social organisations and co-operatives, as well as private enterprises. 14 for trainees.
	Hazardous work. Minimum age of 18 for work that is physically arduous or harmful to health, underground work, and the lifting and transporting of weights that are heavier than fixed standards.
ALBANIA	Basic minimum age. 15 in state and social undertakings, institutions and organisations, and for members of handicraft co-operative societies.
	Hazardous work. Minimum age of 18 for underground work, and for work declared to be particularly arduous or unhealthy in the relevant occupational safety and health regulations.
ALGERIA	Basic minimum age. 16 for all individual and collective employment relationships, except for persons employed in air and sea transport, the crews of merchant and fishing vessels, homeworkers, journalists, performers, commercial travellers, championship athletes, and domestic staff. Exceptions also include work performed under an apprenticeship contract. A worker who is under age may be recruited upon submission of written authorisation by his or her legal guardian.
	Hazardous work. Minimum age of 16 for work that is dangerous, unhealthy or detrimental to morals. 18 for work in the maritime industry.
ANGOLA	Basic minimum age. 14, with the permission of the father, mother or legal guardian, in all sectors except family undertakings.
	Hazardous work. Minimum age of 18 (16 for apprentices) in work or circumstances that may cause physical or mental harm to young persons or affect their normal development, particularly underground work, work in mines and quarries, power stations and furnaces, and work in places of entertainment or connected with the sale or publicity of pharmaceutical products; all kinds of work specified by the schedule to the relevant decree, including the production or handling of various acids, tar, asphalt, bitumen, rubber, cement, crystal and glass, alcohol, electricity, mirrors, explosives, gypsum, glue, marble and stone, or varnishes.
ANTIGUA AND BARBUDA	Basic minimum age. 16 in public or private agricultural or industrial undertakings and on ships. Exceptions include undertakings and ships where adult members of the same family are employed at the same time and place, subject to restrictions on working hours, and members of recognised youth organisations engaged collectively in such employment for fund raising.
	Light work. A minimum age of 14 applies to young persons who work in factories, whether or not they receive wages, in the collection, carrying or delivery of goods, carrying messages or running errands.

Minimum age for admission to employment: Legal provisions

ARGENTINA

Basic minimum age. 14 for work of any kind, with exceptions for family undertakings on condition that the work is not harmful or dangerous and that the hours do not interfere with primary schooling. Other exceptions may be authorised by the competent authority for young persons who have not completed compulsory schooling if the work is indispensable for the young worker's maintenance and/or that of his or her family, on condition that the minimum period of education has been completed.

Hazardous work. Minimum age of 18 for work specified by regulations as arduous, dangerous or unhealthy. Prohibited occupations include the loading of ships, work in underground mines and quarries, loading by means of cranes and hoists, working as a mechanic or stoker on locomotives, greasing or cleaning machinery in motion, operating circular saws or other dangerous machines, smelting metal, melting glass, transporting radioactive substances, or working on premises where alcoholic beverages are sold.

AUSTRALIA

Basic minimum age. No general minimum age. Certain states and territories impose a minimum age (15, 16 or after the completion of compulsory schooling) in certain sectors; others merely prohibit work during school hours.

Hazardous work. Minimum ages of 16-18, depending upon the jurisdiction and sector of activity. For example, 16 for work at sea, work associated with oil and gas burners and oxy-acetylene blow pipes in all jurisdictions; underground mining (Northern Territories, Queensland, Tasmania, New South Wales); lead processing (Western Australia); and work involving contact with asbestos or cement (Victoria). 17 for the use of agricultural chemicals (Queensland), subject to regulations; underground mining (Victoria). 18 for underground mining (South and Western Australia); lead processing (Queensland and Victoria); trimmers and stokers in all jurisdictions; use of explosives, power tools, circular saws, guillotines or similar machinery, or working on premises where alcoholic beverages are sold (Victoria).

AUSTRIA

Basic minimum age. 15, or upon completion of compulsory schooling, for all industrial and commercial sectors and agriculture, excluding employment for the exclusive purpose of training or education. The competent authority may permit the use of children in musical, theatrical and other artistic performances as well as in films, with the agreement of the school authority and, in some cases, of the labour inspectorate as well as the legal guardians.

Light work. Minimum age of 12 for non-agricultural work; no minimum age specified for agricultural work. Light work of an occasional nature may be carried out outside school hours in enterprises; at home; as a messenger; on sports fields and playgrounds; collecting flowers, herbs, mushrooms and fruit or similar activities, if it does not endanger the child's physical, mental and moral health and development, does not expose the child to the risk of accidents or the harmful effects of the heat, cold, humidity or of substances, rays, dust, gases or steams endangering health. It must not interfere with school instruction or the observance of religious obligations. The work must not exceed two hours a day and, on school days, the combined total of hours of school attendance and work must not exceed seven. Occasional light work may not be performed on Sundays or statutory holidays, or without the consent of a legal guardian, who must be satisfied that there are no grounds for objecting to the child's employment on health grounds or for reasons of schooling. Occasional light tasks and occupations are permitted in agriculture only in the case of children who work for their own parents, provided that the work is of limited duration and that due care is taken to avoid prejudicing the child's health and safety.

Minimum age for admission to employment: Legal provisions

AUSTRIA (continued)

Hazardous work. Minimum ages of 16 to 18. 18 for work in variety shows, cabarets, bars, sexshops, dance halls, discotheques, cinemas, circuses or similar enterprises where work may prejudice the minor's health or morals; work involving exposure to various substances or composites which are harmful to the health, in particular noxious or corrosive substances or substances which may cause irritation to the skin or mucuous membranes (in such cases, the minimum age can be reduced to 16 for young persons who have completed half their vocational training, and who work under supervision and after medical examination; stricter regulations apply to women workers); various types of work with substances or composites where there is a risk of explosion oir which are inflammable; various types of work involving exposure to hazardous levels of vibration, lasers and ionising rays (can be reduced for young persons undergoing vocational training under certain conditions); work involving particular physical strain (the transport of heavy loads; work involving exposure to heat, cold, high or low air pressure; diving; etc.); the operation of various motor-driven and other machinery, if no appropriate measures have been taken to reduce the danger of accidents (can be reduced to 16 in connection with vocational training or to 17 in some cases); work with enterprise fire brigades and gas rescue services; underground work (17 for men undergoing training, altogether prohibited for women); work in brick kilns; construction work; work on roofs or at exposed heights; railway work; operating lifts; operating vehicles, cranes and excavators; work as a member of the crew of a ship (unless undergoing training); various types of metal work (unless undergoing training; may be reduced to 17 if medically certified fit); work involving exposure to risks of infection; and itinerant trades among others. Minimum age of 17 for scheduled work in quarries, certain work related to glass, spray and dip painting, among others. Minimum age of 16 for piece-rate work.

BAHAMAS

Basic minimum age. 14 in a broad range of industrial undertakings, including mines and quarries, agricultural undertakings, utilities and transportation, excluding transport by hand and work in family undertakings.

Hazardous work. Minimum age of 16 for work aboard ships if certified medically fit; 18 without medical certificate. Minimum age of 18 for work in the engine room of a ship.

BAHRAIN

Basic minimum age. 14 for employment in private industry and occupations that are not hazardous or unhealthy, excluding agriculture, the maritime sector, family undertakings (provided work is under the immediate supervision of the family), domestic service, and certain temporary and casual work.

Hazardous work. Minimum age of 16 for work in quarries and work pertaining to the prospecting of minerals and stones; work involving any material connected with radiation or X-rays; work resulting in exposure to the dust of asbestos or cotton; work in industries engaged in prospecting and refining oil; work such as in bakery ovens or such other furnaces that are used for melting metallurgical materials or refining or smelting them; the aluminium industry; occupations related to the production or storage of explosives; the glass industry; the manufacture of bricks, tiles and the cutting of marble and other stones; forging, filing and fitting as well as auto-mechanical work; work connected with materials or components provided for in the schedule for occupational diseases attached to the Social Insurance Law and which may result in poisoning due to their use or handling or exposure to their dust, vapours or fumes; welding with oxy-acetylene and arc welding; spray painting; the operation and control of mixing and pasting in the manufacture and repair of electrical batteries; the operation, control, repair and cleaning of machinery while it is in motion; work on cranes; casting of metals; carpentry; skinning and butchering of animals; construction, renovation, repair or pulling down of any building, port, dock, berth, canal, quay, highway, tunnel, breach, major drainage complex, drains, wells, cables, telephone installations, and plants for the generation of gas, water desalination and distribution; work involving the generation, distribution or transmission of electricity and any type of mechanical energy; the manufacture of ice; freezing operations; the filling of gas cylinders under pressure; carrying weights of more than 20 kilograms.

Minimum age for admission to employment: Legal provisions

BANGLADESH

Basic minimum age. 14 for any factory; 12 for tea plantations, shops and establishments. Agriculture is generally excluded, as well as factories with less than ten workers and tea plantations with less than 30 workers. 15 for work in any capacity on any ship, except on a school or training ship, or on a ship in which all persons employed are family members, or where the young person is employed on nominal wages and shall be under the protection of his father or other close male relative.

Hazardous work. Minimum ages of 16 to 18. 16 for work in factories where the machinery is in motion or in places where a cotton opener is operated. 17 for work in mines either below or above ground. 18 for trimmers or stokers, with exceptions under specified circumstances for those over 16, and for work on factory machinery unless the worker receives instruction on the dangers and is sufficiently trained and supervised by an experienced and qualified machine operator. In general, "where the provincial Government is satisfied that any operation ... exposes any person employed to serious risk of bodily injury, poisoning or disease, it may make rules ... prohibiting or restricting employment of ... adolescents or children".

BARBADOS

Basic minimum age. 15 for industrial undertakings or ships. Industrial undertakings include mines and quarries, manufacturing, construction and other prescribed undertakings as well as the transportation of passengers or goods by road or rail and the handling of goods at docks, warehouses or airports, except for technical training ships under approved supervision and family undertakings. Children of compulsory school age, up to 16, are prohibited from employment "in any undertaking whatever during school hours".

Hazardous work. Minimum age of 18 for "any work that by its nature or the circumstances under which it is done is likely to cause injury to ... health, safety or morals", including certain processes connected with the manufacture of lead.

BELGIUM

Basic minimum age. 14 and completion of compulsory schooling for all employment generally. Applies to fishing during school holidays, provided there is no danger and the vessel belongs to the minor's family or only employs family members. 15 for full-time students working under student contracts of employment. Individual exceptions may be granted to child performers.

Hazardous work. Minimum ages of 16 to 21, depending upon the activity. Generally the age is 18 for work in underground or surface mines or quarries, work as trimmers and stokers, work exceeding the strength of young persons or endangering their health or morals. Such work includes the manufacture or production of flammable liquids or gases or other processes involving danger of fire or explosion, the use of white lead, or radiation.

BELIZE

Basic minimum age. 12 to 15. 14 for public and private industrial undertakings, including mines and quarries, manufacturing, shipbuilding, power utilities, construction, transportation and specially designated agricultural undertakings, but excluding approved and supervised work in technical schools and entertainment where the child is not compensated and the net proceeds are devoted to charity, education or purposes other than the private profit of the promoter. 12 for all occupations not specified or regulated, subject to restrictions on hours of work. 15 for employment at sea, unless a medical practitioner has certified not more than one year previously that the person is fit for the proposed employment. The restriction is not applicable to vessels where only members of the same family are employed and to work on school or training ships, provided they are approved and supervised by a public authority. 14 on ships if authorised by the competent authority on the grounds that the work is beneficial to the minor.

Minimum age for admission to employment: Legal provisions

BELIZE (continued)	Light work. The Minister may authorise the employment of children under the age of 12 by their parents or guardians in light agricultural or horticultural work only in the parents' or guardians' lands or gardens. Hazardous work. Minimum age of 18 for trimmers and stokers on ships, unless only persons under 18 are available, in which case persons over the age of 16 may be employed provided two are engaged for each position. Children are prohibited from lifting, carrying or moving anything so heavy as to be likely to cause injury. Nor shall they be employed in occupations likely to be prejudicial to their life, health or education.
BENIN	Basic minimum age. 14 for all undertakings. Light work. Minimum age of 12 for domestic work and light work in plantations. Hazardous work. Minimum age of 18 for certain undertakings. "The types of work and categories of undertakings on and in which young people shall not be employed, and the age up to which the prohibition shall apply shall be specified by decree". For undertakings in the private sector, "the conditions of work ... of young persons under the age of 18 years shall be determined in accordance with the law".
BOLIVIA	Basic minimum age. 14 for all employment, except apprentices. Hazardous work. Minimum age of 18 for work exceeding the physical strength of young persons or likely to endanger their normal physical development; for dangerous, unhealthy or heavy work; or any occupation which is prejudicial to the morals or good conscience of the young person. The following work is prohibited: underground work in quarries and mines; handling of moving footways and conveyor belts; work with circular saws and other dangerous machines; work related to the smelting of metals or glassblowing by mouth; transport of inflammable materials; bricklaying or painting walls involving the use of ladders and scaffolding; work in plants distilling alcohol or mixing spirits; the manufacture of white lead and colouring products, as well as the use of paint, enamel or varnish containing lead or arsenic; work in factories or workshops where explosives and inflammable or caustic materials are produced or stored; work in locations where irritants or toxic dust, gases or vapours are usually produced or where temperatures are too high, low or the air is humid or poorly ventilated; work in places where obscene performances take place or where pornographic material is produced; places where there are games of chance, billiards or betting; night clubs, dance halls, etc., where alcohol is sold; work in the streets and plazas and kiosks which function late at night; and artistic performances requiring strength or violence or which use hypnotism.
BOTSWANA	Basic minimum age. 15 for industrial or agriculture undertakings, excluding family undertakings and work approved by the Commissioner of Labour. No employer may continue to employ a child or young person after oral or written notice has been received of an objection from a parent or guardian, except for employment under a written contract approved by the Commissioner. Light work. Minimum age of 14 provided that the child is not attending school; for light work that is not harmful to the child's health and development if performed for a member of the family, or where, other than domestic service for which suitable accommodation is provided, the child may readily return home each night. Light work is restricted to no more than six hours a day or 30 hours a week. Children of at least 14 years of age who are still attending school may perform light work during their vacation for no more than five hours a day between 6:00 and 16:00.

Minimum age for admission to employment: Legal provisions

BOTSWANA (continued)	Hazardous work. Minimum ages of 15 to 18. 18 for underground work and work which is harmful to a young person's health and development, or which is dangerous or immoral. The Commissioner may notify employers that the kind of work being performed by a young person falls within such categories and thus must be terminated. 15 for work involving lifting, carrying or moving anything so heavy as to be likely to endanger a child's physical development.
BRAZIL	Basic minimum age. 14 for employment in general, but 12 for apprentices.
	Hazardous work. Minimum age of 18 for dangerous, unhealthy or heavy work; work in areas prejudicial to schooling and to the young person's physical, psychic, moral and social development; work according to schedules and in localities that make school attendance impossible; and in workplaces or types of work that are prejudicial to a young person's morals, such as employment in variety theatres, cinemas, night clubs, casinos, cabaret shows, dance halls or similar establishments; employment in various circus acts; work involving the production, composition, delivery or sale of written or printed matter or materials which a competent authority deems prejudicial; and the retail sale of alcoholic beverages. Employment in streets, squares and other public places is subject to a permit from the Juvenile Court showing that the young person's employment is essential for his or her maintenance or that of the family and not prejudicial to morals. 21 for stevedoring and for underground work.
BULGARIA	Basic minimum age. 16 for all sectors. Persons below 15 may be hired for films and rehearsing and performing theatrical and other performances, "but under alleviated conditions and in accordance with the requirements for their proper physical, mental and moral development". Medical examinations and a certificate of fitness for employment pursuant to individual permits is required for the employment of all young persons.
	Light work. Minimum age of 15 for jobs which are light and pose no hazard or harm to the health or proper physical, mental and moral development of the young person. A 1987 document authorising a special work scheme for 15 year olds, with the consent of their parents or guardian, provides that there shall be quarterly medical exams, a maximum of four hours work a day, rest periods and a rest period of at least 14 hours between days of work.
	Hazardous work. Minimum age of 18 for heavy, harmful and hazardous jobs. The list of such jobs is to be approved, and is to be updated to reflect changes in working conditions and reviewed at least once every three years.
BURKINA FASO	Basic minimum age. 14 for all sectors. Exclusions may be authorised, provided they do not affect school attendance.
	Light work. Minimum age of 12 for domestic work and light agricultural work, such as harvesting and tending animals.
	Hazardous work. Minimum ages of 16 to 18. 16 for underground work (men only), work on scaffolding, with mechanical saws and in exterior stalls of shops. 18 for work exceeding the strength of young persons and work harmful to their morality. Limits are established for the loads young persons aged 14 to 18 may carry, pull or push.

Minimum age for admission to employment: Legal provisions

BURUNDI

Basic minimum age. 16 for all sectors, subject to individual exceptions granted by the Labour Inspector. Exclusions include technical and professional schools where work is essentially of an educational nature, is limited and is performed with the agreement and surveillance of a competent authority; family undertakings; and domestic work in the family.

Light work. 12 with the permission of the parent or guardian, provided the work does not interfere with the health or development of the child or interfere with progress in school. This covers domestic work, harvesting, horticulture and other light agricultural work, or work authorised by the labour inspector. Such work may not exceed six hours a day, whether on school or vacation days. Farm products weighing more than 15 kilograms may not be lifted.

Hazardous work. 18 for work of an immoral nature or in establishments where alcohol is consumed; operation of machines or moving mechanisms, especially where dangerous parts are not adequately protected; mining; transportation; work with explosives or flammable substances; construction or utilities; specified maritime tasks.

BYELORUSSIAN SSR

Basic minimum age. 16 for all sectors generally; 15 in exceptional cases with the agreement of the factory or labour union.

Hazardous work. 18 for arduous work or employment in unhealthy or dangerous working conditions and underground work.

CAMEROON

Basic minimum age. 14 for all sectors. Exceptions may be authorised by the ministry in charge of employment and social insurance and after consultation with the National Labour Council, taking account of local circumstances and the type of job.

Hazardous work. Minimum age of 14 to 18 for carrying, pulling or pushing objects beyond the strength of children, according to the weight and sex of the child. Minimum age of 18 for underground work in mines, quarries or galleries (except for boys 16 years of age undergoing vocational training); greasing, cleaning, inspecting or repairing machines or mechanisms in motion; work on premises with dangerous hand- or power-driven machines not covered by protective shields; work with shears, sharp mechanical blades, circular saws, band saws and presses of all kinds (except for boys 16 years of age undergoing training); work in connection with compressed air; the manufacture, handling or use of explosives; handling electrical cables, apparatus and machines of all kinds exceeding 600 volts for direct current and 150 volts for alternating current; work in bars, restaurants and similar establishments where alcoholic beverages are served; the production, handling and sale of literature, drawings, photographs, etc., injurious to the morality of young persons. Minimum age of 16 for operating steam valves; operating wheels, winches or pulleys; work on flying scaffolding; etc. Minimum age of 16 for girls for work with pedal-operated sewing machines. Minimum age of 18 for all kinds of work specified by the schedule to the relevant decree, including work with various acids, lead, enamel, glass, metals, bleaching, zinc, lead ores and many other substances. 16 for work with blast furnaces, chemical matches, gypsum and lime kilns, tobacco, inter alia.

Minimum age for admission to employment: Legal provisions

CANADA

Basic minimum age. At the federal level there is no absolute minimum age. An employer may employ a person under 17 years of age only in such occupations and subject to such conditions as are specified by regulation. By regulation, persons under 17 may work in offices and plants, transport, communications, maintenance or repair services; construction work; or other employment in a federal job, undertaking or business, only if not required to be in attendance at school under the law of the province of residence and provided that the work falls outside certain excluded categories and is not likely to endanger health or safety. At the provincial level, ages vary generally between 14 and 17, with exclusions covering various sectors and occupations, such as agriculture or family undertakings.

Hazardous work. At the federal level, minimum age of 17 in underground mining; in places prohibited to minors under the Explosives Regulations; as atomic energy workers; in work prohibited under the Canadian Shipping Act; and work likely to injure health or endanger safety. Various provincial provisions set minimum ages that are generally between 16 and 18 in underground or surface mining, certain construction work, such as hoisting, and in work that is detrimental to the safety, health, welfare or moral well-being of the child.

CAPE VERDE

Basic minimum age. 14 under contract as a permanent worker. 15, or upon completion of schooling, for public or private industrial establishments or any ancillary premises. Establishments employing only family members are excluded.

Light work. Minimum age of 12 for light work in agriculture.

Hazardous work. Minimum age of 16 for work which by its nature or the conditions in which it is performed is dangerous to life, health or morals; 18 for underground work.

CENTRAL AFRICAN REPUBLIC

Basic minimum age. 14 (15 during the school term for children who are still attending school) for all sectors, unless an exemption has been issued by the Minister of Labour after consulting the Labour Consultative Committee, taking into account local circumstances and conditions. Exceptions include family undertakings. Prohibited categories of employment are to be fixed by Decree of the Council of Ministers acting on the proposal of the Minister of Labour, after consulting the Labour Consultative Commission.

Light work. Minimum age of 12 for light domestic work and other light work (except in industry) by authorisation; and light harvesting work in agriculture, subject to the consent of the parents or guardian and to the written authorisation of the Inspector of Labour and Social Laws, issued upon presentation of a medical certificate which must be registered by the employer.

Hazardous work. Minimum ages of 16 to 18. 16 for work using crank- or pedal-operated machines, including jigs and shaking tables, mechanical saws, shearing machines and emery wheels; construction, except finishing jobs not requiring scaffolding. 18 for work that is prejudicial to the moral well-being, and work done under dangerous or unhealthy conditions or which demand great strength or attention; work with machinery that is in motion and near exposed machinery; the operation of lifting equipment; in slaughterhouses; in mines and quarries, and earth-moving work; and the operation of vehicles and motors. Limits are established on the loads young persons may carry, drag or push.

Minimum age for admission to employment: Legal provisions

CHAD

Basic minimum age. 14 for all undertakings, except for establishments in which only members of the same family are employed where the work is performed under the authority of the father, mother or guardian. 12 for specified agricultural tasks, with the consent of the parents or legal guardian.

Light work. Minimum age of 12 for light domestic work, such as kitchen help, valet or babysitter, and light work of a non-industrial nature, with the authorisation of the labour inspector and the consent of a parent or legal guardian.

Hazardous work. Minimum age of 18 for work with machinery that is in motion or machines with dangerous parts that are insufficiently protected; the operation of lifting equipment; the handling or use of explosives, irritating, corrosive or poisonous materials; work in tanneries or related occupations; the extraction of minerals or other raw materials from underground mines or quarries, as well as other excavations; the operation of specified motor vehicles or mechanical engines; all work that is of an immoral nature; and transportation by cabriolet or similar two-wheeled vehicles. 16 for work in the vicinity of mechanical equipment involving pedals, wheels, etc., operated by foot or hand; the use of circular, band or multiple-lanced saws, shears or grinding equipment or mechanical machinery; building work, except work that does not require the use of scaffolding; lifting of heavy weights, unless within the limits specified. Children shall not be required to perform work that is beyond their strength.

CHILE

Basic minimum age. 15 or upon completion of compulsory schooling, provided the minors have been authorised to work by one of their parents, a grandfather, a legal guardian or, failing them, a labour inspector. In specific cases, the legal guardian or a juvenile court may authorise work in the theatre, cinema, radio, television, circus or similar activities.

Light work. Minimum age of 14, provided compulsory schooling has been completed and with appropriate authorisation, as indicated above. The work must not prejudice the health or morals of the child nor impede his or her progress at school, or his or her participation in educational programmes.

Hazardous work. Minimum ages of 18 to 21, depending on the sector. 18 for underground work, work requiring excessive force, and for activities that are dangerous to the health, safety or morals. 21 for work in cabarets and other establishments presenting live performances and offering alcoholic beverages to be consumed on the premises, subject to expressly authorised exceptions.

CHINA

Basic minimum age. 16 in all undertakings, except for work in family undertakings, and combined work/study activities organised by the school.

Hazardous work. Minimum age of 18 for work that is harmful to the health, extraordinarily heavy physical labour, and work as stokers and trimmers.

COLOMBIA

Basic minimum age. Minimum age of 14, below which minors must attend school. In order to work, minors less than 18 must have written authorisation from the labour inspector or local authority or protector of the family. Indigenous minors must be authorised to work by the governor for the indigenous people or the traditional authority of the community concerned.

Light work. A minimum age of 12 may be allowed under special circumstances specified by the protector of the family and provided the total working time per day does not exceed four hours on light work.

Minimum age for admission to employment: Legal provisions

COLOMBIA (continued)

Hazardous work. Minimum age of 18 (except for apprentices) for work in connection with toxic or noxious substances, under extreme temperatures, in workplaces where there is a risk of contamination or insuffcent ventilation, or in mines where a combination of noxious or contaminated substances, unsuitable temperatures, oxygen deficiency, oxidation or gaseous substances create hazardous conditions; work exposing the minor to high voltages or to noises above 80 decibels; work involving the handling of radioactive substances, luminiscent paints, or exposure to X-rays, ultra-violet and infra-red rays and radio-frequency emissions; work invovling exposure to high voltage currents; underwater work; work exposing the minor to dangerous biological agents; work requiring the handling of explosive, flammable or caustic substances; storekeeping or stoking fires aboard maritime vessels; industrial paint work involving the use of white lead, lead sulphate or any product containing these substances; work with grinding or polishing machines, sharpening tools, high-speed sharpening stones, etc.; work with very hot furnaces, smelting metals, in steel factories, laminating workshops, silversmiths' forges and pressing heavy metals; work and operations involving the manipulation of heavy loads; work involving changing transmission belts, oiling and greasing or other related work involving heavy or high-speed machinery; work in relation to shearing, cutting, laminating, lathing, winching, milling, stamping machinery and other particularly dangerous machines; work connected with glass and pottery making, in engraving workshops and in the ceramics industry; work involving gas and arc welding, cutting when using oxygen tanks or in confined spaces, on scaffolding or in pre-heated architectural moulds; work in brick, pipe and similar factories, making of bricks by hand, working with presses and ovens for making bricks; work in operations and processes where there are high levels of heat and humidity; work in the steel industry and with other metals where the operations and/or processes produce toxic vapours and dust; work in cement plants; agricultural work and work in the agro-industry which have high health risks; and work likely to put the minor under moral risks, in particular in brothels and places of entertainment where alcoholic drinks are consumed; the use of minors to represent pornographic scenes, violent deaths, the justification of crimes and other similar scenes.

COMOROS

Basic minimum age. 15 in all enterprises. The nature of the work prohibited to children is fixed by law.

Hazardous work. Upon receipt of the views of the Supreme Works Council, the nature of work and categories of enterprises prohibited to adolescents and the age limits to which such prohibitions shall apply shall be determined by ministerial decision. (Formerly, a basic minimum age of 18 was set for hazardous work.)

CONGO

Basic minimum age. 16 in all enterprises, unless an exception is authorised by the national Minister of Education.

Light work. Minimum age of 12 for light domestic service; certain agricultural work as long as the health and safety of the children are protected; and light non-industrial work which can only be performed by children, with authorisation. The written authorisation of the competent authority and the consent of the parents or legal guardian are required for the employment of children from 12 to 14 years.

Hazardous work. Minimum ages of 16 to 18. 18 for work in the vicinity of machinery in motion and other dangerous machinery; the operation of lifting and loading equipment; handling explosive, irritant, corrosive and toxic substances; work in slaughterhouses; work in mines, quarries and earth-moving operations; the operation of motors, vehicles and mechanical equipment; work likely to be harmful to morals; and as trimmers and stokers on ships. 16 for pedal- and crank-operated equipment; work with circular and band saws, cutting and shearing machines, and emery wheels; construction, except light work not requiring scaffolding. In addition, limits are established for the loads young persons aged 12 to 18 may carry, pull or push.

Minimum age for admission to employment: Legal provisions

COSTA RICA

Basic minimum age. 12 (but in agriculture and stock-raising children of this age may only perform light work compatible with the physical and mental health and morals of the minor), although employment is generally prohibited when compulsory schooling has not been completed or when work would prevent its completion; work is prohibited in excess of five hours a day and 30 hours a week (between the ages of 12 and 15), except for domestic service. 15-18 for employment not exceeding seven hours a day and 42 a week. 15 for acting or other work in public performances at theatres, broadcasting studios and similar places of amusement, except for performances during scholastic ceremonies or for religious purposes or charity.

Hazardous work. The minimum age of 18 applies to contracts of employment for work which is classified as unhealthy, physically or morally dangerous or too heavy, as determined by regulations, including those processes, installations or industries which can endanger or injure workers' health because of the materials used, produced, emitted or stored (work in agricultural and stock-raising undertakings is permitted only in well-defined exceptional cases); night work; work during the day in hotels, clubs, public houses and other places where intoxicating beverages are sold and consumed on the premises. 15 (men) and 18 (unmarried women) for self-employment in street trades.

COTE D'IVOIRE

Basic minimum age. 14 in all sectors, except for 12 in domestic work, and 16 for public performances and girls working in street stalls or using pedal-driven sewing machines.

Light work. Minimum age of 12 for light agricultural work on plantations. Rest breaks are to be established in each case individually and may be reviewed by the Inspector of Labour and Social Laws. The employment authorisation for the entire establishment may be revoked if it is proved that children less than 14 years have been employed in a capacity for which they are not physically fit. Children aged 12 to 14 years must have the explicit authorisation of their parents or legal guardian, unless the work is in the same establishment as their parents and at their side. Children aged 12 to 14 years employed in light work may not work more than 4:30 hours a day.

Hazardous work. Minimum ages of 16 to 18. 16 for light underground work and work on scaffolding. 18 for trimmers and stokers on ships; work with machinery in motion, shearing and cutting machines, presses, explosives, vertical wheel winches and pulleys; in glassworks; operating steam engines; handling materials harmful to morality and other work on premises where such materials are handled. Weight limits are established for loads that young persons aged 14 to 18 may carry, pull or push.

CUBA

Basic minimum age. 17 is the age at which a contract of employment may be concluded, but young persons of 15 and 16 years may, for exceptional reasons related to vocational training, be authorised to take employment with employing bodies, subject to medical confirmation that the adolescent is physically and mentally fit for work.

Hazardous work. Minimum ages of 17 to 18. 17 for stevedoring or handling excessively heavy weights; extraction of minerals; work at heights; work in places in which harmful, reactive or toxic substances are used; and work in which the young person's safety or that of others depends on their responsibility. 18 for work underground or on work handling substances that may affect their general health or development. It is also specified that young persons shall be employed on work appropriate to their physical and mental development.

Minimum age for admission to employment: Legal provisions

CYPRUS

Basic minimum age. 13 in general. 14 for employment in any industrial undertaking, including mines, quarries and other related work; various construction activities and transport, including the handling of goods at docks, warehouses, airports, etc. 16 for employment on vessels, except for vessels employing only members of the same family, and street trading. Excluded are family undertakings that are not dangerous; work in technical or professional schools; work on school or training ships, subject to approval and conditions prescribed by the Commissioner; domestic service and agriculture. Children under 16 may not be employed more than six hours a day, 36 hours a week in any industrial undertaking, unless it is a family undertaking, and then only if the Commissioner is satisfied that the conditions and nature of employment are such as to justify an extension of the normal hours; or work more than 4:30 hours without an interval of at least 30 minutes for a meal or rest; they may not be employed for more than two hours on Sundays or after 16:00 on days of evening school attendance; they may not be employed between 19:00 and 6:00 (20:00 to 6:00 from June to September) unless the work, in the interest of art, science or education, is in a duly licensed place of public entertainment.

Light work. Employment of those under age 13 is allowed in occupations where only members of the same family are employed and which involve light work of an agricultural or other character, with the approval of the Commissioner. Children who have not completed the sixth grade may not be employed more than two hours per day nor before the close of school hours on any day of school attendance.

Hazardous work. Minimum ages of 16 to 18 for work set out in a schedule. Examples include the following: 16 for specified employment in shipbuilding; heading of yarn dyed by a lead compound; enamel or tin manufacture; lead processing; the handling of cellulose solutions; and work in any process in the manufacture of rubber. Minimum age of 18 for cleaning machinery in motion; specified railway tasks; signaling crane drivers on a construction project; working underground or with specified minerals, such as zinc or lead, and chemical products, rubber, potassium, sodium or substances used in making explosives, insulating mattresses or handling asbestos; carrying clay scraps in the manufacture or decoration of pottery; and lifting, carrying or otherwise moving loads so heavy as to be likely to cause injury. 18 (women only) for specified work connected with the manufacture of glass and in brine and salt processes, brass casting and lead processes. The employment of children under the age of 16 and young persons under 18 in any dangerous trade or occupation is subject to the conditions prescribed by the Commissioner.

CZECHOSLOVAKIA

Basic minimum age. Upon completion of compulsory schooling (16) for all sectors, whether or not governed by an employment contract, with an absolute minimum age of 16 for piece work.

Hazardous work. Minimum age of 18 for work not suited to the young person's physical or mental development or in occupations that are unsafe, dangerous or unhealthy, considering the person's physical and mental development at that age and exposure to the risk of accidents. 16 if the work forms part of professional training. Schedules issued by the competent authorities have indicated that the following types of work are prohibited to young persons: underground work; work involving exposure to ionising radiation; work involving exposure to the harmful effects of vibration or excessive noise; work involving continued exposure to high frequency electro-magnetic waves; work involving continued exposure to excessive heat, cold or temperature changes; work involving exposure to markedly high or low atmospheric pressure; work involving exposure to infectious diseases or in a particularly repulsive environment; work involving exposure to noxious substances (benzene, mercury and its compounds, lead and its compounds, coal tar and other especially carcinogenic substances); work in an environment affected by noxious gases or dust exceeding prescribed concentrations; work with poisons, drugs and other substances harmful to the health; work involving excessive physical effort, particularly in lifting and handling heavy loads; and work involving a high risk of bodily harm.

Minimum age for admission to employment: Legal provisions

DENMARK

Basic minimum age. 15 generally for all work done for an employer, and for agricultural and horticultural work in family undertakings (except work with dangerous materials and substances).

Light work. The Minister of Labour may establish rules for young persons under 15 to be employed on lighter forms of gainful activity and to appear in public performances, films and the like. Such rules are to take into account the person's age, development and state of health and their schooling or other form of instruction. Types of work allowed for those under 15 have been established by Order. Minimum age of 10 for light feeding and cleaning in agriculture, minding small animals, weeding, planting, picking fruit and running errands. Minimum age of 13 for activities such as shop assistants, work in laundries, labelling goods, working in kiosks, bakeries and greengrocers, packing and sorting light articles, light domestic chores, light manual assembly, painting with safe materials, and newspaper sale and delivery. The maximum number of hours is two a day on school days, eight on Sunday and a total of 12 a week. Continuous rest of at least 12 hours in 24, normally between 20:00 and 6:00, is also required.

Hazardous work. Minimum ages of 16 to 18 for work with technical equipment, substances or materials and other work dangerous to the health, safety and development of young persons. 16 for agricultural and horticultural work with mechanically or electrically-driven machines, such as tractors, etc.; employment at sea, except for family undertakings, provided the work does not involve dangerous technical equipment, devices or substances; and domestic service in private households. 18 for mechanically or electrically-driven cutting and stamping machines, machines with open wheels or which are used for mixing, grinding and mincing; certain work involving the use of tractors unless the young person has a license; the operation of transportation and lifting equipment; work involving repairing, servicing and surveillance of machinery that may cause physical damage; work with substances and materials that are classified as toxic, acidic or explosive, unless the substances and materials are in a closed system; underground mining and mining activities above ground if they involve danger of falling materials; and trimmers. 19 for stokers on ships. Exceptions are permitted if the work is part of vocational training. The Minister of Labour may lay down rules prescribing a lower age limit than 18 for employment on work with substances and materials, and may lay down rules to declare other materials and substances hazardous.

DJIBOUTI

Basic minimum age. 14 in all sectors.

Hazardous work. Minimum age of 16 for work such as operating steam engines; work with vertical wheel winches and pulleys; for women operating pedal-operated sewing machines and in street trading; work on scaffolding; and for public performances. Minimum age of 18 for work as trimmers and stokers; work with machinery in motion, including woodworking machinery; use of industrial paints containing white lead; underground work; work with mechanical cutting and shearing machines and presses; work in connection with molten glass and explosives; the handling of materials prejudicial to morals and other work in premises where such materials are handled; other work in specified establishments. Weight limits are set for the manual transport of loads by young persons aged 14 to 18.

Minimum age for admission to employment: Legal provisions

DOMINICA

Basic minimum age. 15 in public or private industrial undertakings or branches thereof, including mining, manufacturing, shipbuilding, electrical utilities, construction, transportation by road, rail or ship. Exceptions are family undertakings; ships employing only family members; manual labour under order of detention in reformatory institutions; work or industrial schools or institutions; manual labour in any school approved and supervised by a public authority; commerce and agriculture.

Hazardous work. Minimum age of 18 for cleaning dangerous parts of machinery in motion.

DOMINICAN REPUBLIC

Basic minimum age. 14, excluding agriculture, unless dangerous or unhealthy work is involved.

Hazardous work. Minimum age of 18 for dangerous or unhealthy work as determined by the Minister of Labour. A minor less than 18 cannot work as a messenger in the distribution or delivery of goods or messages; and cannot be employed in the retail sale of intoxicating beverages. Minors between 14 and 18 may be employed in artistic performances until midnight with the prior authorisation of the Department of Labour or local authority. Minors less than 16 may not engage in hawking or peddling without the previous authorisation of the Department of Labour.

ECUADOR

Basic minimum age. 14, except for apprentices, domestic work and the self-employed. Between 12 and 14 with authorisation from the Juvenile Court as long as the legal minimum schooling has been completed or is attending a night school, workers' institute or elementary education establishment, and as long as the minor is clearly obliged to work for his/her living or to maintain parents or grandparents unable to work or younger brothers or sisters. Anyone employing a minor less than 18 who has not completed elementary schooling must release that person for two hours a day during working hours in order to attend school. 15 for work on fishing vessels except occasionally during school holidays and as long as such work is not harmful to health or normal development and does not prejudice attendance at school and is not intended for commercial profit.

Hazardous work. Minimum age of 18 for work deemed dangerous or unhealthy as listed in regulations. Prohibited work includes distillation of alcohol and manufacturing or mixing of distilled liquors and retail sale of alcoholic beverages; manufacture of lead and other poisonous pigments and handling of products containing salts of lead or arsenic; work with or around explosives or inflammable or caustic substances; work involving melting of glass and metals, glass cutting and polishing, metal polishing with emery, and work in any place habitually generating dust, irritants or poisonous fumes; loading or unloading ships, with or without cranes and winches; work underground or in quarries; work as enginemen and stokers; operation of drive belts, circular saws and other dangerous machinery; transporting substances in a state of incandescence; any other work involving serious danger to the morals or physical development; work in dance halls, bars, cafés, gaming houses and similar places; work involving the production, distribution and sale of offensive material; work in the streets or public places may be authorised for men between 14 and 18 and for women between 14 and 21, only if necessary for the subsistence of the minor. Weight limits are set for manual transport of loads by young persons.

EGYPT

Basic minimum age. 12, except for the public sector, domestic service, family undertakings and agriculture.

Hazardous work. The Minister of Manpower and Training has authority to make regulations covering the employment of young persons between 12 and 17 years of age, and to fix the circumstances, conditions and cases in which employment is permitted and the jobs, occupations and industries in which each age category of young persons may be employed.

Minimum age for admission to employment: Legal provisions

EL SALVADOR	Basic minimum age. 14, or age of having completed compulsory schooling requirements, unless authorised by the Minister of Labour and Social Security because the work is necessary for the subsistance of the child or of his/her family, provided that it does not interfere with minimal education requirements. Hazardous work. Minimum age of 18 for unhealthy or dangerous work, or work endangering young persons' morals. Dangerous work is that capable of causing death or immediate physical injury, because of its nature, the substances used or residues produced, or because of the need to handle or store corrosive, inflammable or explosive substances. It includes the operation of machinery in motion or designated mechanical tools and equipment which require special precautions; work underground or under water; the manufacture or use of explosives, detonators, inflammable substances and similar work; general construction and demolition; work in mines and caverns; maritime employment, including loading and unloading ships; and such other types of work as may be specified by law, regulations, collective agreements, individual contracts or work rules. Unhealthy work is that which is capable by its nature of being detrimental to the worker's health or of causing injury by virtue of the type of substance used or produced, including toxic materials, harmful gases, vapours or effluvia and dangerous or noxious dust, and any other type of work specified in relevant laws, regulations, collective agreements, individual contracts or work rules. Work in bars, canteens, billiard parlours and similar establishments is considered unhealthy.
EQUATORIAL GUINEA	Basic minimum age. 14, with the express authorisation of the parent or guardian. Light work. Minors above 13 may perform light work as long as it is not prejudicial to their health or development and their attendance at school. Minimum age of 12 for certain jobs or light tasks in artisenal or agricultural work as indicated by the labour authorities, who will first consult workers' organisations, where they exist, and will take special care to safeguard the health, physical and moral integrity, and education of minors. Hazardous work. Minimum age of 16 for work which is detrimental to the health, safety or morals of young persons. Where they exist, workers' organisations must be consulted. Labour authorities must ensure adequate protection and that minors receive adequate vocational training before starting work. The labour authorities may raise the minimum age to 18 as long as the principle of equal employment opportunities is not undermined.
ETHIOPIA	Basic minimum age. 14 for employment in all sectors on the basis of a contract of employment or apprenticeship. Hazardous work. Minimum age of 18 for work in dangerous trades.
FIJI	Basic minimum age. 12 for all sectors, except industrial undertakings, if the parent or guardian does not object. 15 for industrial undertakings, including mining, quarries, factories for mineral extraction, manufacturing, shipbuilding, utilities, construction, transport, and any factory or other prescribed undertaking. Excluded are family undertakings, ships on which only members of the same family are employed, school institutions or training ships which have received special authorisation, and other work authorised by the Governor in Council. The Commissioner must give written approval for a child over 14 to be employed on a ship. A child shall be employed only for a daily wage and on a day-to-day basis, and on condition that he or she returns each night to the parent or guardian's residence.

Minimum age for admission to employment: Legal provisions

FIJI (continued)

Light work. Is permitted for children under 12, where the work is suited to the child's capacity, in agricultural undertakings run and operated by the family.

Hazardous work. Minimum ages of 16 to 18 depending upon the sector. 16 for the operation of certain factory machinery. 18 for employment in mines, unless a certificate attesting to the young person's fitness for such work has been signed by a medical officer; and for trimmers and stokers.

FINLAND

Basic minimum age. 15, including those who will reach the age of 15 during the calendar year, provided compulsory school attendance has been completed. Exclusions include work on board ship and unsupervised home work which is not detrimental to physical, mental or moral development and is appropriate to the worker's age and strength.

Light work. Minimum age of 14, including those who will reach the age of 14 within the calendar year, for very light work carried out during the school holidays and for not more than two-thirds of the holiday period. Hours of work are not to exceed seven a day or 36 a week, and must be between 7:00 and 19:00, and include at least 14 hours of consecutive rest in every 24. Where work exceeds five hours a day, a one-hour rest period in the course of the work is required. Disputes over whether employment should be regarded as very light work are to be submitted to the Labour Council. While medical examinations are generally required, they need not be obtained for light shop or office work. For domestic workers under 15, work is permitted between 6:00 and 19:00 with a continuous weekly rest period of at least 38 hours, preferably on Sunday. Restrictions on the working hours of workers under 15 are subject to exceptions for emergency situations.

Hazardous work. Minimum ages of 16 to 18. 16 if the work is not dangerous, and in merchant shipping and fishing. The employer must notify the labour inspectorate. 18 for work which puts unreasonable pressure or responsibility on the young person; which implies responsibility for other persons' safety or financial responsibility; work alone if it involves a risk of accidents or criminal acts; care for mentally disturbed persons; handling and transport of corpses; work in slaugherhouses; manufacture or transport of explosives; work involving radioactive substances or ionising radiation; and other work that may be further regulated, except when undergoing vocational training. Exemptions may be granted by the labour authority.

FRANCE

Basic minimum age. Not before completion of compulsory schooling. 16 in industrial and commercial establishments of all kinds, legal offices and other professions, non-trading corporations, trade unions and associations of all kinds. Child performers and models under school-leaving age may be exempted only with individual authorisation and under certain conditions restricting their hours of work, etc. Parents performing in circuses may not employ their children under the age of 12 in their performances. Excluded from the minimum age provisiona are children working in establishments where only members of the same family are employed, if they are working under the authority of a parent or legal guardian.

Minimum age for admission to employment: Legal provisions

FRANCE (continued)

Light work. Minimum ages of 12 to 14. 14 for light work during school holidays provided a rest period is guaranteed of at least one-half of the holiday period. 12 where such light work is performed under the supervision of a parent or guardian employed in the same undertaking, provided such work does not conflict with compulsory schooling. Permissible light agricultural work includes caring for plants, weeding, flower cutting, fruit harvesting by hand - provided it is not accomplished from a height necessitating the use of a ladder or other equipment which expose the child to the risk of falling - grape picking and similar activities.

Hazardous work. Minimum ages of 16 to 18, depending upon the sector and occupation. 16 for performances including dangerous feats of strength or contortions or work that is dangerous to the life, health or morals of the child; performances in circus acts with persons other than the child's parents. In addition, those under 16 may not perform work requiring the operation of verticle wheels, winches or pulleys designed to lift certain loads or weights; machines run by motorised pedals as well as hand-operated presses or other similar tools; specified agricultural tasks, such as pruning; work in glassworks; and work involving exposure to or use of compressed liquids or sprays, as prescribed by special decree. 17 for cutting and blowing glass, operating machines in glassworks where production is mechanical and where the weight of glass required to be lifted is above a certain specified level.

Those employing workers under the age of 18 in industrial or commercial establishments must ensure that propriety is maintained and public decency observed. Regulations determine for establishments, including mines and quarries, transport undertakings and family undertakings, the types of work that involve the risk of danger, excessive strain or are prejudicial to morals and which are prohibited to young workers under 18 or are subject to special conditions. These types of work include the operation of moving machinery, various cutting and shearing tools or instruments, and specified agricultural tractors and forestry equipment; work in glassworks involving exposure of the face to heat or dangerous particles without adequate protection; work involving steam equipment other than onboard ship; work involving laminating and stitching of wire; work in agriculture and construction at heights which has not been medically approved as suitable for the young worker; demolition work; specified underground work; specified work with electric currents; work in tanneries; work with specified chemicals and other substances including acids, explosives, lead and radioactive materials.

GABON

Basic minimum age. 16 for all sectors, excluding family undertakings, except during school hours. Exemptions may be allowed by decree.

Hazardous work. Minimum age of 18 for unhealthy or particularly dangerous work or any type of work liable to be detrimental to morals. Dangerous work includes work with moving machinery, unguarded machinery, lifting and handling equipment; work in slaughterhouses, tanneries and similar work; underground or surface work in mines and quarries; the operation of motors, vehicles, and manually or pedal-operated equipment, including jigs and shakers, mechanical saws, shearing and cutting machines or emery wheels; construction, except finishing that does not involve the use of scaffolding; trimmers and stokers on ships; work involving weights in excess of established limits or transporting loads by means of a two-wheeled hand trolley or other similar vehicle; handling of white lead.

Minimum age for admission to employment: Legal provisions

GERMANY

Basic minimum age. 15, unless no longer subject to compulsory schooling and then only for vocational training or light work. Applies generally to all sectors and work except insignificant and occasional assistance provided as a favour, on the basis of family law provisions, in youth assistance institutions, in institutions for the rehabilitation of the disabled, or in the family. The supervisory authority may grant exceptions for certain performances subject to the written consent of the persons responsible for the child's care, and the obtention of a medical certificate, provided that the work is not prejudicial to the health and physical, psychological and mental development and welfare of the child, and does not interfere with progress at school and subject to rules on hours of work and rest periods. Those over 6 years may be allowed to work in theatrical performances up to four hours a day between 10:00 and 23:00. Those between the ages of 3 and 6 may work up to two hours a day between 8:00 and 17:00. Those over 6 years may work up to three hours a day between 8:00 and 22:00 in musical and other performances and certain other activities, such as radio, television, films, photography and public displays.

Light work. Children under 15 who are no longer liable to full-time compulsory schooling may perform light and suitable work for up to seven hours a day and 35 hours a week. Children over 13 years of age, subject to the consent of the person responsible for their care, may work up to three hours a day during the harvest, up to two hours a day delivering newspapers and up to two hours a day for minor services in connection with sporting events, to the extent that such employment is light and suitable. They shall not be employed between 18:00 and 8:00, nor before or during school hours. Their progress in school must not be adversely affected.

Hazardous work. Workers under 18 are prohibited from work which is beyond their strength; exposes them to moral dangers; involves a risk of accidents due to their lack of safety consciousness or experience; is hazardous on account of exceptional heat, cold or humidity; involves exposure to the harmful effects of noise, vibration, radiation or poisonous, caustic or irritant substances; and work underground. The latter four types of work may be authorised for persons over 16 if necessary for their training and with proper supervision that ensures their safety and, in the case of underground work, if they have received special training. Piece work is prohibited for those under 18, unless necessary for vocational training and properly supervised.

GHANA

Basic minimum age. 15. Employment is prohibited for those "apparently less than 15 years" of age. 15 for merchant shipping. These limits do not apply to family undertakings or ships upon which only members of the same family are employed, or on school or training ships, provided such work is approved and supervised by a public authority.

Light work. Children "apparently less than 15" working under the supervision of the family may perform only light tasks of an agricultural or domestic nature.

Hazardous work. Minimum age of "apparently" 18 in mines or other underground work.

Minimum age for admission to employment: Legal provisions

GREECE	Basic minimum age. 15 for all types of employment and self-employment, except farming, forestry or cattle-breeding activities within a family business. With the permission of the Labour Inspectorate, the employment of young persons who have not completed their 15th year is permited for theatrical productions, concerts of music or other artistic performances, advertising, fashion modelling, radio or television recordings or broadcasts, video recordings and films. They may be employed as models, provided that their physical and mental health and their morals are not prejudiced. Hazardous work. Minimum ages of 16 to 18 as provided by legislation or regulations to protect the safety, health and morals of the young person. 16 in the manufacture of lead accumulators. 18 for work which is dangerous, heavy or unhealthy, or which in general hinders the free development of the personality.
GUATEMALA	Basic minimum age. 14, except for well-defined cases authorised by the general labour inspectorate. These include apprenticeships or where the minor has to contribute to the family income on account of extreme poverty. The work must be light in duration and intensity, be compatible with the physical and mental health and the moral welfare of the minor, who must receive the minimum legal level of education. Hazardous work. Minimum age of 16 for unhealthy or dangerous work as classified by the regulations or the general labour inspectorate, excluding agriculture or stock-raising except in exceptional circumstances. Includes work during the day in canteens or other similar establishments where alcoholic beverages are sold for consumption on the spot.
GUINEA	Basic minimum age. 16 for all industrial undertakings and individual employment relationships governed by an employment contract.
GUINEA BISSAU	Basic minimum age. 14, or upon completion of compulsory schooling, except where such schooling is not available or for similar reasons certified by the Ministry of Education. Hazardous work. 18 for heavy work, work under unhealthy or dangerous conditions, and underground work.
GUYANA	Basic minimum age. 14 under the Education Act for industrial undertakings, ships, factories (including docks), buildings, engineering, construction and mines. Excluded from specific coverage are commerce and industrial undertakings and ships employing only members of the same family, technical schools where work is approved and supervised by the competent public authority, and services rendered by children to their parents, except during school hours. Hazardous work. Minimum ages of 16 to 18. 16 for cleaning or oiling any dangerous part of moving machinery powered by mechanical power or any machine that exposes the worker to the risk of injury, and for all work involving exposure to radiation.

Minimum age for admission to employment: Legal provisions

HAITI	Basic minimum age. 15 for industrial, agricultural and commercial undertakings. 12 for domestic service, provided the employer meets specified criteria, obtains a permit and provides the required care. Children shall not be employed on domestic tasks liable in any way to harm their health or normal development or interfere with their regular attendance at school. Hazardous work. 18. "Minors shall not be employed in unhealthy or ardous work endangering their health, physical development or morals nor in places where alcoholic drinks are sold."
HONDURAS	Basic minimum age. 14, provided compulsory schooling has been completed, in any kind of work for all undertakings, businesses, establishments and individuals, excluding day work in agricultural and stock-raising enterprises with no more than ten workers. Work may be authorised by the competent authority if it is deemed essential to the subsistence of the young person or his/her family and does not affect compulsory schooling. Written permission by a competent authority is required for workers under 16 and may be given only if the official is of the opinion that the young person will not suffer any obvious physical or moral harm by engaging in the occupation in question. 16 on ships, except for training ships and ships supervised by the Ministry of Education. Hazardous work. Minimum age of 16 for work declared unhealthy or dangerous by the Labour Code, the Health Code or the health and safety regulations; for employment in clubs, theatres, circuses, cafés, canteens, places where intoxicating liquor is consumed on the premises and bawdy houses. 16 for males and 18 for females in work involving printed matter, advertisements, drawings, engravings, paintings, emblems or images which may be regarded as prejudicial to morality and decency. The Labour Code deems any process, plant or industry to be unhealthy if it is capable of giving rise to conditions that could threaten or impair the worker's health due to the substances used, manufactured or emitted, or due to the waste matter produced in the form of solids, liquids or gases, and deemed to be dangerous if it may be immediately and seriously prejudicial to the life of the workers, whether by its nature or due to the substances used, manufactured or emitted, to the waste matter produced or to the storage of toxic, corrosive, flammable or explosive substances in any form.
HUNGARY	Basic minimum age. 15, provided that compulsory schooling has been completed or a dispensation obtained from regular school attendance for all employment relationships. Those under 16 entering an employment relationship with a handicraft co-operative must have the consent of a legal representative. There is no minimum age for work during school vacations; agricultural and industrial co-operatives may be subject to special decree respecting minimum age, as may workers employed by private employers. Light work. 14 during school holidays. Hazardous work. 16 for underground work in mines. 18 for any work which may have adverse effects on the young person's constitution or physical development.

Minimum age for admission to employment: Legal provisions

ICELAND	Basic minimum age. 15 in factories and transport, provided the child has completed compulsory schooling. Light work. Minimum age of 14 for light work. Hazardous work. Minimum age of 18 or 19 for some work on ships. 19 as a trimmer or stoker.
INDIA	Basic minimum age. 14 for employment in designated occupations connected with rail transport and for work for port authorities within the limits of any port and in workshops where the following processes are carried out: making bidis; carpet weaving; cement manufacture, including the bagging of cement; cloth printing, dyeing and weaving; manufacture of matches, explosives and fireworks; mica-cutting and splitting; shellac manufacture, soap manufacture, tanning, wool-cleaning; and building and construction. The central government, after giving notice, may add occupations and processes to the prohibited list. Prohibitions do not apply in workshops where processes are carried out with the assistance of the operator's family or to schools established by or receiving assistance or recognition from the government. The minimum age does not apply in establishments where none of the above occupations or processes are carried out. In establishments including shops, commercial establishments, workshops, farms, residential hotels, restaurants, eating houses, theatres or other places of public amusement or entertainment, the employment of children is subject to regulations, including the following: a maximum of three hours for each period of work without a rest interval of one hour; daily hours restricted to a maximum of six; prohibition of overtime and night work; weekly rest of one whole day; and the requirement for employers to maintain a register containing particulars on child workers and the work that they perform. Hazardous work. The appropriate government may, after giving notice, make rules for the health and safety of children who are permitted to work concerning such matters as work on or near machinery in motion; the employment of and the instruction, training and supervision of children for work on dangerous machines; the transport of excessive weights; and work in the vicinity of explosives or involving exposure to inflammable substances, dust, gas or other materials. 18 for mining, work involving exposure to radiation and work on or near machinery in motion or on dangerous machines in factories.
INDONESIA	Basic minimum age. 14. Children younger than 14 may work with the permission of parents or guardians up to four hours a day, except in underground work, on ships (unless supervised by their parents or relatives), carrying or loading heavy goods, and work with dangerous production tools and harmful substances. The employer must report such child employment to the Ministry of Manpower. Hazardous work. Minimum age of 18 for underground work or work that is dangerous to the health (to be specified by Government Order).
IRAN	Basic minimum age. 15 for all sectors, with the requirement of a pre-employment medical examination by the social security organisation. Hazardous work. Minimum age of 18 for all arduous, harmful and dangerous types of work, and work that is prejudicial to the health or ethical principles.

Minimum age for admission to employment: Legal provisions

IRAQ

Basic minimum age. 15 for any employment generally. Excluded are family undertakings, provided the work is supervised by the spouse, father, mother or brother.

Hazardous work. Minimum age of 18 for any work which is arduous or harmful to the health or morals; such types of work are to be determined by instructions issued by the Ministry of Labour and Social Affairs. This includes work in quarries, mines, and archaeological or other excavations; the driving or operation of mechanical or steam engines, river- or sea-going ships or steamers, whether as members of the crew, stokers, trimmers or their assistants (medical certificates are required); and in work where benzene or its component materials are used.

IRELAND

Basic minimum age. 15, and having completed schooling, for work in industry and commerce, subject to exclusions. Exclusions cover work in the defence forces and as fishermen, lighthouse keepers, outworkers or seafarers.

Light work. Minimum age of 14 for light non-industrial work outside school hours and for no more than 14 hours in any week.

Hazardous work. Minimum age of 18 for work as trimmers or stokers unless on a training ship or ship propelled by means other than steam; underground work in a mine; work with moving machinery; work relating to the process of melting or blowing glass other than lamp-blown glass; annealing glass other than plate or sheet glass; the evaporating of brine in open pans or the stoving of salt; any work to do with lead or zinc processing; mixing or pasting in connection with the manufacture or repair of electric accumulators; the cleaning of workrooms where any lead or zinc processing is carried on.

ISRAEL

Basic minimum age. 15 and on completion of compulsory schooling, except for apprentices in a state-supervised vocational training programmes in all sectors, except agriculture and commerce.

Hazardous work. Minimum age of 16 to 18 (14 to 17 for the transport of loads of a specified weight). 16 for driving motor vehicles; driving a locomotive; operating a goods lift, a crane dragline and a gantry crane in order to lift or to transport loads and signalling for these operations; operating a goods transporter, pulley-block or overhead transporter that is powered mechanically. 17 for employment in hospitals involving contact with tuberculosis, leprosy or mental patients. 18 for employment underground in a mine or quarry.

ITALY

Basic minimum age. 15 for all employment generally and for maritime work. 14 for agriculture or domestic work inherent in family life, as long as this is compatible with the standards for the protection of the minor's health and on condition that such employment does not interfere with school attendance. Minors under 15, with the written consent of a parent or legal guardian, may help in preparing or act in theatrical performances or films, provided that the work is not dangerous and does not continue after midnight; that 14 consecutive hours of rest are assured; and that standards guaranteeing the protection of health, morals and school attendance are met.

Light work. Minimum age of 14 in "non-industrial branches of activity [commerce and agriculture] where such work is compatible with the standards required for protection of the health and does not interfere with school attendance, on condition that it is not performed at night or on a public holiday". A Presidential Decree defines permissable light work.

Minimum age for admission to employment: Legal provisions

ITALY (continued)	Hazardous work. Minimum ages of 15 to 18. 15 for men and 18 for women for hazardous, arduous and unhealthy work as specified by decree of the President of the Republic on the recommendation of the Minister of Labour and Social Welfare, after consultation with the Higher Health Board and the trade union associations; work cleaning and operating motors, transmission machinery and machinery in motion. Minimum age of 16 for itinerant trades, and 18 for underground work and open-face mineral extraction; lifting and transporting specified weights if under conditions of hardship or danger; work with the cinema, theatre or other performances (subject to the exception cited above); and the retail sale of alcoholic beverages. Periodic medical examinations are required to ensure the fitness of young persons to do the work they are required to perform.
JAMAICA	Basic minimum age. 15 for any industrial undertaking, trade or occupation (including work in quarries; distilleries and breweries; sugar, spirit compounds, match, soap, cigar or cigarette factories, or the manufacture thereof; cleaning, alteration, repair or demolition work; shipbuilding; electrical or motive power generation; construction and transport), or work in or upon any ship, other than a ship where only members of the same family are employed. Agricultural undertakings are excluded. Minimum age of 12 for other sectors. Light work. Under 12 when employed by parents or guardians in light domestic, agricultural or horticultural work, or in prescribed occupations, provided the work is not at night and is not with an industrial undertaking. Hazardous work. Minimum age of 16 for work related to the operation of a sugar mill, or cleaning dangerous parts of machinery in motion. 17 for work in underground mining operations.
JAPAN	Basic minimum age. 15 for all sectors, including manufacturing, mining, construction, transport, agriculture and forestry, livestock and fisheries, service industries, entertainment, utilities, education and research facilities, health and sanitation services, hotels and restaurants, incineration, cleaning and butchery enterprises, public offices and any others defined by Ordinance. Exclusions cover any enterprise, office or sailing vessel employing only those relatives living with the employer as a family member and domestic employees in the home. Exempted from the minimum age requirement are children (under 12) employed in motion-picture production and theatrical performance enterprises, provided the work is not injurious to their health or welfare, is outside school hours and is authorised by the administrative office. Light work. Minimum age of 12 provided the work is not injurious to the health and welfare of the child, is outside school hours and authorised by the administrative office. Specified enterprises in which light work is permitted include agriculture and forestry, stock and fish breeding, commodities trading and hairdressing, banking, insurance and other service industries, entertainment industry, public utilities, education and research facilities, hospitals, nursing homes and other health and sanitation services, hotels, restaurants and related food industry establishments, enterprises engaged in incineration, cleaning and butchering, and public offices. Children may work a maximum of seven hours a day, 40 hours a week, including hours of school attendance. The employer must keep at the workplace a certificate from the child's teacher stating that the work does not hinder his or her school performance. Parents or a legal guardian must give their written consent and may cancel (as may the administrative office) any labour contract which they consider unfair. Persons violating the provisions concerning employment of children in light work shall be subject to imprisonment for up to one year or a fine of up to 100,000 yen.

Minimum age for admission to employment: Legal provisions

JAPAN (continued)	Hazardous work. Minimum age of 18 for handling dangerous parts of any machinery or power-transmission apparatus that is in operation (including driving belts or ropes); operating a power-driven crane or other similar tasks prescribed by Ordinance; conveying specified heavy goods; handling poisons, powerful drugs or other injurious substances, or explosive, inflammable or combustible goods; working where dust, powder or harmful gases or radiation are generated, high temperatures and pressures exist or other places that are dangerous or injurious to the safety, health and welfare of the minor; underground work; trimmers and stokers, and as further specified by Ordinance.
JORDAN	Basic minimum age. 13 for any establishment, provided that the child has obtained and the employer has kept an authorised medical certificate showing his or her age and fitness for the work (based upon a reliable birth certificate or an educated guess). Exclusions cover those employed in agricultural work (except those employed in government organisations and institutions, on mechanical equipment or in permanent irrigation work); domestic servants, gardeners, cooks and similar work; and family undertakings. Hazardous work. Minimum age of 15 for any process specified in regulations issued by the Council of Ministers on the recommendation of the Minister of Social Affairs and Labour as hazardous for women or children. 18 for underground work.
KENYA	Basic minimum age. 16 for industrial undertakings (mines, factories, construction, demolition, transport), except for employment as an apprentice or as an indentured learner, or for children working with their families. Hazardous work. Minimum age of 16 for work in connection with machinery and in any open-cast workings or sub-surface workings which are entered by means of a shaft or adit. 18 as a trimmer or stoker. No person under 15 may be employed on any vessel unless it is a training ship, a family vessel or unless a medical certificate has been obtained.
KUWAIT	Basic minimum age. 14 in all sectors. A permit from the Ministry of Social Affairs and Labour is required for 14 to 18 year olds, as well as a medical certificate. Hazardous work. Minimum age of 18 in hazardous and noxious trades and industries which are set down by an order issued by the Ministry of Social Affairs and Labour.
LAO PEOPLE'S DEMOCRATIC REPUBLIC	Basic minimum age. 15 in all sectors. Persons below the age of 18 may not work more than six hours in a day and 36 hours in a week. Hazardous work. 18 for all types of work which are heavy and dangerous to the health, including mining and quarrying; work with chemical and leather products; work with corpses and city cleaning; work with radioactivity; work with gas and smoke which affects the health; work with explosives; underground or underwater work.

Minimum age for admission to employment: Legal provisions

LEBANON	Basic minimum age. 13 in industry, commerce, agriculture and the corporations of the liberal professions, except for domestic work, family undertakings, government and municipal services, and agricultural corporations having no connection with commerce or industry. The employment of any child under the age of 8 years is absolutely prohibited. Hazardous work. Minimum age of 16. A medical certificate is required for work in industries involving the boiling of blood, bones and soap, the melting of tallow and the production of fertilisers.
LESOTHO	Basic minimum age. 15 in commercial or industrial undertakings. An exception is made for private family undertakings, technical schools or similar institutions. Hazardous work. Minimum age of 16. Young males over the age of 16 employed on the surface of mines or quarries must be covered by an apprenticeship agreement and obtain a medical certificate approved by the Labour Commissioner.
LIBERIA	Basic minimum age. 14 in any activity carried out for the purpose of profit or earning a livelihood. 15 on fishing vessels, except fishing in ports and harbours, or in estuaries of rivers, or fishing for sport or recreation; on school ships or training ships, subject to the approval and supervision by a public authority; in activities on board fishing vessels during school holidays if the activities are not harmful to the health or normal development of the young person and are not intended for commercial profit. 16 in industry, agriculture and ships, except family vessels, school ships or training ships. Hazardous work. Minimum age of 18 on coal-burning fishing vessels as trimmers or stokers.
LIBYAN ARAB JAMAHIRIYA	Basic minimum age. 15 in all sectors, except family undertakings, domestic service, agriculture and seafaring. Hazardous work. Minimum age of 18 in prohibited jobs and industries prescribed by order of the Ministry of Labour and Social Affairs. A birth certificate or best estimate by a physician is required as proof of age.
LUXEMBOURG	Basic minimum age. 15, or until compulsory education is completed, in all sectors, except work performed in technical and vocational schools; help with domestic work at home; or public performances in the interests of art, science or education, authorisation for which is to be granted by the Minister of Education (the minimum age for this work is 6 years). 18 on ships, except training ships. Hazardous work. Minimum age of 18 for types of work that are beyond the capabilities or harmful to the development of young persons, which require them to make efforts out of proportion to their strength or are likely to be detrimental to their physical, mental or moral health. Classes of work prohibited to adolescents under 18 years include foundry work where the melting of metals may involve the risk of inhaling or absorbing toxic fumes or substances; work in extremes of heat or cold; work with corrosive substances; work with soldering irons; tar production; work with asbestos or other products likely to harm the lungs; working with machinery in motion; work involving exposure to radiation; the manufacture or transport of explosives, chemically unstable or inlfammable substances; underground work in mines and quarries; the operation of cranes and heavy transport vehicles; work in sewers; work in areas of high infection; loading and unloading ships; demolition work and work with potentially dangerous machinery, such as chainsaws, roadmaking equipment and external scaffolding. The law also specifically prohibits employment in any profession considered to be potentially harmful to the moral development of the child, such as work in cabarets and bars, gambling halls, liquor retailing and in slaughterhouses (except under an apprenticeship agreement).

Minimum age for admission to employment: Legal provisions

MADAGASCAR	Basic minimum age. 14, including apprenticeships, in all sectors, except for officials, who are subject to or governed by the special rules laid down for public services, and establishments or persons governed by the Merchant Shipping Code (the minimum age for seafarers is 15). Other exceptions may be granted by the labour authority after consultation with the National Labour Council. Hazardous work. Minimum age of 16 to 18 on work exceeding the strength of the young persons, involving danger or which, on account of its nature or of the conditions in which it is carried out, is liable to endanger their morals. Prohibited activities include work on machines in motion; use of circular or band saws; glass-blowing; handling of explosives; work on scaffolding; the operation of winches and steam engines; dangerous circus tricks; work involving the risk of danger from harmful dust, vapours, emanations, lead, infections, poisons, or which require special care and attention.
MALAWI	Basic minimum age. 14 in industry, except for family undertakings and light work. 15 on ships, except for family ships where the child is employed for nominal wages and is under the responsibility of his father or another close adult male relative. Light work. Minimum age of 12 in employment involving light work of a character approved by the Minister and notified in the Gazette. Hazardous work. Minimum age of 18 for work as a trimmer or stoker on any ship; work done on machinery in motion, such as the examination, lubrication, adjustment, mounting or shipping of belts.
MALAYSIA	Basic minimum age. 14 for work as a domestic servant; in an industrial undertaking suitable to the young person's capacity; in an office, shop (including hotels, bars, restaurants and stalls), godown, factory, workshop, store, boarding house, theatre, cinema, club or association; and on any vessel under the personal charge of the young person's parent or guardian. No young woman may be employed in hotels or bars unless they are managed by her family. The minimum age does not apply to work undertaken in connection with vocational training. Young persons between 14 and 16 may not work more than seven hours a day, and their combined hours of school and work may not exceed eight hours a day. Light work. Children under 14 may be engaged in employment involving light work suitable to their capacity in any undertaking carried on by their family for a maximum of six hours a day. Combined hours of school and work may not exceed seven a day. Hazardous work. Minimum age of 16 on work involving the management of, or attendance on or proximity to, any machinery, unless undergoing vocational training, in which case the minimum age is 14 or 15.
MALI	Basic minimum age. 14 in all sectors except family undertakings, domestic work within the family, non-commercial work in vocational training establishments. Exceptions are authorised by order of the Minister of Labour. Light work. Minimum age of 12 on work suitable to the child's health or physical and moral development, such as agricultural work, domestic service, other non-industrial work with the written permission of the labour inspectorate and for a maximum of 4.5 hours a day. Children younger than 14 and attending school may only work two hours a day during school holidays. No child may work on Sundays, public holidays or at night (between 20:00 and 8:00).

Minimum age for admission to employment: Legal provisions

MALI (continued)	Hazardous work. Minimum age of 18 on work exceeding the strength of the young persons, involving danger or which, on account of its nature and the conditions in which it is carried out, is liable to endanger their morals. 16 for work on pedal- and crank-operated equipment, including jiggers, shaking tables and hand-operated looms.
MALTA	Basic minimum age. 16 in all sectors, except shipping and family undertakings. 15 on ships, except family ships and school or training ships.
	Hazardous work. Minimum age of 18 for the cleaning of machinery in motion and for training on dangerous machinery; trimmers and stokers and other types of work which are potentially injurious; work with lead and electric accumulators, and work involving exposure to ionising radiation.
MAURITANIA	Basic minimum age. 14 in all sectors except seafaring, for which the minimum age is 15; exceptions may be authorised by order of the Minister of Labour.
	Hazardous work. Minimum age of 18 on tasks which exceed the strength of minors or which, by their nature or the conditions in which they are carried out, are liable to injure their health, endanger their life or limbs or affect their morals.
MAURITIUS	Basic minimum age. 15 in all sectors, except seafarers.
	Hazardous work. Minimum age of 18 on work at any machine specified by decree. These include brick and tile presses, carding machines and gill boxes used in wool and textile manufacture, lifting equipment, meat-mincing machines, woodworking machines, softening and stripping machines used in fibre processing, milling machines, guillotines, power presses, steam boilers, wire stitching machines and washing machines. The cleaning of machines while they are in motion is prohibited.
MEXICO	Basic minimum age. 14 in all sectors. A medical certificate confirming aptitude for work is required by law for persons 14 to 16 years of age.
	Hazardous work. Minimum age of 16 for work which, on account of its nature or the physical, chemical or biological conditions of the environment in which it is performed or the composition of the raw materials used, is liable to affect the life, development and physical and mental health of young persons. Prohibited activities include work with acids, lead, benzene, explosives, electric wires, petroleum, blast furnaces, wild animals, rubber, solvents and work in tanneries, and any activities that may involve exposure to noxious dust and fumes. The minimum age of 16 also applies to the sale of liquor and to employment underground and underwater.
MONGOLIA	Basic minimum age. 16 in various sectors of the national economy and culture, except agriculture. In exceptional cases and subject to the consent of the trade union committee, the employment of persons over 15 is permitted.
	Hazardous work. Minimum age of 18 for arduous work, work in which the working conditions are hazardous, and underground work.

Minimum age for admission to employment: Legal provisions

MOROCCO

Basic minimum age. 12 in all sectors.

Hazardous work. Minimum age of 16 for types of work involving danger, excess strain or that may be harmful to the morals. Prohibited operations include work in workshops and buildings that are under repair or where painting is carried out; greasing, cleaning, inspecting or repairing machines or appliances in motion; operations causing harmful emanations, dust or vapours, or where there is a danger of fire, burns, explosions or poisoning.

MOZAMBIQUE

Basic minimum age. 15 in all sectors.

Hazardous work. Minimum age of 18 in unhealthy or dangerous work, or in work which requires great physical effort.

MYANMAR

Basic minimum age. 13 for factories, shops, commercial establishments or entertainment establishments, excluding factories using motive power with fewer than ten workers and those without motive power with less than 20 workers and public enterprises.

Hazardous work. Minimum ages of 15 to 18. 15 for general employment or work requiring presence in an underground mine; work near cotton openers or the lifting, carrying or moving of loads of such a weight that they are likely to cause injury. 17 for work below ground, unless the young person is certified fit for such work by a qualified medical authority. 18 for work on moving machinery and other dangerous machinery, unless the young person is properly trained and supervised, and for trimmers and stokers. The President may restrict or prohibit employment of children in operations in factories that could expose them to a risk of bodily injury, poisoning or disease.

NAMIBIA

Basic minimum age. 14 for work in any factory or mine, under conditions and circumstances regulated by an Act of Parliament.

Hazardous work. 16 for work that is likely to be hazardous or to interfere with education, or to be harmful to the health or physical, mental, spiritual, moral or social development of the child.

NEPAL

Basic minimum age. 14 in any factory, as long as the work is between the hours of 6:00 and 18:00. Provision is made for the Government to exempt any factory that it may deem appropriate from this restriction.

Hazardous work. Minimum age of 18 for work on hydraulic and other machine-operated presses, milling machines used in metal industries, guillotines, circular saws, printing machines, etc.

NETHERLANDS

Basic minimum age. 15 in all sectors.

Light work. Minimum age of 13 on light work as an assistant in agriculture or in a shop thatforms an integral part of a dwelling, and provided that work is not carried out during school hours and is less than two hours a day on any school day and less than five hours on other days. 15 for light non-industrial work (must not be performed during school hours); newspaper delivery (not during school hours, on Sundays, for more than two hours a day or between 19:00 and 6:00); and public performances, films and radio broadcasts (not during school hours).

Minimum age for admission to employment: Legal provisions

NETHERLANDS (continued)	Hazardous work. Minimum age of 18 for work that is dangerous to life and health. A detailed list of prohibited occupations is laid down in the legislation, including work involving contact with benzene or substances emitting ionising radiations; work involving contact with harmful substances or infectious diseases; work involving the risk of damage to the eyes or ears or organs of the body; transporting or lifting heavy loads; work in contact with moving machinery; the operation of cranes or hoists; demolition work; felling trees; looking after dangerous animals; work involving the risk of explosions or fire.
NEW ZEALAND	Basic minimum age. On completion of compulsory schooling for all employment. Hazardous work. There is no general minimum age. Different minimum ages (from 15 to 21) are specified for different types of work which are considered likely to jeopardise the health, safety or morals of young persons.
NICARAGUA	Basic minimum age. 14 in industry. In other sectors, employers must allow children between 12 and 14 years of age to attend primary school. Hazardous work. Minimum age of 18 in work underground, and in industrial paint work involving toxic materials or products. 14 for artistic performances, work in cafés or any other place of entertainment which could be dangerous to the health or the physical, intellectual or moral development of the young person.
NIGER	Basic minimum age. 14 in all sectors. Exceptions may be authorised by Decree of the Ministry of Labour, such as for child performers. Light work. 12, provided work is performed outside school hours and does not by its nature impede performance at school, does not exceed two hours a day (whether a school day or day of rest), and provided that the daily number of hours devoted to school and light work does not exceed seven. During vacation periods, such work is limited to 4:30 hours a day. Light work is defined as domestic tasks, such as cleaning and work as a kitchen aide, valet or babysitter; light agricultural tasks, such as cutting, gathering or picking; non-industrial light work designated by special authorisation in writing by the labour inspector. All light work on Sundays and legal holidays as well as night work (between 20:00 and 8:00) is prohibited for this age group. Hazardous work. Minimum age of 16 to 18. Limits are established for the loads young persons aged 14 to 18 may carry, pull or push.
NIGERIA	Basic minimum age. 12 in all sectors. 15 in industry and shipping, except technical schools or similar institutions and family undertakings. A person under 14 may be employed only on a daily wage, on a day-to-day basis, provided that he or she returns each night to the place of residence of his or her parents or guardian or a person approved by his or her parents or guardian. Light work. A child under 12 may be employed by a member of his or her family on light work of an agricultural, horticultural or domestic character approved by the Commissioner for Labour. Hazardous work. Minimum age of 18 for any employment which is potentially injurious to the health or morals of a child. 18 in a vessel as a trimmer or stoker. However, two young persons of 16 years can be employed for each trimmer or stoker required where no trimmer or stoker is available. 16 for underground work and the operation of machines.

Minimum age for admission to employment: Legal provisions

NORWAY	Basic minimum age. 15, provided that compulsory education has been completed, in all sectors. Exceptions are made for seafaring, fishing, and work related to education and vocational training. Minimum age is 16 on merchant ships. Light work. Minimum age of 13 for light work that is not detrimental to the health, development or school attendance. The Directorate of Labour Inspection may make rules fixing the length of the hours of work and the conditions in which the work is to be performed. Hazardous work. Minimum age of 18 for work which may be harmful to the health, safety and development of the child; and for work involving contact with white lead in painting. 16 for boys and 18 for girls for service at sea.
PAKISTAN	Basic minimum age. 14 in industry, shops and commerce, and for work at sea (except on a school ship, family ship, or if the young person is in the charge of a relative). 15 for mines, rail transport and as pledged labour, except in a factory with less than ten workers. Hazardous work. Minimum age of 17 on dangerous machines (provided there is adequate training and supervision), machinery in motion or underground work. 18 for road transport service or as a trimmer or stoker on a vessel. (Two 16 year olds may do the work of one trimmer and stoker.) 21 to drive a vehicle for the purposes of road transport.
PANAMA	Basic minimum age. 14 (or 15 if primary education is still being completed) in all sectors. 16 on ships, except training ships. Light work. Minimum age of 12 for light farm work in agricultural and stock-raising undertakings and farms; and as a domestic employee performing light work. The work must be performed outside school hours with the prior authorisation of the Ministry of Labour and Social Welfare. Hazardous work. 18 on work which, on account of its nature or due to the conditions in which it is carried out, endangers the life, health or morals of the persons performing it. Especially prohibited is work in the following areas: clubs and establishments selling alcohol; the transport of passengers or merchandise; the generation of electricity; handling explosives or inflammable materials; mines, quarries or sewers; work involving exposure to radiation.
PAPUA NEW GUINEA	Basic minimum age. 16 in all sectors. (A person over 11 but under 16 may be employed in a family undertaking. A person of 14 or 15 may be employed in any industry other than in an industrial undertaking or the fishing industry, if the employer is satisfied that the child no longer attends school and has the written permission of the child's parent or guardian. A medical certificate is also required.) Hazardous work. Minimum age of 16 in any employment or in any place or under working conditions that are likely to be injurious to the health of the person. 18 for employment on board ship.

Minimum age for admission to employment: Legal provisions

PARAGUAY	Basic minimum age. 15 for all sectors, except family undertakings and vocational schools. However, work below the age of 18 must be authorised by parents or guardians and an annual medical certificate indicating physical and mental aptitude to work must be issued by the competent health authority. Minors up to 18 years cannot work more than six hours a day or 36 a week. Light work. Minimum age of 12 in agriculture under the following conditions: completion of legally-required minimum level of education or that the work does not hinder attendance at school; medical certificate indicating physical and mental fitness to work; work is not dangerous or unhealthy; authorisation of parents or guardian endorsed by the competent authority; working hours to be no longer than four per day or 24 per week (for minors attending school, no more than two hours of work a day; combined school and working hours are not to exceed seven); no work on Sundays or public holidays. Hazardous work. 18 for work endangering the life, health or morals of the young person as specified in laws and regulations.
PERU	Basic minimum age. 14 to 16 by sector. 14 for agriculture; 15 for industry; 16 for deep-sea fishing. With special authorisation from the labour authorities, minors of 13 may work as long as they are able to read, write and count, and have obtained a medical certificate indicating their physical capacity to work. Exceptions to minimum requirements include family undertakings, domestic service and agricultural work, if mechanical devices are not used. Limit of six hours per day for 14 year olds and younger. Hazardous work. Minimum age of 18 for work underground; machinery in motion; work on scaffolding; loading and unloading ships; work in ports and seafaring; work in foundries; the use of circular saws; handling inflammable, toxic, caustic or explosive materials; driving vehicles; work in places of public entertainment or where alcoholic beverages are consumed; handling materials offensive to morality; work in the street, except with authorisation from the labour authority and when warranted by economic necessity (for female minors, the minimum age is 21).
PHILIPPINES	Basic minimum age. 15 in all sectors, except for work in family undertakings and employment which does not interfere with schooling. Light work. Children below 15 may be employed to perform light work which is not harmful to their safety, health or normal development and which is not prejudicial to their studies. Hazardous work. Minimum age of 18 in an undertaking in which the work is hazardous. Occupations listed as hazardous include fishing, logging, mining, quarrying, transport, communications, crafts and related occupations, sports and related occupations, bars, production of chemicals, explosives, poisons and flammable liquids, manufacture of radioactive substances.
POLAND	Basic minimum age. 15 in all sectors. In exceptional cases, children who have not yet reached 15 but have completed their basic schooling, may be employed. Light work. Minimum age of 15. Young persons may be employed on light seasonal and intermittent work prescribed by the competent ministries in agreement with the Minister of Labour, Wages and Social Affairs and the appropriate trade union organisation. Hazardous work. Minimum age of 18 on prohibited types of work drawn up by order of the Council of Ministers. In some cases, exceptions may be made to allow young persons over 16 to work in these areas.

Minimum age for admission to employment: Legal provisions

PORTUGAL	Basic minimum age. 14 in all sectors. Hazardous work. Minimum age of 18 in underground work; in workplaces where there is a danger of noxious dust, fumes, liquids or gases; in the distillation of liquors; the production of explosives, fireworks or inflammable liquids or materials.
QATAR	Basic minimum age. 12 in all sectors, except family undertakings and domestic service.
ROMANIA	Basic minimum age. 16 in all sectors, but persons may be appointed for temporary work from the age of 14 (or 15 in industrial units) with the consent of their parents or guardians, but only for work compatible with their physical development, aptitudes and attainments. Hazardous work. Minimum age of 18 for work in unhealthy, arduous or dangerous conditions; as seamen, trimmers or stokers.
RWANDA	Basic minimum age. 14 in all sectors, including apprentices. Hazardous work. The types of work and categories of undertakings prohibited for minors shall be specified by order of the Minister, made on the advice of the Labour Advisory Committee.
SAINT LUCIA	Basic minimum age. 12 in all sectors. 14 in industry and ships, except work in recognised schools, family industrial undertakings or ships, work in technical schools or work on school ships or training ships. No work is to be performed during school hours if the child is still completing his/her education. Light work. The Governor in Council may make regulations with respect to the employment of children under the age of 12 years by their parents or guardians in light agricultural or horticultural work on the land or garden of the said parent or guardian or any other work of a like nature. Hazardous work. Minimum age of 14 to lift, carry or move anything so heavy as to be likely to cause injury, or in any occupation likely to be injurious to life, limb, health or education. Minimum age of 16 for men for cleaning any dangerous parts of any machinery while the machine is in motion.
SAO TOME AND PRINCIPE	Basic minimum age. 14 for work under contract as a permanent worker. 15 in all public or private industrial establishments, except light work in agriculture, technical schools and family establishments. Work in technical schools must be approved by the competent authority. Light work. Minimum age of 12 for light work in agriculture. Hazardous work. Minimum age of 16 for work which, by its nature or by reason of the conditions in which it is performed, is dangerous to the life, health or morals of the persons doing it. 18 for work underground.

Minimum age for admission to employment: Legal provisions

SAUDI ARABIA

Basic minimum age. 13 in all sectors, except family undertakings, domestic service and persons employed in pastures, animal husbandry or agricultural enterprises which do not process their own produce.

Hazardous work. Persons under 18 shall not be employed in hazardous operations or harmful industries, such as operating power-operated machinery, mines, quarries and the like.

SENEGAL

Basic minimum age. 14 in all sectors, even as an apprentice; exceptions to this rule may be authorised by order of the Minister of Labour and Social Security. 15 for work at sea.

Light work. Minimum age of 12 for light work of a seasonal nature, with the consent of the parents and for a maximum of seven to ten hours per day.

Hazardous work. The types of work and the categories of undertakings on and in which young persons under 16 or 18 may not be employed are determined by order of the Minister of Labour and Social Security. It is prohibited to employ any children in any work which may damage their morals. Activities prohibited to children under 16 include piloting ships; cleaning or repairing moving machinery; work with saws, on scaffolding and with water under pressure. Persons under 18 are prohibited from work in glassblowing and annealing and work with explosives.

SEYCHELLES

Basic minimum age. 15 in all sectors.

Light work. Children aged 12 to 14 may participate in work schemes, run occasional errands and do odd jobs, provided the duties are light and not recurrent.

Hazardous work. No person under 18 may be employed in a hotel, guest house, boarding house, or any place where tourists are accommodated; restaurants, shops, bars, nightclubs, dance halls, discotheques or similar places of entertainment; courts, prisons or as probation officers. Persons under 21 may not be employed in a gaming house or casino.

SIERRA LEONE

Basic minimum age. 12. 15 for industry and work at sea, except on a family vessel, school ship or training vessels approved by the government. Minimum age of 16 (men) for mines.

Light work. No minimum age for light work of an agricultural or domestic nature for the family which has been approved by the competent government authority. No work shall be performed before 6:00 or after 20:00 on any day or for more than two hours on any day.

Hazardous work. Minimum age of 16 for underground work in mines (men only). Those who are 16 but not yet 18 may be employed in mines if medically certified fit. 18 for work on vessels as trimmers or stokers. Where only young persons of less than 18 years are available, two young persons of at least 16 years may be employed in the place of the trimmer or stoker.

Minimum age for admission to employment: Legal provisions

SINGAPORE

Basic minimum age. 12 to 14.

Light work. Children who have completed their 12th year may be employed in light work suited to their capacity. A medical certificate is required.

Hazardous work. Minimum age of 16 to 18. Young persons under 16 may not be employed in any occupation or in any place or under working conditions injurious or likely to be injurious to their health. Industries and jobs prohibited to young persons include operation of machinery in motion, shipping (except on family vessels), underground mines, any industrial undertakings (unless the young person has a valid certificate of registration). Persons under 18 may not be employed as a trimmer or stoker or in places where asbestos dust is generated.

SOLOMON ISLANDS

Basic minimum age. 12 in all sectors or activities. 15 in industrial undertakings and work at sea, except school ships, training ships or technical schools.

Light work. A child below the age of 12 may be employed by and in the company of a parent or guardian on light work of an agricultural, domestic or other character which has been approved by the Commissioner.

Hazardous work. Minimum age of 16 for underground work in any mine (a medical certificate is required). 18 for work on any ship as a trimmer or stoker, unless in possession of a special medical certificate.

SOMALIA

Basic minimum age. 15 for all sectors, except the armed forces, police forces and para-military forces of the state; pupils attending public and state-supervised trade schools or non-profit-making training workshops; family undertakings.

Light work. Minimum age of 12 years, on condition that the work is compatible with the proper protection, health and moral welfare of the child, and in cases where it is necessitated by special business or local conditions and by the special technical requirements of the work, or is essential to the learning of a trade.

Hazardous work. Persons under 16 shall not be employed in work on flying scaffolds or portable ladders in connection with the construction, demolition, maintenance or repair of buildings. Persons under 18 shall not be employed on a vessel as a trimmer or stoker or in underground work in quarries or mines.

SPAIN

Basic minimum age. 16 in all sectors, except public entertainment by authorisation in exceptional cases.

Hazardous work. Minimum age of 18 for machinery in motion; use of cutting machines, presses, saws and other dangerous mechanical equipment; or on scaffolding. Limits are established for the loads young persons may carry, pull or push. Activities and industries prohibited to men under 18 and women under 21 include certain agricultural processing industries; forestry; stone working; metalworking; chemical industries; the construction industry; the timber and textile industries; printing trades; the production of alcohol or paper; the water and gas industries; transport and any other industries where the work may be dangerous, arduous or entail risks from noxious dust, vapours, explosions or infection.

Minimum age for admission to employment: Legal provisions

SRI LANKA

Basic minimum age. 14 in all sectors, except for work at sea (15), in family undertakings, in technical schools or on training ships.

Light work. The employment of children below the age of 14 by their parents or guardians in light agricultural or horticultural work is permitted for less than one hour on any day before school. Light work is also permitted in any school or institution for training purposes, or in any dramatic performance.

Hazardous work. Persons under 14 shall not be employed in street trading; persons under 16 in any public performance in which life or limbs are endangered; persons under 18 as a trimmer or stoker.

SUDAN

Basic minimum age. 12 in all sectors, except for the vocational schools of the state, non-profit-making training workshops, family undertakings, and work undertaken under apprenticeship contracts.

Hazardous work. Juveniles under 18 shall not be employed in dangerous industries and work that is injurious to the health or which requires physical effort, or in jobs which are potentially injurious to their morals. Work prohibited includes work with steam boilers and pressure receptacles; blast furnaces and foundries; underground or underwater work; work with lead in its various forms; work involving exposure to poisonous materials, acids, mercury, petrol and its compounds, and radiation.

SWAZILAND

Basic minimum age. 13 in all commercial undertakings. 15 in all industrial undertakings, except family undertakings and technical schools. Exemptions may be granted in the interests of art, science, education or entertainment. No child under 15 shall be employed during school hours, for more than six hours a day and 33 hours a week, or at night (between 18:00 and 7:00).

Hazardous work. Minimum age of 18 for work which is likely to cause injury to morals or conduct; the sale of intoxicating drinks; work underground; dangerous or unhealthy work; and any other employment prescribed by the Commissioner.

SWEDEN

Basic minimum age. 16 in all sectors, or after completion of compulsory schooling, as long as it is not detrimental to the young person's health or development. The labour inspectorate may prohibit employment or lay down restrictions on the employment of young persons.

Light work. Minors over 13 may be employed on light work as long as it is not detrimental to the young person's health, development and schooling.

Hazardous work. Young persons under 18 shall not be employed on work that involves a substantial risk of accidents, excess strain or any other harmful effect on their health or development. Two schedules of dangerous jobs are issued by the National Board of Occupational Safety and Health and in the Ordinance Prohibiting the Employment of Minors on Certain Types of Work. Prohibited activities include work involving exposure to dangerous fumes or dust; welding; work with gas appliances; work involving exposure to lead, toxic substances or fumes; work with machinery in motion; work on electrical installations; work with explosives; underwater work.

Minimum age for admission to employment: Legal provisions

SWITZERLAND	Basic minimum age. 15 (14 if compulsory schooling has been completed) in all sectors, except agriculture, horticulture, fishing, private households and government undertakings. Light work. Minimum age of 13. Types of work permitted include light work in connection with sporting activities, in shops and forestry enterprises, as long as the health and school work of the young persons are not harmed and their morals are protected. Maximum hours of work are two a day and nine a week during the school term, and three a day and 15 a week during school vacations. Work between 20:00 and 6:00 is prohibited. Hazardous work. Minimum age of 16 to 18. 18 for operating or servicing moving or dangerous machinery; work involving possible danger of fire, explosion, accident, infection, poisoning, burning vapours; work in hotels, restaurants or entertainment establishments; and work in underground mines. 16 for work with heavy loads; work involving exposure to extreme heat or cold; and work in circuses.
SYRIAN ARAB REPUBLIC	Basic minimum age. 12 in all sectors, except industry, undertakings with fewer than ten employees and domestic service. Minimum age of 13 for industry. Hazardous work. Minimum age of 15. Employment below this age is prohibited in establishments involving mining or processing mineral ores; work involving exposure to mercury or lead; glass melting; welding; the operation of power engines in motion; tanneries; manufacture of asphalt; production of tobacco or fertilisers.
TANZANIA	Basic minimum age. 12 in all sectors, but 15 in industry and work at sea, except on a training ship or family vessel. Light work. Children aged 10 to 12 may be employed by and in the company of their parents (or one of them) or their guardian on light work of an agricultural or other character, approved by the proper authority. Such work includes harvesting, drying, cleaning and grafting agricultural produce, planting and animal husbandry. Working hours must be less than four hours a day; night rest from 17:30 to 5:30. Hazardous work. No young person under 18 shall be employed in any employment which is injurious to health, dangerous or otherwise unsuitable. This includes work as a trimmer or stoker on any ship.
THAILAND	Basic minimum age. 12 in all sectors, except agricultural activities if the work is not detrimental to the child's health and physical development and for which permission has been obtained from a permit-issuing officer. Work at night (between 22:00 and 6:00) and on holidays is prohibited. Light work. Minimum age of 12, unless a permit is obtained to work at a lower age, for light work in commercial undertakings, except where alcohol is sold; newspaper delivery services; employment relating to sports; picking and delivery of fruit and flowers; lifting of weights not exceeding 10 kg. Hazardous work. Minimum age of 15 for liquor stores or pubs; places of entertainment as specified by law; massage parlours; places of gambling. 18 for cleaning machinery or engines while in operation; underground or underwater work; manufacture or transport of dangerous chemicals, poisonous substances, explosives or inflammable materials; work involving exposure to radioactivity; other work as stipulated by the Ministry of the Interior.

Minimum age for admission to employment: Legal provisions

TOGO	Basic minimum age. 14 in all sectors. Exceptions are authorised by decree of the Ministry of Labour after consultation with the National Labour Council. 15 for apprenticeship, except for children who have left the education system or who were unable to be educated who may begin an apprenticeship at 14. Hazardous work. Minimum age of 18 for dangerous work, including work involving exposure to lead, explosives, chemicals; melting of animal fats; and any other activities where there may be risks from noxious fumes, gases, dusts and absorption of poisons.
TRINIDAD AND TOBAGO	Basic minimum age. 12. 14 in industrial undertakings. A certificate of fitness for work is required. Exceptions include undertakings and vessels where only family members are employed, work done by children under order of detention in a certified industrial school or certified orphanage, or by children receiving instruction in manual labour in any school supervised by the public authorities. 16 on any ship, except for school ships or training ships or ships on which only family members are employed. Hazardous work. Minimum age of 14. 18 for work on dangerous machines and in the engine room of any ship.
TUNISIA	Basic minimum age. 13 in agricultural undertakings and activities. 15 in industrial establishments and work at sea, except for family establishments, apprenticeships and technical schools. Light work. Minimum age of 13 for light work in non-industrial and non-agricultural activities, on condition that it is not harmful to the child's health or normal development and is not such as to prejudice his or her attendance at school. 14 on light work of less than two hours per day. The hours spent both at school and on light work must be less than seven a day. Light work is prohibited on weekly rest days and statutory public holidays. Hazardous work. Minimum age of 18 in unhealthy or dangerous establishments, such as in any establishment or worksite where scrap metal is salvaged, processed or dumped; underground work; seafaring.
TURKEY	Basic minimum age. 15 in all sectors, except for agricultural work; work performed at home by the members of a family or close relatives; domestic service; any construction work that falls within the scope of the family economy; janitorial services in dwellings. Light work. Minimum age of 13 where there is no danger to the child's health or development or where the work does not interfere with the child's education or hamper opportunities of following vocational guidance and training programmes. Hazardous work. Minimum age of 18 for underground and underwater work, cable laying, and the construction of sewers and tunnels (men only; women are prohibited from work in these areas, irrespective of their age).

Minimum age for admission to employment: Legal provisions

UGANDA	Basic minimum age. A person under the apparent age of 18 years shall not be employed other than as provided by decree. Light work. Minimum age of 12 years for such light work as the Minister may from time-to-time prescribe by statutory order. Hazardous work. Minimum age of 16 for underground work. 18 for any employment which is injurious to the health, dangerous or otherwise unsuitable.
UKRAINIAN SSR	Basic minimum age. 16 in all sectors, although young persons aged 15 years may be employed with the consent of the factory, works or local trade union committee. Hazardous work. Minimum age of 18 on arduous work or work in unhealthy or dangerous working conditions; underground work; or the lifting or carrying of weights exceeding the prescribed limits. The types of work and jobs prohibited for young persons under 18 are listed by decree. The separate divisions of the list have notes indicating the conditions under which minors over 17 are permitted to work in certain types of agricultural work, such as work on tractors and other machines.
UNITED ARAB EMIRATES	Basic minimum age. 15 in all sectors, except for family establishments, domestic service, agriculture, or establishments employing a maximum of five employees. Exempted from this provision are registered educational and charitable institutions providing vocational training for young persons. Hazardous work. The law states that no young person may be employed on dangerous, arduous or unhealthy operations defined by order of the Ministry of Labour and Social Affairs.
UNITED KINGDOM	Basic minimum age. 13 in all sectors. End of compulsory schooling (normally 16) for employment in industrial undertakings, particularly in mines and quarries, manufacturing, construction and transport industries, unless as an apprentice in the last year of compulsory schooling. Children below the age of 16 may not work before the close of school hours or for more than two hours on any day on which the child is required to attend school or on any Sunday. No work before 7:00 or after 19:00 on any day. A child may not be employed to lift, carry or move anything so heavy as to be likely to cause injury. Light work. Children under 13 may be employed in artistic performances and in light agricultural or horticultural work in the company of their parents. Hazardous work. Minimum age of 16 (local authorities may raise the minimum age to 18) for work in especially hazardous industries or involving exposure to dangerous substances. These include work involving exposure to asbestos, lead, zinc ores, rubber, ionising radiation; blasting of castings; work with dangerous chemicals; chromium plating; work with dangerous machines or as machinery attendants; work with circular saws; work on offshore installations; street trading; and in specified agricultural operations.

Minimum age for admission to employment: Legal provisions

UNITED STATES

Basic minimum age. 16 in all sectors except agriculture, unless otherwise provided by regulation or order of the Secretary of Labor provided that the employment (a) is not in the manufacturing or mining sectors; (b) is determined by the Secretary of Labor not to be oppressive child labour; and (c) is confined to periods which will not interfere with the minor's schooling, health or well-being. Categories excluded are employment by parent or child custodian, provided employment is in a sector other than manufacturing or mining and is not deemed by the Secretary of Labor to be particularly hazardous or detrimental to the health and well-being of children under 18; delivery of newspapers; acting or other types of performing; domestic service, sucy as babysitting, companionship for the elderly or yard work on a casual basis.

Hazardous work. Minimum age of 16 to 18. 18 for work in manufacturing and mining sectors, such as manufacturing or storing explosives or articles containing explosive components; motor vehicle driver and outside helper; coal mining; logging, saw/lathe/shingle milling or cooperage; power-driven woodworking machines; exposure to radioactive substances and to ionising radiations; power-driven hoisting apparatus; power-driven metal forming, punching and shearing machines; mining other than coal; slaughtering, meat packing or processing; bakery machine operation; paper product machine operation; brick, tile, and related product manufacture; circular or band saws, guillotine shear operation; wrecking, demolition, shipbreaking operations; roofing; excavation. 16 for agricultural activities, such as operating or assisting in the operation of certain specified machinery and equipment, such as tractors over 20 horsepower; cotton or corn picking work with grain combines, hay mowers, potato diggers, feed grinders; power post-hole diggers, trenchers or earthmoving equipment; forklifts; power-driven circular, band or chain saws; working in a farmyard, pen or stall occupied by certain specified animals; certain lumberjacking activities; working from a ladder or scaffold at a height greater than 20 feet (six metres); driving a bus, truck or automobile when transporting passengers, or riding on a tractor as a passenger; working inside specified fruit, forage or grain storage facilities; handling or applying specified agricultural chemicals and blasting agents; transporting, transferring or applying anhydrous ammonia.

URUGUAY

Basic minimum age. 15 in all sectors as a general principle.

Light work. Minimum age of 12 for light, non-industrial work, provided that a certificate is furnished stating that the child has completed primary school and that the work is essential to the existence of the family.

Hazardous work. Minimum age of 18 to 21 by sector. 18 for handling articles that are harmful to the young person's morals; work in forestry; work in the electricity, gas and sanitation services. 21 for work in places of entertainment; other work detrimental to health and safety; and other heavy agricultural work; work in bakeries; handling industrial paints containing white lead and lead sulfate; handling heavy loads; work involving exposure to benzene; work in cotton mills; operation of machinery in motion. 20 for work in cold stores. Limits are established for the loads that young persons aged 15 to 18 may lift and carry.

USSR

Basic minimum age. 16 in all sectors. In exceptional cases, the employment of persons over 15 may be allowed with the consent of the factory, works or local trade union committee.

Hazardous work. Minimum age of 18 for arduous work or work in unhealthy or dangerous working conditions; underground work; transporting or moving any load whose weight exceeds the limits prescribed for young persons.

Minimum age for admission to employment: Legal provisions

VENEZUELA

Basic minimum age. 14 in industrial, commercial or mining undertakings, businesses and establishments. The National Institute for Minors, or the labour authorities, may authorise minors between 12 and 14 to work in specific justifiable circumstances, as long as the work they perform corresponds to their physical capacity and their education is guaranteed.

Hazardous work. Minimum age of 18 in mines, foundries, undertakings in which there is a risk to life or health, work beyond the strength of the young persons or such as to prevent or retard their normal physical development, work prejudicial to their intellectual or moral development and in the retail sale of spirits (hotels, restaurants, restaurants on ships and aeroplanes, and similar places are not covered by the prohibition of work in the retail sale of spirits).

YEMEN

Basic minimum age. 12 in all sectors, except for temporary workers, agricultural workers and household servants.

YUGOSLAVIA

Basic minimum age. 15 in all branches of economic and non-economic activity.

Hazardous work. Minimum age of 18 on work of a particularly arduous nature, or other types of work capable of having a harmful influence on, or involving a particular risk for life or mental or physical health; underground work; work as stokers on vessels.

ZAIRE

Basic minimum age. 14 in all sectors, including apprenticeships.

Light work. Minimum age of 14 for light and healthy work as defined by decree, on condition that the work is for less than four hours a day on school days and holidays, and that it does not infringe the law respecting school attendance.

Hazardous work. Minimum age of 16 to 18. 18 for work on machinery in motion; machinery whose dangerous parts are not covered; the operation of lifting machinery; work in abattoirs or tanneries; mines and quarries; driving vehicles and engines; work with circular or chain saws; work involving exposure to explosives or inflammable materials; work in connection with electrical systems; work with lead; stokers or trimmers on ships. It is also prohibited for children under 18 to work in bars or public places or in any businesses selling alcohol or producing materials which may be harmful to the individual's moral well-being. Weight limits are established for loads that young persons may carry, pull or push.

ZAMBIA

Basic minimum age. 14 in public or private industrial undertakings or their branches, except undertakings employing only family members; technical schools or similar institutions approved and supervised by the Permanent Secretary, Ministry of Education or an appointed person; commercial or agricultural undertakings. Until age 16 any work contract is deemed to be a daily contract.

Hazardous work. Minimum age of 18 for work done on machinery in motion, such as the lubrication, examination and operation of machines; underground work. A young person shall not be employed in any type of employment or work which, by its nature or the circumstances in which it is carried out, is likely to jeopardise the health, safety or morals of that young person.

List of legislative sources used

Afghanistan

- Ordinance No. 103 of the Presidium of the Revolutionary Council of the Democratic Republic of Afghanistan adopting the Labour Code of the Democratic Republic of Afghanistan, dated 11 June 1987 (Official Gazette, No. 645, 23 August 1987, pages 1-106).

Albania

- Act No. 4170 to promulgate a Labour Code for the People's Republic of Albania, dated 12 September 1966 (Gazeta Zyrtare, No. 6, 29 September 1966, page 140) [LS 1966 - Alb.1].

Algeria

- Act No. 90-11 respecting labour relations, dated 21 April 1990 (Journal Officiel, No. 17, 25 April 1990, pages 488-501) [LLD 1990-DZA4].

- Ordinance No. 76-80 establishing a Maritime Code, dated 23 October 1976 (Journal Officiel, No. 29, 10 April 1977, page 398).

Angola

- Decree No. 58 to provide for certain measures to be taken for the protection of young persons, dated 9 July 1982 (Diário da República, No. 160, 9 July 1982, page 873) [LS 1982-Ang.1C].

Antigua and Barbuda

- Antigua Labour Code, Act No. 14, dated 19 September 1975 (Official Gazette, No. 14, Extraordinary, 1975).

- Factories Ordinance 1957, Ordinance No. 12, dated 1 January 1957 (Official Gazette, 1957), as amended up to Act No. 16, dated 5 September 1973 (Official Gazette, Extraordinary, 1973).

Argentina

- Act No. 20,744 to approve the rules governing contracts of employment, dated 11 September 1974 (Boletín Oficial, No. 23,003, 27 September 1974), as amended up to Decree No. 390, dated 13 May 1976 (Boletín Oficial, No. 23,410, 21 May 1976, page 2) [LS 1974-Arg.2; 1976-Arg.1].

- Act No. 22,248 to approve nation-wide rules governing agricultural work, dated 3 July 1980 (Boletín Oficial, No. 24,461, 18 July 1980, page 2) [LS 1980-Arg.1].

- Act No. 11,317 to regulate the employment of women and young persons, dated 30 September 1924 (Crónica Mensual del Departamento Nacional del Trabajo, Vol. 7, No. 81, September 1924, page 1417), as amended up to Act No. 18,624, dated 13 March 1970 (Boletín Oficial, No. 21,893, 20 March 1970, page 2) [LS 1924-Arg.1; 1943-Arg.2; 1970-Arg.2].

Part V: National legal provisions on the minimum age for admission to employment

---

Australia

- Commonwealth Navigation Act 1912 (Acts of the Parliament, 1912, printed separately, 12 pages), as amended up to Act No. 57, dated 15 June 1988 (Acts of the Parliament, 1988).

- West Australian Child Welfare Act 1947 (Government Gazette of Western Australia, 1947), as amended up to Act No. 31, dated 15 June 1984 (Government Gazette of Western Australia, 1984, printed separately, 4 pages).

- Commonwealth Health Amendment Act 1987, Act No. 22 on application of agricultural chemicals by persons under 17 and new provisions on hazardous substances, dated 23 April 1987 (Acts of the Parliament, 1987, printed separately).

Austria

- Federal Act respecting the employment of children and young persons, dated 1 July 1948 (Bundesgesetzblatt, No. 146, 19 August 1948), as amended up to Act dated 4 December 1987 (Bundesgesetzblatt, No. 222, Text 599, 18 December 1987) [LS 1948-Aus.3; 1952-Aus.1; 1962-Aus.1; 1969-Aus.4B; 1982-Aus.1].

- Agricultural Labour Act 1948, dated 2 June 1948 (Bundesgesetzblatt, No. 140, 12 August 1948, page 515), as amended up to Act dated 9 July 1984 (Bundesgesetzblatt, No. 129, Text 287, 18 July 1984, page 1771).

- Ordinance of the Minister for Social Administration and Commerce, Trade and Industry respecting types of employment prohibited to and restricted for young persons, dated 2 October 1981 (Bundesgesetzblatt, No. 206, Text 527, 3 December 1981, page 2201) [LS 1954-Aus.3].

Bahamas

- Employment of Young Persons Act 1939, dated 27 February 1939 (Official Gazette, 1939), as amended up to Chapter 246 of 1965 (Official Gazette, 1965, printed separately).

- Employment of Children Prohibition Act 1938, dated 27 February 1938 (Official Gazette, 1938), as amended up to Act No. 6, dated 27 April 1966 (Official Gazette, 1966, printed separately).

- Merchant Shipping Act 1976, Act No. 16, dated 29 November 1976 (Official Gazette, Supplement, Part I, 16 December 1976), as amended up to Act No. 6, dated 7 July 1989 (Official Gazette, 14 July 1989, Extraordinary).

Bahrain

- Amiri Decree-Law No. 23 to promulgate the Labour Law for the private sector, dated 16 June 1976 (Official Gazette, No. 1184, Supplement, 15 July 1976), as amended up to Amiri Decree-Law No. 3, dated 25 February 1984 (Official Gazette, 1984) [LS 1976-Bah.1].

- Ministerial Order No. 6 respecting industries and dangerous occupations harmful to health of juveniles, dated 16 August 1976 (Official Gazette, 1976).

Bangladesh

- East Pakistan Factories Act 1965, Act No. 4, dated 1 September 1965 (Dacca Gazette, 1 September 1965, Extraordinary, page 1535) [LS 1965-Pak.2].

- Employment of Children Act 1938, Act No. 26, dated 1 December 1938 (Gazette of India, 1938), as amended up to Act No. 15, dated 8 April 1939 (Gazette of India, 1939) [LS 1938-Ind.5; 1939-Ind.3].

- Tea Plantation Labour Ordinance 1962, Ordinance No. 29, dated 1 June 1962 (Gazette of Pakistan, 4 June 1962, Extraordinary, page 864) [LS 1962-Pak.1].

- East Pakistan Shops and Establishments Act 1965, Act No. 7, dated 1 September 1965 (Dacca Gazette, 1 September 1965, Extraordinary, page 1641).

- Indian Mines Act 1923, dated 23 February 1923 (Gazette of India, 1923), as amended up to Act No. 65 of 1973 (Bangladesh Gazette, 1973).

- Bangladesh Merchant Shipping Ordinance 1983, Ordinance No. 26, dated 30 June 1983 (Bangladesh Gazette, 30 June 1983, Extraordinary, pages 3551-3734).

Barbados

- Employment (Miscellaneous Provisions) Act 1977, Act No. 6, dated 24 March 1977 (Official Gazette, 24 March 1977, Supplement).

- Factories Act 1982, Act No. 17, dated 29 April 1983 (Official Gazette, 9 May 1983, Supplement, pages 1-186).

- Education Act 1981, Act No. 25, dated 7 May 1981 (Official Gazette, 14 May 1981, Supplement).

Belgium

- Labour Act, dated 16 March 1971 (Moniteur Belge, No. 62, 30 March 1971, page 3931), as amended up to Act of 4 February 1987 (Moniteur Belge, No. 57, 21 March 1987, page 4323) [LS 1971-Belg.2].

- Seaman's Act 1928, dated 5 June 1928 (Moniteur Belge, No. 208, 26 July 1928, page 3321) [LS 1928-Bel.5].

- Royal Order governing circumstances in which services of young persons aged 15 and over may be hired under student contracts, repealing Order of 28 June 1984, dated 19 June 1985 (Moniteur Belge, No. 123, 28 June 1985, page 9746).

- Act respecting contracts of employment, dated 3 July 1978 (Moniteur Belge, No. 160, 22 August 1978, page 9299) [LS 1978-Bel.1].

- Royal Order concerning circumstances under which exceptions to the minimum age for apprentices (18) can be made, dated 11 August 1987 (Moniteur Belge, No. 173, 9 September 1987, pages 13,217-13,218).

Belgium (continued)

- Royal Decree to prohibit certain underground work for workers under 21 years of age in mines, surface mines and quarries, dated 17 April 1972 (Moniteur Belge, No. 101, 26 May 1972, page 6195).

- Royal Decree to prohibit employment of young workers under 16 in underground work, dated 4 April 1972 (Moniteur Belge, No. 79, 21 April 1972, page 4761).

- Decision modifying and complementing Title III, Chapter II of the General Regulations for the protection of workers regarding dangerous substances (Moniteur Belge, No. 61, 27 March 1986, pages 4031-4065).

Belize

- Labour Ordinance 1960, Ordinance No. 27, dated 1 August 1960 (Official Gazette, Cap. 234, 1960), as amended up to Act No. 11, dated 27 March 1986 (Official Gazette, Cap. 234, 1986).

Benin

- Ordinance No. 33 PR/MFPT to promulgate a Labour Code, dated 28 September 1967 (Journal Officiel, No. 27, 15 December 1967, page 831), as amended up to Ordinance No. 74-38, dated 9 May 1974 (Journal Officiel, No. 11, 1974) [LS 1967-Dah.1; 1974-Dah.1].

- General collective labour agreement applicable to undertakings in Dahomey in the private sector (Journal Officiel, No. 20, 1 October 1974, page 969) [LS 1974-Dah.2].

- Order No. 1781 ITLS/D respecting the employment of children and young persons, dated 12 July 1954 (Journal Officiel, Special issue, 16 July 1954).

- Order No. 1783 ITLS/D respecting derogation from the minimum age for children, dated 12 July 1954 (Journal Officiel, Special issue, 16 July 1954).

Bolivia

- Labour Decree, dated 24 May 1939, as amended up to 1990, in I. Sandoval Rodriguez and A.R. Arenas de Sandoval (editors): Legislación del Trabajo (Ministero del Trabajo, La Paz, 1990) [LS 1939-Bol.1].

- Minors' Code, Law No. 12,538, dated 30 May 1975 (Gazeta Oficial, 1976, page 11).

Botswana

- Employment Act 1982, Act No. 9, dated 30 November 1982 (Government Gazette, Extraordinary, Supplement A, 1982).

- Apprenticeship and Industrial Training Act 1983, Act No. 34, dated 21 December 1983 (Government Gazette, Supplement, 1983, pages A147-A174).

Brazil

- Decree No. 5452 to approve the consolidation of Labour Laws, dated 1 May 1943 (Diario Oficial, No. 108, 5 June 1943, page 7945), as amended up to Act No. 7305, dated 2 April 1985 (Diário Oficial, No. 64, 3 April 1985, page 5761) [LS 1985-Bra.1].

- Act No. 8069 to provide for the status of children and adolescents, and to make other provisions, dated 13 July 1990 (Diário Oficial, No. 135, 16 July 1990, page 13,563; errata: ibid., No. 187, 27 September 1990, page 18,551).

Bulgaria

- Labour Code, Decree No. 940, dated 24 March 1986 (D'rahaven Vestnik, No. 26, 1 April 1986, pages 1-32; No. 27, 4 April 1986, pages 1-24), as amended up to Ordinance No. 72, dated 30 December 1986 (D'rzhaven Vestnik, No. 6, 23 January 1987, pages 5-8; No. 8, 30 Janaury 1987, page 7) [LS 1951-Bul.2; 1957-Bul.2; 1968-Bul.1A].

Burkina Faso

- Act No. 26/62/AN to establish the Labour Code, dated 7 July 1962 (Journal Officiel, No. 33bis, Special, 18 August 1962), as amended by Act No. 9/73/AN, dated 7 June 1973 (Journal Officiel, No. 31, 26 July 1973, page 418).

- Order No. 539/ITLS/HV respecting the employment of children, dated 29 July 1954 (Journal Officiel, 15 August 1954, Extraordinary, page 349).

- Order No. 545/ITLS/HV to provide for exceptions to the rules governing the age for admission to employment, dated 2 August 1954 (Journal Officiel, 15 August 1954, Extraordinary).

Burundi

- Law No. 001/31 to promulgate a Labour Code, dated 2 June 1966 (Bulletin Officiel, 15 September 1966), as amended up to Act No. 1/04, dated 19 February 1980 (Bulletin Officiel, No. 5, 1 May 1980, page 159).

- Ministerial Ordinance No. 630/1 regulating child labour, dated 5 January 1981 (Bulletin Officiel, 1981, printed separately).

Byelorussian SSR

- Labour Code of 1972, dated 23 June 1972.

- Order No. 283/P-9 of the State Labour and Social Affairs Committee of the USSR and the Presedium of the All-Union Central Council of Trade Unions respecting a list of processes, occupations and jobs involving arduous and harmful conditions of work in which it is prohibited to employ persons under 18 years of age, dated 10 September 1980 (Byulleten Gosudarstvennogo Komitetu SSR po Trudu i Sotsialnym Voprosom, No. 3, 1981, pages 7-21).

Cameroon

- Law No. 74-14 instituting the Labour Code, dated 27 November 1974 (Official Gazette, Supplement, 5 December 1974) [LS 1974-Cam.1].

- Order No. 17 relating to the employment of women and children, dated 27 May 1969 (Official Gazette, No. 10, 1 June 1969) [LS 1969-Cam.2B].

Canada

- Canada Labour Standards Code 1970, 13-14 Eliz. II, Chap. 38, 18 March 1965 (Acts of the Parliament, 1964-65, Part I, page 307), as amended up to 35-36-37 Eliz. II, Chap. 33, 21 July 1988 (Canada Gazette/Gazette du Canada, Part III, Vol. 11, No. 7, 3 November 1988, page 871) [LS 1965-Can.1A; 1971-Can.3; 1972-Can.1].

- Canada Labour Standards Regulations, SOR/72-7, dated 12 January 1972 (Canada Gazette, No. 2, Part II, 26 January 1972, page 118) [LS 1972-Can.1].

- For a summary of provincial legislation on minimum age for industrial employment through 1 January 1987, see CCH Canadian Master Labour Guide: 1987, 841 CCH Canadian Labour Law Reports (CCH) (extra edition 30 January 1987), paragraphs 2015-2250.

Cape Verde

- Rural Labour Code, Decree No. 44,309, dated 27 April 1962 (Boletim Oficial, No. 95, 1962), as amended up to Decree No. 47,590, dated 16 March 1967 (Boletim Oficial, No. 16, 1967) [LS 1962-Por.1].

Central African Republic

- Act No. 61/221 to establish the Labour Code of the Central African Republic, dated 2 June 1961 (Journal Officiel, Special issue, August 1961).

- Decree No. 837/ITT, dated 22 November 1953 (Journal Officiel AEF, 15 December 1953), as amended by Order No. 42 respecting the conditions of employment of young workers, dated 24 January 1959 (Journal Officiel AEF, 15 March 1959, page 534).

Chad

- Act No. 7/66 to establish a Labour and Social Welfare Code, dated 4 March 1966 (Journal Officiel, No. 7, Extraordinary, 24 March 1966, page 353) [LS 1966-Chad 1].

- Decree No. 55/PR-MTIS, DTMOPS concerning child labour, dated 8 February 1969 (Textes d'Application du Code de Travail, 1971, page 44).

Chile

- Act No. 18,620 approving the Labour Code, dated 27 May 1987 (Diario Oficial, No. 32,812, 6 July 1987, pages 3633-3656; errata, No. 32,830, 27 July 1987, page 4021), as amended up to Act No. 18,752, dated 18 October 1988 (Diario Oficial, No. 33,207, 28 October 1988, page 1).

China

- Tentative rules for study duration and living subsidies for apprentices in enterprises and undertakings run by the State, State-private and individuals (1958), as noted in the report by the Government to the ILO Committee of Experts on Conventions Nos. 7 and 15, dated 5 December 1984.

- Notice on implementation of all-round appraisal recruitment of workers (1979), as noted in the report by the Government to the ILO Committee of Experts on Conventions Nos. 7 and 15, dated 5 December 1984.

- Order No. 81 of the State Council on implementation of the Regulation on the prohibition from hiring child labour, dated 15 April 1991.

Colombia

- Decree No. 2737 to promulgate a Minors' Code, dated 27 November 1989 (Diario Oficial, No. 39,080, 27 November 1989).

Comores

- Act No. 84-018/PR establishing the Labour Code, dated 18 February 1984 (Official Journal, 1984, printed separately, 62 pages).

- Order No. 60/130/IT-C to provide for exceptions to the rule governing the age for admission to employment for children, dated 1 August 1960 (Official Journal, 16 August 1960, page 8).

Congo

- Act No. 45-75 to establish the Labour Code, dated 15 March 1975 (Journal Officiel, 17 March 1975, special edition).

- Order No. 2224 to provide for exceptions to the rules governing the employment of young persons, the types of employment and the categories of undertakings permitted to them, dated 24 October 1953 (Journal Officiel, 1953).

Costa Rica

- Act No. 2 to promulgate the Labour Code, dated 27 August 1943 (La Gaceta, Vol. 65, No. 192, 29 August 1943, page 1169), as amended up to 1984 [LS 1943-CR1; 1944-CR1A-C; 1947-CR1; 1949-CR2; 1951-CR2; 1955-CR1].

- Decree No. 2601-TSS prohibiting the employment of young persons under the age of 18 years as shovellers, stokers and trimmers on coal-fired fishing boats, dated 13 October 1972 (La Gaceta, No. 206, 31 October 1972, page 4861).

Côte d'Ivoire

- Act No. 64-290 to establish a Labour Code, dated 1 August 1964 (Journal Officiel, No. 44, Extraordinary, 17 August 1964), as amended up to Act No. 75-496, dated 10 July 1975 (Journal Officiel, No. 41, 21 August 1975, page 1480) [LS 1964-IC1; 1974-IC1; 1975-IC1].

- Decree No. 67-265 codifying the regulations issued in application of Title V (Conditions of Work) of the Labour Code, dated 2 June 1967 (Journal Officiel, No. 22, 30 April 1968).

Cuba

- Act No. 49 to promulgate a Labour Code, dated 28 December 1984 (Gacete Oficial, No. 2, 23 February 1985, page 17) [LS 1984-Cuba 1].

- Decree No. 883 to complete and bring together the laws respecting the employment of young persons and to give effect to the international labour Conventions ratified by Cuba, dated 27 May 1953 (Gacete Oficial, No. 42, 30 May 1953, page 8) [LS 1953-Cub.1].

Cyprus

- Children and Young Persons (Employment) Law 1953, dated 30 September 1953 (Ephemeris tes kybernesseos, 1953), as amended up to Law No. 18 of 1968 (Ephemeris tes kybernesseos, 12 December 1968, Supplement No. 1, page 23) [LS 1953-Cyp.2].

Czechoslovakia

- Labour Code, dated 16 June 1965 (Sbirka Zákonu, No. 32, Text 65, 30 June 1965), as amended up to 5 December 1990 (Sbirka Zákonu, Part 1, 31 January 1991, pages 17-30) [LS 1965-Cz.1].

- Decision No. 32 on principles governing the preparation of lists of employments prohibited to women and young persons, dated 7 December 1966 (Sbirka Zákonu, 1967).

Denmark

- Act No. 681 respecting the working environment, dated 23 December 1975 (Lovtidende A, No. 65, 1975, page 1951), as amended up to Notification No. 646, dated 18 December 1985 (Lovtidende A, No. 89, 1985) [LS 1975-Den.1].

- Notification No. 25 regarding children in public performances, dated 22 January 1964 (Lovtidende A, No. 2, 1964, page 52), as amended up to Order No. 611, dated 18 December 1985 (Lovtidende A, No. 87, 1985, pages 1939-1953).

- Notification No. 333 on the performance of light, paid work by children, dated 23 June 1977 (Lovtidende A, No. 32, 1977, page 968).

- Notification No. 400 for Greenland respecting ligth work performed by children, dated 24 June 1986 (Lovtidende A, No. 44, 1986, pages 1260-1261).

- Notification No. 465 regarding night work by young persons, dated 25 October 1985 (Lovtidende A, No. 73, 1985, pages 1503-1504).

- Merchant Shipping (Masters and Seamen) Act 1973, Act No. 420, dated 13 June 1973 (Lovtidende A, No. 37, 1973, page 1351), as amended up to Act No. 519, dated 4 December 1985 (Lovtidende A, No. 81, 1985, pages 1757-1769) [LS 1973-Den.2].

- Notification No. 103 respecting dangerous work performed by children, dated 15 February 1989 (Lovtidende A, No. 17, 1989, pages 404-410), as amended up to Notification No. 883, dated 21 December 1989 (Lovtidende A, No. 126, 1989).

Djibouti

- Act No. 52-1322 establishing a Labour Code in overseas territories, dated 15 December 1952 (Journal Officiel de la République Française, No. 298, 15-16 December 1952, page 11,541) [LS 1952-Fr.5].

- Decision No. 786 concerning the employment of children, dated 7 June 1955 (Journal Officiel de la Côte française des Somalis, 1 July 1955).

- Order No. 1012/SG/CG to amend and repeal two previous orders concerning the employment of children, dated 3 July 1968 (Journal Officiel, No. 14, 25 July 1968, page 253).

Dominica

- Employment of Children Prohibition Ordinance, Ordinance No. 5, dated 29 December 1939 (Laws of Dominica, Vol. II, Cap. 110, 1941, page 1027).

- Employment of Women, Young Persons and Children Ordinance, Ordinance No. 16, dated 1 February 1938 (Laws of Dominica, Vol. II, Cap. 111, 1941, pages 1029-1034).

Dominican Republic

- Act No. 2920 to promulgate the Labour Code, dated 11 June 1951 (Gaceta Oficial, Vol. 72, No. 730bis, 23 July 1951), as amended up to 1984 [E.A. Gautreaux Sanchez: Codigo de Trabajo de la Republica Dominicana (Libreria Dominicana, Santo Domingo, 1984)] [LS 1951-Dom.1; 1961-Dom.1].

- Order No. 4/58 respecting intermittent work and work constituting a danger to the lives and health of women workers and persons under 18 years of age, dated 30 April 1958 (Gaceta Oficial, 1958).

Ecuador

- Labour Code, dated 30 June 1978 (Registro Oficial, No. 650, 16 August 1978, page 6), as amended up to an Act dated 13 November 1989 (Registro Oficial, No. 316, 16 November 1989, page 2) [LS 1978-Ec.1].

- Act No. 187 to promulgate the Minors' Code, dated 19 August 1969 (Registro Oficial, No. 320, 3 December 1969, page 2397), as amended up to Act No. 83, dated 9 July 1990 (Registro Oficial, No. 486, 25 July 1990, page 3).

Egypt

- Act No. 137 to promulgate a Labour Code, dated 6 August 1981 (Al-Jarida al-Rasmiya, No. 33, 13 August 1981) [LS 1981-Egypt 2].

- Decree No. 55 concerning the conditions and measures of protection necessary to ensure safety and health at work, dated 17 May 1983 (Al-waqai al-misriya, No. 210, 12 September 1983).

El Salvador

- Decree No. 38 to promulgate the Constitution of the Republic of El Salvador, dated 15 December 1983 (Diario Oficial, No. 234, 16 December 1983).

- Decree No. 15 to promulgate a Labour Code, dated 31 July 1972 (Diario Oficial, Book 236, No. 142, 31 July 1972, page 7061).

Equatorial Guinea

- Act No. 2 to promulgate the Labour Code, dated 4 January 1990 (Bolétin Oficial, Extraordinary, 1990, pages 1-39) [DDS 1990-GNQ1].

Ethiopia

- Labour Proclamation No. 64, dated 6 December 1975 (Negarit Gazette, No. 11, 6 December 1975, page 55) [LS 1975-Eth.1].

Fiji

- Employment Ordinance, Ordinance No. 15, dated 23 July 1964 (Fiji Gazette, No. 15, 1964), as amended up to Act No. 31, dated 18 December 1975 (Fiji Gazette, 1975).

- Factories Act 1971, Act No. 56, dated 23 December 1971 (Fiji Gazette, Vol. 99, 17 January 1972, page 28).

Finland

- Act No. 669 respecting the protection of young workers, dated 29 December 1967 (Suomen Asetuskokoelma-Finlands Författningssamling, No. 669, 1967, page 1516), as amended up to Act No. 908, dated 24 November 1983 (Suomen Asetuskokoelma-Finlands Författningssamling, No. 908, 1983) [LS 1967-Fin.3].

- Act No. 951 respecting conditions of employment of domestic workers, dated 16 December 1977 (Suomen Asetuskokoelma-Finlands Författningssamling, No. 951, 1977) [LS 1977-Fin.1].

- Ordinance No. 508 respecting the protection of young workers, dated 27 June 1986 (Suomen Asetuskokoelma-Finlands Författningssamling, No. 508, 1986, pages 1100-1101).

France

- Labour Code, Act No. 73-4, dated 2 January 1973 (Journal Officiel, No. 2, 3 January 1973, page 52; errata: ibid., No. 160, 11 July 1973, page 7489), as amended up to Act No. 90-603, dated 12 July 1990 (Journal Officiel, No. 161, 13 July 1990, page 8273) [LS 1981-Fr.1; 1982-Fr.2; 1983-Fr.2; 1984-Fr.1; 1987-Fr.1; 1987-Fr.2].

- Ordinance No. 67-830, dated 27 September 1967 (Journal Officiel, 28 September 1967, pages 9557-9560), as amended up to Decision of 13 July 1977 (Journal Officiel, 14 July 1977).

Gabon

- Act No. 5-78 to promulgate a Labour Code, dated 1 June 1978 (Journal Officiel, No. 25, 28 November 1978, Extraordinary, page 1) [LS 1978-Gab.1].

- Decree No. 275/PR to provide for exceptions to the rules governing the employment of young persons, dated 5 December 1962 (Journal Officiel, No. 5, 15 February 1963, page 185) [LS 1962-Gab.2].

Germany

- Young Persons (Protection of Employment) Act, dated 12 April 1976 (Bundesgesetzblatt, Part I, No. 42, 15 April 1976, page 965), as amended up to the Young Persons (Protection) Act, dated 15 October 1984 (Bundesgesetzblatt, Part I, No. 43, 20 October 1984, page 1277) [LS 1976-Ger.FR2].

Ghana

- Labour Decree 1967, National Liberation Council Decree No. 157, dated 10 April 1967 (Ghana Gazette, 1967), as amended up to Decree No. 368, dated 8 July 1969 (Ghana Gazette, 1969) [LS 1967-Ghana 1].
- Merchant Shipping Act, Act No. 183 of 1963 (Ghana Gazette, 1963).

Greece

- Act No. 1837 for the protection of young persons in employment and other provisions, dated 22 March 1989 (Ephemeris tes kyherneseos, Part I, No. 85, 23 March 1989, pages 1105-1109).
- Act No. 1182 incorporating ILO Convention No. 138, dated 24 July 1981 (Ephemeris tes Kyherneseos, 1981).
- Act No. 1414 respecting the application of the principle of equality of the sexes in employment relationships and to make other provisions, dated 30 January 1984 (Efemeris tes kyherneseos, Part I, No. 10, 2 February 1984, page 1) [LS 1984-Gr.1].
- Regulation of work in mines and quarries, dated 9 September 1972 (Efemeris tes kyherneseos, 9 September 1972).

Guinea

- Ordinance No. 003/PRG/SGG/88 issuing the Labour Code, dated 28 January 1988 (printed separately) [LS 1988-Gui.1].

Guinea Bissau

- General Labour Act No. 2, dated 5 April 1986 (Boletim Oficial, No. 14, 5 April 1986, 3rd supplement, pages 1-29).

Guatemala

- Constitution of the Republic of Guatemala, dated 31 May 1985 (Diario de Centro América, No. 41, 3 June 1985, page 897) [LS 1985-Gua.1].
- Decree No. 1441 to promulgate the consolidated text of the Labour Code, dated 5 May 1961 (El Guatemalteco, No. 14, 16 June 1961, page 145), as amended up to Agreement No. 1234 of 1987 [Codigo del Trabajo (Jimenez and Ayala, Guatemala, 1991)] [LS 1961-Gua.1].

Guyana

- Education Act 1877, Act No. 3, dated 3 February 1877 (Laws of Guyana, Cap. 39:01, LRO 1/1973), as amended up to Act No. 4 of 1972 (Official Gazette, 1972).

- Employment of Women, Young Persons and Children Act 1933, Act No. 14 of 1933 (Official Gazette, 1933), as amended up to Act No. 7, dated 23 March 1940 (Official Gazette, 1940).

- Factories Act 1947, Act No. 30 of 1947 (Official Gazette, 1947), as amended by Act No. 4 of 1972 (Official Gazette, 1972).

- Recruiting of Workers Act 1943, Act No. 9, dated 5 June 1943 (Official Gazette, 1943).

Haiti

- Act to promulgate the Labour Code, dated 6 October 1961 (Le Moniteur, Nos. 1-A, 1-B, 1-C and 1-D, Extraordinary, 19 October 1961), as amended up to Decree, dated 24 February 1984 (Le Moniteur, No. 18A, 5 March 1984, page 1) [LS 1961-Hai.1; 1984-Hai.1].

Honduras

- Decree No. 131 to promulgate the Constitution of the Republic of Honduras, dated 11 January 1982 (La Gaceta, Extraordinary, 1982).

- Decree No. 189 to promulgate a Labour Code, dated 1 June 1959 (La Gaceta, Nos. 16,827-16,834, 15-18 and 20-23 July 1959), as amended up to Decree No. 927, dated 7 May 1980 (La Gaceta, 1980) [LS 1959-Hon.1].

Hungary

- Labour Code 1967, dated 8 October 1967 (Magyar Közlöny, No. 67, 8 October 1967, page 907), as amended up to Decree No. 29, dated 1 December 1979 (Magyar Közlöny, No. 84, 1 December 1979, page 1304) [LS 1967-Hun.2A; 1979-Hun.1].

- Decree No. 12 of the Ministry of Industry modifying Decree No. 9 of 23 June 1982 establishing the minimum age and duration of training in certain branches, dated 21 October 1984 (Magyar Közlöny, No. 44, 21 October 1984, page 751).

- Decree No. 6 of the Minister of Health relative to the protection of women and young persons, dated 12 June 1982 (Magyar Közlöny, No. 35, 12 June 1982, pages 661-665).

- Decree No. 4 of the Minister of Labour, dated 5 April 1962 (Magyar Közlöny, No. 22, 5 April 1962, page 212).

Iceland

- Act No. 53 on protection of children and young persons, dated 13 May 1966 (Stjórnartídindi, 1966).

- Act No. 46 on facilities, hygiene and safety at workplaces, dated 28 May 1980 (Stjórnartídindi, 1980).

India

- Child Labour (Prohibition and Regulation) Act 1986, Act No. 61, dated 23 December 1986 (Gazette of India, Part II, Extraordinary, 23 December 1986, page 292).

- Factories Act 1948, Act No. 63, dated 23 September 1948 (Gazette of India, Part IV, Extraordinary, 23 September 1948, page 292), as amended up to Act No. 94, dated 25 October 1976 (Gazette of India, 1976) [LS 1948-Ind.4; 1954-Ind.1].

- Plantation Labour Act 1951, Act No. 69, dated 2 November 1951 (Gazette of India, Part II, No. 50, Extraordinary, 1951, page 457), as amended up to Act No. 61, dated 23 December 1986 (Gazette of India, Part II, Extraordinary, 23 December 1986, page 292) [LS 1951-Ind.5].

- Motor Transport Workers Act 1961, Act No. 27 of 1961 (Gazette of India, 1961), as amended up to Act No. 61, dated 23 December 1986 (Gazette of India, Part II, Extraordinary, 23 December 1986, page 292).

- Indian Merchant Shipping Act 1958, Act No. 44, dated 30 October 1958 (Gazette of India, 1958), as amended up to Act No. 61, dated 23 December 1986 (Gazette of India, Part II, Extraordinary, 23 December 1986, page 292) [LS 1958-Ind.2].

- Mines Act 1952, Act No. 35, dated 15 March 1952 (Gazette of India, Part II, No. 18, Extraordinary, 17 March 1952, page 155), as amended up to the Mines (Amendment) Act 1983 (Gazette of India, 1983) [LS 1952-Ind.3; 1959-Ind.2].

Indonesia

- Law No. 1 to bring the Labour Code of 1948 into operation throughout Indonesia, dated 6 January 1951 (Lembaran Negara, No. 2, 1951) [LS 1951-Indo.1].

- Ordinance on Employment of Women, Children and Young Persons, dated 17 December 1925 (Lembaran Negara, No. 647, 1925), as amended up to Ordinance No. 9, dated 17 January 1949 (Lembaran Negara, No. 8, 1949).

- Ordinance on Work of Children and Young Persons aboard Ships, dated 27 February 1926 (Lembaran Negara, No. 87, 1926) [LS 1926-DEI1].

- Ministerial Decree No. PER-01/MEN/1987 regarding the protection of forced working children, dated 7 February 1987 (Lembaran Negara, 1987)

Iran

- Labour Code, dated 20 November 1990 (Official Gazette, No. 13,387, February 1990, pages 1-14).

Iraq

- Act No. 71 promulgating the Labour Code, dated 27 July 1987 (Al-Waqayi'u al'Iraqiya, printed separately, 1987) [LS 1987-Iraq 2].

- Revolutionary Council Resolution No. 150, dated 30 March 1987 (Alwaqai Aliraqiya, No. 3143, 30 March 1987; Official Gazette, No. 17, 29 April 1987, pages 6-7).

Ireland

- Protection of Young Persons (Prohibition of Employment of Children) Order, Statutory Instrument No. 429, dated 17 December 1981 (Statutory Instruments, No. 429, 1981).

- Protection of Young Persons (Employment) Act 1977, Act No. 9, dated 6 April 1977 (Acts of the Oireachtas, 1977).

- Protection of Young Persons (Employment) (Exclusion of Close Relatives) Regulations 1977, Statutory Instrument No. 303, dated 26 September 1977 (Statutory Instruments, No. 303, 1977).

- Protection of Young Persons (Employment) (Agricultural Workers) Regulations 1977, Statutory Instrument No. 220, dated 4 July 1977 (Statutory Instruments, No. 220, 1977).

- Conditions of Employment Act 1936, Act No. 2, dated 14 February 1936 (Public Statutes of the Oireachtas, 1936), as amended up to Act No. 12, dated 26 April 1944 (Acts of the Oireachtas, 1944) [LS 1936-Ire.2; 1944-Ire.2].

- Merchant Shipping (International Labour Conventions) Act 1933, Act No. 29, dated 22 August 1933 (Public Statutes of the Oireachtas, 1933) [LS 1933-IFS2].

- Mines and Quarries Act 1965, Act No. 7, dated 11 May 1965 (Acts of the Oireachtas, 1965).

- Factories Act 1955, Act No. 10, dated 9 June 1955 (Acts of the Oireachtas, 1955).

Israel

- Youth Labour Law, dated 15 July 1953 (Sefer Hakhukim, No. 128, 1953, page 115) [LS 1953-Isr.2].

- Youth Labour (Prohibited and Restricted Work) Regulations of 1954 (Kovet Hatakamot, No. 419, 1954).

Italy

- Act No. 977 respecting the protection of children and young persons in employment, dated 17 October 1967 (Gazzetta Ufficiale, No. 276, 6 November 1967, page 6105) [LS 1967-It.1].

- Act No. 929 incorporating the European Social Charter, dated 3 July 1965 (Gazzetta Ufficiale, No. 193, 3 August 1965, Supplement).

- Act No. 233 concerning maritime, dated 15 May 1954 (Gazzetta Ufficiale, 1 June 1954).

- Presidential Decree No. 36 regulating light work, dated 4 January 1971 (Gazzetta Ufficiale, No. 66, 15 March 1971, page 1563).

- Decree No. 432 on dangerous and unhealthy work, dated 20 June 1976 (Gazzetta Ufficiale, No. 165, 24 June 1976).

Jamaica

- Juveniles Act, dated 1 July 1951 (Gazette of Jamaica, Chap. 189, 1975, page 5).

- Factories Regulations, dated 1 September 1961 (Gazette of Jamaica, Chap. 124, Vol. 84, No. 18, 1 September 1961).

- Mining (Safety and Health) Regulations, No. 114, dated 30 December 1977 (Gazette of Jamaica, 1977).

Japan

- Labour Standards Law No. 49, dated 5 April 1947 (Kampoo, No. 303, 1947, page 1), as amended up to Law No. 99, dated 1 September 1987 (Kampoo, 26 September 1987, pages 9-11) [LS 1947-Jap.3; 1987-Jap.1].

- Mariners' Law No. 100, dated 1 September 1947 (Kampoo, 1947) [LS 1947-Japan 5].

- Ordinance No. 13 on labour standards for women and minors, dated 19 June 1954 (Kampoo, 1954).

Jordan

- Law No. 21 to promulgate a Labour Code, dated 14 May 1960 (Al-jarida al-rasmiya, No. 1491, 1960, page 511), as amended up to Law No. 2, dated 2 January 1965 (Al-jarida al-rasmiya, No. 1818, 18 January 1965, page 52) [LS 1960-Jor.1; 1965-Jor.2].

- Mining Regulations No. 63 of 1964 (Official Gazette, No. 1, 1 November 1964, page 803).

Kenya

- The Employment (Children) Rules 1977, Statutory Instrument No. 155, dated 6 June 1977 (Kenya Subsidiary Legislation, 1977, page 373).

- The Employment of Juveniles at Sea (Medical Examination) Rules 1977, dated 6 June 1977 (Kenya Subsidiary Legislation, 1977, page 376).

- Employment Act 1976, Act No. 2, dated 12 April 1976 (Kenya Gazette, No. 16, 15 April 1976, Supplement No. 19, page 51) [LS 1976-Ken.1].

Kuwait

- Law No. 38 pertaining to work in the national sector, dated 13 January 1964 (Official Journal, 1964).

Lao People's Democratic Republic

- Labour Code 1990, Decree No. 10/90/ASP, dated 24 December 1990 (printed separately).

Lebanon

- Labour Code Act, dated 23 September 1946 (Al-jarida al-rasmiya, 1946), as amended up to 30 September 1988 (Argus de la législation libanaise, No. 3, 1988, pages 8-39) [LS 1946-Leb.1].

Lesotho

- Employment Act 1967, Act No. 22, dated 1 June 1967 (Government Gazette, No. 20, Supplement, 16 June 1967), as amended up to Act No. 14, dated 10 October 1977 (Government Gazette, No. 14, 1977) [LS 1967-Les.1].

Liberia

- Liberian Codification Project: Labour Law Statutes (Monrovia, January 1976), 132 pages.

- Liberian Maritime Law, dated 1 January 1981, as amended up to 28 August 1986.

Libyan Arab Jamahiriya

- Act No. 58-2970 to promulgate a Labour Code, dated 1 May 1970 (Al-Jarida al-Rasmiya, 1 May 1970, Special supplement) [LS 1970-Libya 1].

- Order of the Minister of Labour and Social Affairs, dated 18 October 1972 (Al-Jarida al-Rasmiya, No. 23, 31 May 1973).

Luxembourg

- Act respecting the protection of children and young workers, dated 28 October 1969 (Mémorial, Series A, No. 55, 28 October 1969, page 1263), as amended up to Act of 30 July 1972 (Mémorial, Series A, No. 54, 31 August 1972, page 1331) [LS 1969-Lux.1; 1972-Lux.2].

- Act respecting the establishment of a Luxembourg Maritime Public Register, dated 9 Novmeber 1990 (Mémorial, Series A, No. 58, 12 November 1990, pages 808-831).

Madagascar

- Ordinance No. 75-013/DM to promulgate a Labour Code, dated 17 May 1975 (Journal Officiel, No. 1059, 5 June 1975) [LS 1975-Mad.1].

- Decree No. 62-152 to prescribe the conditions of work of children, women and pregnant women, dated 28 March 1962 (Journal Officiel, No. 216, 7 April 1962) [LS 1962-Mad.2].

- Ordinance No. 60-047 to promulgate a Merchant Marine Code, dated 15 June 1960 (Journal Officiel, No. 105, 25 June 1960).

Malaysia

- Children and Young Persons (Employment) Act 1966, Act No. 40, dated 28 April 1966 (Government Gazette, No. 10, Act Supplement No. 4, 12 May 1966, page 377) [LS 1966-Mal.1].

- Factory and Machinery Act 1967, Act No. 64, dated 26 September 1967 (Government Gazette, 1967).

Malawi

- Employment of Women, Young Persons and Children Ordinance, Ordinance No. 22, dated 20 November 1939 (Nyasaland Gazette, 1939), as amended up to Act No. 22, dated 6 February 1963 (Nyasaland Gazette, 1963).

- Shipping Ordinance 1951, Ordinance No. 13, dated 2 April 1951 (Nyasaland Gazette, 1951).

- Factories Ordinance 1964, Ordinance No. 21, dated 17 March 1964 (Nyasaland Gazette, 20 March 1964).

Mali

- Decree No. 98/PG-RM to determine the nature of the work and the categories of undertakings prohibited to young people, dated 5 June 1975 (Journal Officiel, 1975).

- Act No. 62-67/AN-RM to promulgate a Labour Code for the Republic of Mali, dated 19 August 1962 (Journal Officiel, No. 128, 15 October 1962, page 708) [LS 1962-Mali 1].

Malta

- Education Act 1988, Act No. 24, dated 9 August 1988 (Acts of the Parliament, Vol. 121, Part I, 1988, pages A277-A301).

- Merchant Shipping Act 1973, Act No. 11, dated 6 April 1973 (Government Gazette, No. 12,804, 6 April 1973, Supplement, page A232).

- Factories (Health, Safety and Welfare) Regulations 1986, Legal Notice No. 52, dated 2 September 1986 (Government Gazette, No. 14,635, 2 September 1986, Supplement).

- Work Books Order, Legal Notice No. 110, dated 25 September 1974 (Government Gazette, No. 13,006, Supplement, 1 October 1974, page B345), as amended up to Order No. 2 (Legal Notice No. 78), dated 1 June 1990 (Government Gazette, No. 15,285, Supplement, 1990, pages B455-B456).

Mauritania

- Act No. 63-023 to establish a Labour Code, dated 23 January 1963 (Journal Officiel, No. 106, 20 February 1963), as amended up to Act No. 76-016, dated 27 January 1976 (Journal Officiel, Nos. 416-417, 25 February 1976, page 65) [LS 1963-Mau.1; 1970-Mau.1; 1974-Mau.1; 1976-Mau.1].

- Act No. 78-043 establishing a Maritime Code, dated 28 February 1978 (Journal Officiel, No. 466-467, 29 March 1978).

Mauritius

- Labour Act 1975, Act No. 50, dated 4 December 1975 (Government Gazette, No. 90, Legal Supplement, 1975, page 165) [LS 1975-Maur.1].

- Merchant Shipping Act 1986, Act No. 28, dated 26 July 1986 (Government Gazette, 28 July 1986, Legal Supplement), as amended up to Act No. 5, dated 14 April 1989 (Government Gazette, No. 26, Legal Supplement, 15 April 1989, pages 7-9).

- Occupational Safety, Health and Welfare Act 1988, Act No. 34, dated 2 December 1988 (Government Gazette, No. 76, Legal Supplement, 3 December 1988, pages 133-215).

Mexico

- Federal Labour Act, dated 2 December 1969 (Diario Oficial, No. 26, 1 April 1970, page 1; errata: ibid., No. 51, 10 April 1970, page 2; errata: ibid., No. 29, 5 June 1970, page 16), as amended up to Decree, dated 16 December 1987 (Diario Oficial, No. 14, 21 January 1988, pages 19-24) [LS 1969-Mex.1; 1973-Mex.2; 1979-Mex.1A-D].

- Regulations respecting the employment of women and children in dangerous and unhealthy occupations, dated 31 July 1934 (Diario Oficial, No. 36, 2 August 1934, page 740) [LS 1934-Mex.3].

- Constitution of the United States of Mexico, dated 5 February 1917 (printed separately), as amended up to an Act dated 29 December 1983 (Diario Oficial, No. 44, 30 December 1983, pages 28-32) [LS 1929-Mex.3; 1934-Mex.1; 1960-Mex.1; 1962-Mex.1].

Mongolia

- Act to promulgate a Labour Code, dated 3 July 1973 [LS 1985-Mong.1]

- Decree No. 202/138 by the State Committee on Labour and Wages of the Council of Ministers of the Mongolian People's Republic and the Central Council of Mongolian Trade Unions respecting the adoption of a list of jobs in which women and minors undcer 18 years of age may not be employed, dated 27 December 1973.

Morocco

- Decree to regulate employment, dated 2 July 1947 (Bulletin Officiel, No. 1825, 17 October 1947, page 1028), as amended up to 5 August 1950 (Bulletin Officiel, No. 1993, 5 January 1951, page 2) [LS 1947-Mor.1; 1950-Mor.(Fr.)2)].

- Act No. 1-72-219 to determine the conditions of employment and remuneration of agricultural workers, dated 24 April 1973 (Bulletin Officiel, No. 3156, 25 April 1973) [LS 1973-Mor.1].

- Decree No. 2-56-1019 respecting the dangerous operations prohibited to children and women, dated 6 September 1957 (Bulletin Officiel, No. 2343, 20 September 1957, page 1231) [LS 1957-Mor.4].

Mozambique

- Act No. 8 to approve the Labour Act, dated 14 December 1985 (Boletim da República, No. 50, Fifth Supplement, 14 December 1985, page 196) [LS 1985-Moz.1].

Myanmar

- Factories Act 1951, Act No. 65 of 1951 (Burma Gazette, 1951) [LS 1951-Bur.6].

- Labour and Welfare Act 1951 (Burma Gazette, 1951).

- Shops and Establishments Act 1951, Act No. 59 of 1951 (Burma Gazette, Vol. 5, No. 2, 1951, page 3) [LS 1951-Bur.5].

- Mines Act 1923, Act No. 4 of 1923 (Burma Gazette, 1923).

- Merchant Shipping Act 1923 (Burma Gazette, 1923).

Namibia

- Government Notice No. 1: Publication of the Constitution of the Republic of Namibia, dated 9 February 1990 (Government Gazette, No. 2, 21 March 1990, page 80) [LLD 1990-Nam.1].

Nepal

- Nepal Factories and Factory Workers Act 1959, dated 28 June 1959 (Nepal Rajapatra, 28 June 1959), as amended up to 3 May 1978 (Nepal Rajapatra, Vol. 28, No. 7, 3 May 1978).

- Nepal Factories and Factory Workers Rules 1963, dated 20 May 1963 (Nepal Rajapatra, Vol. 13, No. 6, 20 May 1963), as amended up to 27 February 1978 (Nepal Rajapatra, Vol. 27, No. 45, 27 February 1978).

Netherlands

- An Act to amend the Labour Act 1919 (Conditions of employment of young persons), dated 18 May 1977 (Staatsblad, No. 360, 1977) [LS 1977-Neth.1].

- Labour (Young Persons) Decree, dated 21 November 1972 (Staatsblad, No. 652, 1972) [LS 1972-Neth.1].

New Zealand

- Education Act 1964, Act No. 135 of 1964 (Statutes of New Zealand, 1964).

- Factories and Commercial Premises Act 1981, Act No. 25, dated 3 September 1981 (Statutes of New Zealand, 1981) [LS 1981-NZ2].

- Agricultural Workers Act 1977, Act No. 43, dated 19 October 1977 (Statutes of New Zealand, 1977) [LS 1977-NZ1].

Nicaragua

- Decree No. 336 to promulgate the Labour Code, dated 12 January 1945 (La Gaceta, 1945), as amended up to November 1986 (compilation of Labour Code printed by the Ministry of Labour, Managua, November 1986) [LS 1945-Nic.1; 1962-Nic.1; 1969-Nic.1].

Niger

- Act No. 52-12 to establish a Labour Code, dated 13 July 1962 (Journal Officiel, Extraordinary, 25 August 1962).

- Decree No. 67-126/MFP/T establishing regulations pursuant to the Labour Code, dated 7 September 1967 (Journal Officiel, 1 October 1967).

Nigeria

- Labour Decree 1974, Decree No. 21, dated 29 May 1974 (Official Gazette, No. 28, Supplement, 6 June 1974, page A63) [LS 1974-Nig.1].

Norway

- Provisions as to the employment of primary school pupils who have reached the age of 13 years, dated 14 October 1977 (Norsk Lovtidend, Part I, No. 31, 1977).

- Act No. 4 relating to worker protection and working environment, dated 4 February 1977 (Norsk Lovtidend, Part I, No. 4, 1977), as amended up to Act No. 25, dated 5 June 1987 (Norsk Lovtidend, Part I, No. 12, 1987) [LS 1977-Nor.1].

- Seamen's Act, Act No. 18, dated 30 May 1975 (Norsk Lovtidend, Part I, No. 16, 1975) [LS 1975-Nor.1].

- Act No. 3 respecting white lead in painting, dated 24 May 1929 (Norsk Lovtidend, Part I, No. 20, 1929) [LS 1929-Nor.1].

Pakistan

- Employment of Children Act 1991, dated May 1991 (Gazette of Pakistan, 1991).

- Factories Act 1934, Act No. 25, dated 20 August 1934 (Gazette of India, 1934), as amended up to Ordinance No. 9, dated 28 January 1977 (Gazette of Pakistan, Extraordinary, 1 February 1977) [LS 1946-Ind.1].

- West Pakistan Shops and Establishments Ordinance 1969, Ordinance No. 7, dated 3 July 1969 (Gazette of West Pakistan, Extraordinary, 3 July 1969, page 1057), as amended up to Act No. 1 of 1973 (Gazette of West Pakistan, 1973) [LS 1969-Pak.1].

- Merchant Shipping Act 1923, Act No. 21 of 1923 (Gazette of India, 1923).

- Mines Act 1923, dated 23 February 1923 (Gazette of India, 1923), as amended up to Act No. 65 of 1973 (Gazette of West Pakistan, 1973).

- Road Transport Workers Ordinance 1961, dated 7 October 1961 (Gazette of West Pakistan, 1961), as amended up to Ordinance No. 11, dated 27 September 1974 (Gazette of West Pakistan, 1974).

- Children (Pledging of Labour) Act 1933, Act No. 2, dated 24 February 1933 (Gazette of India, 1933) [LS 1933-Ind.1].

Panama

- Decree No. 252 to approve the Labour Code, dated 30 December 1971 (Gaceta Oficial, No. 17,040, 18 February 1972, Extraordinary), as amended up to Act No. 13, dated 11 October 1990 (Gaceta Oficial, No. 21,645, 16 October 1990, page 1) [LS 1971-Pan.1; 1976-Pan.1; 1981-Pan.1A-B; DDS 1990-PAN 1].

Papua New Guinea

- Employment Act 1978, Act No. 54, dated 12 September 1978 (Official Gazette, 1978), as amended up to Act No. 16, dated 30 July 1981 (Official Gazette, No. 16, 1981).

- Merchant Shipping (Crewmen) Regulation 1980 (Official Gazette, 1980).

Paraguay

- Act No. 729 to promulgate the Labour Code, dated 31 August 1961 (Gaceta Oficial, No. 64, 31 August 1961), as amended up to Act No. 506, dated 27 December 1974 (Gaceta Oficial, 1974) [LS 1961-Par.1].

Peru

- Act No. 13,968 to promulgate a Minors' Code, dated 1 February 1962 (El Peruano, 1962).

- Act No. 2851 respecting the employment of women and children, dated 25 November 1918 (Bolétin del Instituto de Reformes Sociales, 1919, page 659), as amended up to Decision No. 434-88-TR, dated 18 October 1988 (El Peruano, No. 2975, 19 October 1988, page 69,317) [LS 1919-Per.1].

- For an overview of Peruvian legislation, see A. Murguía Sanchez and N.A. Voto-Bernales (editors): Sistematización de la legislación laboral peruana; 1: Derecho individual del trabajo [Systematisation of Peruvian labour legislation; 1: Individual right to work] (Ministry of Labour and Social Promotion/ILO-CIAT, Lima, May 1988, 3rd edition).

Poland

- Labour Code Act, dated 26 June 1975 (Dziennik Ustaw, No. 24, Text 141, 1974), as amended up to 24 November 1986 (Dziennik Ustaw, No. 42, Text 201, 6 December 1986) [LS 1974-Pol.1].

- Decision of the Council of Ministers respecting the employment of young persons over the age of 16 years on certain prohibited jobs in coal mining, dated 17 April 1987 (Dziennik Ustaw, No. 14, Text 86, 12 May 1987, pages 169-170).

- Decision of the Council of Ministers respecting young persons' vocational training and remuneration in socialist enterprises, dated 12 October 1989 (Dziennik Ustaw, No. 56, Text 332, 20 October 1989, pages 849-850).

Philippines

- Presidential Decree No. 442 instituting a Labour Code, dated 1 May 1974 (Official Gazette, No. 23, 10 June 1974; No. 24, 17 June 1974; No. 25, 24 June 1974) [LS 1974-Phi.1].

- Child and Youth Welfare Code, Presidential Decree No. 603, dated 10 December 1974 (Official Gazette, 1974).

Portugal

- Decree No. 14,498 to regulate the employment of young persons and women, and to institute a system for safeguarding the health of young persons and women, dated 29 October 1927 (Diário do Governo, No. 240, 1927, page 2134) [LS 1927-Por.6A].

- Decree No. 14,535 to approve the regulations respecting the employment of women and young persons and the relevant schedules, dated 31 October 1927 (Diário do Governo, Part I, No. 240, 5 November 1927) [LS 1927-Por.6B].

Qatar

- Labour Law No. 3 of 1962 (Official Gazette, 1962), as amended up to Labour Law No. 2, dated 31 January 1981 (Official Gazette, No. 2, 11 March 1981).

Romania

- Labour Code of the Socialist Republic of Romania, Act No. 10, dated 23 November 1972 (Buletinul Oficial, Part I, No. 140, 1 December 1972, page 1168) [LS 1972-Rom.1].

- Order No. 29 of the Ministry of Land, Sea and Air Transport, dated 28 January 1955 (Buletinul Oficial, 1955).

Rwanda

- Act to establish a Labour Code, dated 28 February 1967 (Journal Officiel, No. 5, 1 March 1967) [LS 1967-Rwa.1].

Saint Lucia

- Employment of Children (Restriction) Ordinance, Ordinance No. 28, dated 26 December 1939 (Official Gazette, 1939).

- Employment of Women, Young Persons and Children Ordinance, Ordinance No. 22, dated 22 December 1934 (Official Gazette, 1934).

- Factories Regulations 1948, Statutory Rules and Orders No. 8, dated 28 February 1948 (Official Gazette, 1948).

Sao Tomé and Principe

- Decree No. 44,309 to approve a Rural Labour Code for the provinces, dated 27 April 1962 (Diário do Governo, No. 95, 27 April 1962, page 579; errata: ibid., No. 130, 7 June 1962, page 793, and No. 143, 25 June 1962, page 869) [LS 1962-Por.1].

Saudi Arabia

- Labour Code 1969, Royal Decree No. M/21, dated 15 November 1969 (Official Journal, 1969) [LS 1969-Sau.Ar.1].

Senegal

- Act No. 61-34 to establish a Labour Code, dated 15 June 1961 (Journal Officiel, No. 3462, 3 July 1961, Extraordinary), as amended up to Act No. 87-29, dated 18 August 1987 (Journal Officiel, 1987) [LS 1962-Sen.2B; 1971-Sen.1A and 1B; 1975-Sen.1; 1976-Sen.1; 1977-Sen.1A and 1B; 1987-Sen.1].

- Act No. 62-63 to promulgate the Merchant Marine Code, dated 22 March 1962 (Journal Officiel, No. 3527, 14 May 1962, Extraordinary) [LS 1962-Sen.1].

- Order No. 3724 respecting the employment of children, dated 22 June 1954 (Journal Officiel, 8 July 1954).

- Ministerial Decree No. 10,176 regulating the way of implementing hours of work and its derogations in agricultural establishments, dated 16 September 1974 (Journal Officiel, No. 4380, 28 September 1974, page 1606).

Seychelles

- Employment Act 1990, Act No. 9, dated 1 September 1990 (Official Gazette, 15 October 1990, Supplement, pages 71-137).

Sierra Leone

- Employers and Employed Act 1960, Chapter 212 (Sierra Leone Gazette, 1960).

Singapore

- Employment Act 1968, Act No. 17, dated 6 August 1968 (Government Gazette, No. 18, Acts Supplement, 12 August 1968, page 141) [LS 1968-Sing.1].

- Employment of Children and Young Persons Regulations 1976, No. 3, dated 31 December 1975 (Government Gazette, No. 1, 2 January 1976), as amended up to Act No. 97, dated 25 April 1977 (Government Gazette, No. 21, Supplement, 29 April 1977).

- Factory (Asbestos) Regulations 1980, No. 146, dated 16 April 1980 (Government Gazette, No. 27, 12 May 1980, Subsidiary Legislation Supplement).

Solomon Islands

- Labour Act 1969 (Official Gazette, 1969), as amended up to 31 December 1982 (Official Gazette, Extraordinary, 1983).

Somalia

- Labour Code, Law No. 65, dated 18 October 1972 (Bollettino Ufficiale, No. 10, Supplement No. 3, 25 October 1972, page 1114) [LS 1972-Som.1].

Spain

- Act No. 8 to promulgate a Workers' Charter, dated 10 March 1980 (Boletín Oficial, No. 64, 14 March 1980, page 5799), as amended up to Act No. 32, dated 2 August 1984 (Boletín Oficial, No. 1986, 4 August 1984, page 22,731) [LS 1980-Sp.1; 1984-Sp.1].

- Decree respecting the industries and employments prohibited to women and young persons on account of their dangerous or unhealthy nature, dated 26 July 1957 (Boletín Oficial, No. 217, 26 August 1957, page 785; errata: ibid., No. 226, 5 September 1957, page 836) [LS 1957-Sp.1].

Sri Lanka

- Act No. 47 to regulate the employment of women, young persons and children, dated 7 November 1956 (Official Gazette, 1956), as amended up to Act No. 43, dated 12 November 1964 (Official Gazette, 1964) [LS 1956-Cey.2].

- Merchant Shipping Regulations 1975 (Official Gazette, 1975).

Sudan

- Individual Labour Relations Act 1981, Act No. 65, dated 5 June 1981 (Sudan Gazette, No. 1286, 25 June 1981, Supplement No. 1).

- Industrial Safety Act 1976, Act No. 3, dated 3 February 1976 (Sudan Gazette, No. 1180, Legislative Supplement, 15 February 1976).

Swaziland

- Employment Act 1980, Act No. 5, dated 26 September 1980 (Government Gazette, No. 55, Extraordinary, 1980), as amended up to Act No. 4, dated 14 January 1985 (Government Gazette, No. 388, 1985).

Sweden

- Working Environment Act 1977, Act No. 1160, dated 19 December 1977 (Svensk Författningssamling, No. 1160, 1977), as amended up to Act No. 973, dated 25 October 1990 (Svensk Författningssamling, No. 973, 1990) [LS 1977-Swe.4].

- Seamen's Act, Act No. 282, dated 18 May 1973 (Svensk Författningssamling, No. 282, 1973) [LS 1973-Swe.1].

- Order No. 521 to prohibit the employment of young persons on certain types of work, dated 2 September 1966 (Svensk Författningssamling, No. 521, 1966) [LS 1966-Swe.2].

Switzerland

- Federal Labour Act, dated 13 March 1964 (Recueil des lois fédérales, No. 4, 24 January 1966, page 57), as amended up to Ordinance No. 1, dated 27 November 1989 (Recueil des lois fédérales, No. 50, 19 December 1989, page 2483) [LS 1964-Swi.1].

Syrian Arab Republic

- Law No. 91 to promulgate a Labour Code, dated 5 April 1959 (Al-jarida al-rasmiya, No. 71bis, 7 April 1956, page 1), as amended up to Law No. 106, dated 19 March 1960 (Al-jarida al-rasmiya, No. 71, 24 March 1960, page 451) [LS 1959-UAR1; 1960-UAR2].

- Agricultural Labour Code 1958, Act No. 134 to organise agricultural relations, dated 4 September 1958 (Al-jarida al-rasmiya, No. 26, 4 September 1958, page 18) [LS 1963-Syr.1].

Tanzania

- Employment Ordinance 1955, Ordinance No. 47, dated 10 November 1955 (Official Gazette, 1955), as amended up to Ordinance No. 1, dated 3 April 1975 (Official Gazette, No. 14, Supplement, 4 April 1975) [LS 1955-Tan.1; 1960-Tan.1; 1962-Tan.2; 1969-Tan.1].

- Employment of Children, Young Persons and Adolescents (Restriction) Decree, Decree No. 8, dated 9 April 1952 (Revised Laws of Zanzibar, Cap. 56, 1952).

Thailand

- Announcement of the Ministry of the Interior respecting labour protection, dated 16 April 1972 (Government Gazette, No. 61, Special Issue, 16 April 1972) [LS 1972-Thai.2].

Togo

- Labour Code 1974, Act No. 16, dated 8 May 1974 (Journal Officiel, 1974).

- Ordinance No. 884-55/ITLS concerning the work of women and children, dated 28 October 1955 (Journal Officiel, No. 864 bis, 1955).

- Act No. 83-20 concerning the adaption and renewal of apprenticeships, dated 20 June 1983 (Journal Officiel, 1983), as amended up to Act No. 88-16, dated 23 November 1988 (Journal Officiel, No. 37bis, 2 December 1988, pages 12-13).

Trinidad and Tobago

- Occupational Safety and Health Act 1983 (Trinidad and Tobago Gazette, 1983).

- Ordinance No. 20 on the employment of children and young persons, dated 21 December 1936 (Legal Supplement, 1936) [LS 1936-Trin.1].

- Shipping Act 1987, Act No. 24, dated 1 December 1987 (Trinidad and Tobago Gazette, Vol. 26, No. 336, Legal Supplement, Part A, 18 December 1987, pages 119-318).

Tunisia

- Act No. 66-27 to promulgate a Labour Code, dated 30 April 1966 (Journal Officiel, Nos. 21-22, 3-6, 10-13, 17-24 May 1966), as amended up to Act No. 76-84, dated 11 August 1976 (Journal Officiel, No. 51, 13 August 1976, page 1931; errata: ibid., No. 52, 20 August 1976, page 1970) [LS 1966-Tun.1; 1973-Tun.2; 1976-Tun.1].
- Act No. 67-52 to promulgate a Maritime Labour Code, dated 7 December 1967 (Journal Officiel, No. 52, 12 December 1967, page 1563; errata: ibid., No. 2, 16 January 1968, page 30) [LS 1967-Tun.2].
- Act No. 75-17 to promulgate a Fishermen's Code, dated 31 March 1975 (Journal Officiel, No. 22, 1 April 1975; No. 23, 4 April 1975).

Turkey

- Labour Act 1971, Act No. 1475, dated 25 August 1971 (T.C. Resmi Gazete, No. 13,943, 1 September 1971), as amended up to Act No. 2869, dated 29 July 1983 (T.C. Resmi Gazete, No. 18,120, 30 July 1983) [LS 1983-Tur.3].

Uganda

- Employment Decree 1975, Decree No. 4, dated 2 June 1975 (Uganda Gazette, 1975) [LS 1975-Ug.1].

Ukranian SSR

- Labour Code of the USSR, dated 9 December 1971 (Vedomosti Verkhovnogo Soveta RSFSR, No. 50, Text 1007, 16 December 1971), as amended up to 19 November 1982 (Vedomosti Verkhovnogo Soveta RSFSR, No. 47, Text 1725, 25 November 1982) [LS 1971-USSR1; 1976-USSR2; 1980-USSR3; 1982-USSR1].
- Act No. 2-VIII of the Supreme Soviet of the USSR to approve fundamental principles governing the labour legislation of the USSR and the Union Republics, dated 15 July 1970 (Vedomosti Verkhovnogo Soveta SSSR, No. 29, Text 265, 22 July 1970) [LS 1970-USSR1].
- Decree of the State Labour Committee, dated 29 August 1959, as last amended up to 18 November 1970 (Bulletin of the State Labour Committee, No. 7, 1963; No. 3, 1965; No. 1, 1967; No. 1, 1971).

United Arab Emirates

- Federal Law No. 8 to regulate employment relationships, dated 20 April 1980 (Al-Jarida al-Rasmiya, No. 79, 1980) [LS 1980-UAE.1).
- Ministerial Order No. 47/1 to exempt certain establishments from certain provisions of the Labour Relations Act in respect of employment of young persons and women, dated 20 April 1980 (Al-Jarida al-Rasmiya, 1980).

United Kingdom

- Employment of Women, Young Persons and Children Act 1920, 10 and 11 Geo.V, Ch. 65, as amended up to the Employment Act 1989, 37 Eliz. II, Ch. 38, 16 November 1989 (Statutory Instruments, No. 189, 26 February 1990) [LLD 1989-GBR 1].

- Children and Young Persons' Act 1933, Statutory Instrument No. 663, 23 Geo. V, Ch. 12, 1 July 1933 (Statutory Rules and Orders, 1933), as amended up to the Employment Act 1989, 37 Eliz. II, Ch. 38, 16 November 1989 (Statutory Instruments, No. 189, 26 February 1990) [LS 1933-GB1; LLD 1989-GBR 1].

- Children Act 1972, Eliz. II, Ch. 44, 27 July 1972 (Public General Acts and Measures, Part I, pages 817-822).

- Education Act 1973, Eliz. II, Ch. 23, 23 May 1973 (Public General Acts and Measures, Part I, pages 287-288).

- Agriculture (Safety, Health and Welfare Provisions) Act 1956, 4 and 5 Eliz. II, Ch. 49, 5 July 1956 (Public General Acts and Measures, 1956).

- Agriculture (Avoidance of Accidents to Children) Regulations 1958 (Statutory Instruments, No. 366, 1958).

- Agriculture (Circular Saws) Regulations 1959 (Statutory Instruments, No. 427, 1959).

- Agriculture (Poisonous Substances) Regulations 1984 (Statutory Instruments, No. 1114, 1984).

United States

- Fair Labor Standards Act 1938, as amended up to 16 October 1986, 29 United States Code (USC) 201 et seq., 29 Code of Federal Regulations (CFR) 570 et seq. [LS 1966-USA1].

Uruguay

- Act No. 9342 to promulgate a Children's Code, dated 6 April 1934 (Diario Oficial, Book 115, No. 8306, 2 May 1934, page 260) [LS 1934-Ur.4].

- Decree No. 647/978, dated 21 November 1978 (Diario Oficial, No. 20,392, 7 December 1978).

- Decree respecting hygiene, night work, conventions, etc., in bakeries, dated 8 May 1950 (Registro Nacional de Leyes, 1950, page 426).

- Decree respecting the conditions of work in spinning mills, dated 9 January 1942 (Registro Nacional de Leyes, 1942, page 28).

- Decision prescribing the limits of loads which minors may be permitted to lift and carry, dated 4 November 1969 (Diario Oficial, No. 18,202, 26 November 1969, page 518A) [LS 1969-Ur.1].

USSR

- Labour Code of the USSR, dated 9 December 1971 (Vedomosti Verkhovnogo Soveta RSFSR, No. 50, Text 1007, 16 December 1971), as amended up to 19 November 1982 (Vedomosti Verkhovnogo Soveta RSFSR, No. 47, Text 1725, 25 November 1982) [LS 1971-USSR1; 1976-USSR2; 1980-USSR3; 1982-USSR1].

- Act No. 2-VIII of the Supreme Soviet of the USSR to approve fundamental principles governing the labour legislation of the USSR and the Union Republics, dated 15 July 1970 (Vedomosti Verkhovnogo Soveta SSSR, No. 29, Text 265, 22 July 1970) [LS 1970-USSR1].

Venezuela

- Organic Labour Act, dated 27 November 1990 (Gaceta Oficial, No. 4240, 20 December 1990, Extraordinary, pages 1-75) [DDS 1990-VEN 2].

Yemen

- Decree-Law No. 5 concerning the promulgation of the Labour Code, dated 3 October 1970 (Official Gazette, No. 6, 15 October 1970).

Yugoslavia

- Decree No. 921 to promulgate the Act respecting the fundamental rights arising out of the employment relationship, dated 28 September 1989 (Sluzbeni List SFRJ, No. 60, 6 October 1989, page 1469).

- Decree No. 184 respecting mutual relationships of workers in associated labour, dated 25 November 1976 (Sluzbeni List SFRJ, 1976), as amended up to 20 January 1988 (Sluzbeni List SFRJ, No. 11, Text 131, 10 February 1988, pages 293-366).

Zaire

- Legislative Ordinance No. 67/310 to establish a Labour Code, dated 9 August 1967 (Moniteur Congolais, No. 16, 15 August 1967), as amended up to Act No. 73/007, dated 5 January 1973 (Journal Officiel, No. 5, 1 March 1973, page 274) [LS 1967-Congo(Kin.)1; 1973-Zai.1].

- Order No. 68-13 to lay down conditions for the employment of women and children, dated 17 May 1968 (Moniteur Congolais, 1968) [LS 1968-Congo(Kin.)2].

Zambia

- Employment of Women, Young Persons and Children Act 1933, Act No. 10, dated 13 April 1933 (Government Gazette, 1933), as amended up to Act No. 14, dated 15 August 1989 (Government Gazette, 1989) [LS 1933-NR1; 1936-NR1; 1950-NR1].

- Factories Act 1967, Act No. 2, dated 1 May 1967 (Government Gazette, 1967).

- Mining Regulations 1971, Statutory Instrument No. 107, dated 20 May 1971 (Government Gazette, No. 56, Supplement, 21 May 1971, page 301).

Part VI

International standards on child labour

Part VI

International standards on child labour

This part provides the texts of or excerpts from the basic international instruments on child labour. It consists mostly of the principal international labour standards of the ILO on minimum age for admission to employment and conditions of work of children and young persons.

The international labour standards reproduced here consist of Conventions and Recommendations. Conventions are subject to ratification and create binding obligations on the ratifying member States to apply their provisions, while Recommendations complement Conventions and are intended to serve as guidelines for national policy.

The ILO standards are supplemented by excerpts from the well-known Convention on the Rights of the Child, adopted by the UN General Assembly in 1989; the World Declaration on the Survival, Protection and Development of Children and excerpts from the Plan of Action for its implementation, adopted by the World Summit for Children held in New York in 1990, which was organised by the United Nation's Childrens Fund (UNICEF); and an excerpt from the Council of Europe's European Social Charter.

International Labour Organisation (ILO)

The first Convention on child labour was adopted at the first session of the International Labour Conference in 1919. This instrument - the Minimum Age (Industry) Convention, 1919 (No. 5) - fixed at 14 years the minimum age for admission of children to industrial employment. Subsequently, many international labour Conventions and Recommendations were adopted prohibiting the employment of children under a certain age and regulating their conditions of work in particular sectors or occupations. The most recent instruments on the subject are the Minimum Age Convention (No. 138) and Recommendation (No. 146), adopted by the Conference in 1973. Excerpts from these and other Conventions and Recommendations relating to night work, hazardous employment, the handling of heavy weights and medical examinations are reproduced below.

It should be noted that many other international labour Conventions and Recommendations also contain provisions that are relevant to the protection of working children and the abolition of child labour. These include the Labour Inspection Convention (No. 81) and Recommendation (No. 81), 1947; the Discrimination (Employment and Occupation) Convention (No. 122) and Recommendation (No. 122), 1958; the Social Policy (Basic Aims and Standards) Convention, 1962 (No. 117); the Employment Policy Convention (No. 122) and Recommendation (No. 122), 1964; the Co-operatives (Developing Countries) Recommendation, 1966 (No. 127); the Special Youth Schemes Recommendation, 1970 (No. 136); the Workers' Organisations Convention (No. 141) and Recommendation (No. 149), 1975; the Human Resources Development Convention (No. 142) and Recommendation (No. 150), 1975; and the Workers with Family Responsibilities Convention (No. 156) and Recommendation (No. 165), 1981.

Minimum age for admission to employment

Minimum Age Convention, 1973 (No. 138)

The General Conference of the ILO adopted Convention No. 138 in 1973 on a minimum age for admission to employment, stating that "the time has come to establish a general instrument on the subject, which would gradually replace the existing ones applicable to limited economic sectors, with a view to achieving the total abolition of child labour". Articles 1 to 9 are quoted in their entirety.

"Article 1. Each Member for which this Convention is in force undertakes to pursue a national policy designed to ensure the effective abolition of child labour and to raise progressively the minimum age for admission to employment or work to a level consistent with the fullest physical and mental development of young persons.

Article 2. 1. Each Member which ratifies this Convention shall specify, in a declaration appended to its ratification, a minimum age for admission to employment or work within its territory and on means of transport registered in its territory; subject to Articles 4 to 8 of this Convention, no one under that age shall be admitted to employment or work in any occupation.

2. Each Member which has ratified this Convention may subsequently notify the Director-General of the International Labour Office, by further declarations, that it specifies a minimum age higher than that previously specified.

ILO (continued)

Convention No. 138 (continued)

3. The minimum age specified in pursuance of paragraph 1 of this Article shall not be less than the age of completion of compulsory schooling and, in any case, shall not be less than 15 years.

4. Notwithstanding the provisions of paragraph 3 of this Article, a Member whose economy and educational facilities are insufficiently developed may, after consultation with the organisations of employers and workers concerned, where such exist, initially specify a minimum age of 14 years.

5. Each Member which has specified a minimum age of 14 years in pursuance of the provisions of the preceding paragraph shall include in its reports on the application of this Convention submitted under article 22 of the Constitution of the International Labour Organisation a statement - (a) that its reason for doing so subsists; or (b) that it renounces its right to avail itself of the provisions in question as from a stated date.

Article 3. 1. The minimum age for admission to any type of employment or work which by its nature or the circumstances in which it is carried out is likely to jeopardise the health, safety or morals of young persons shall not be less than 18 years.

2. The types of employment or work to which paragraph 1 of this Article applies shall be determined by national laws or regulations or by the competent authority, after consultation with the organisations of employers and workers concerned, where such exist.

3. Notwithstanding the provisions of paragraph 1 of this Article, national laws or regulations or the competent authority may, after consultation with the organisations of employers and workers concerned, where such exist, authorise employment or work as from the age of 16 years on condition that the health, safety and morals of the young persons concerned are fully protected and that the young persons have received adequate specific instruction or vocational training in the relevant branch of activity.

Article 4. 1. In so far as necessary, the competent authority, after consultation with the organisations of employers and workers concerned, where such exist, may exclude from the application of this Convention limited categories of employment or work in respect of which special and substantial problems of application arise.

2. Each Member which ratifies this Convention shall list in its first report on the application of the Convention submitted under article 22 of the Constitution of the International Labour Organisation any categories which may have been excluded in pursuance of paragraph 1 of this Article, giving the reasons for such exclusion, and shall state in subsequent reports the position of its law and practice in respect of the categories excluded and the extent to which effect has been given or is proposed to be given to the Convention in respect of such categories.

3. Employment or work covered by Article 3 of this Convention shall not be excluded from the application of the Convention in pursuance of this Article.

Article 5. 1. A Member whose economy and administrative facilities are insufficiently developed may, after consultation with the organisations of employers and workers concerned, where such exist, initially limit the scope of application of this Convention.

ILO (continued)

Convention No. 138 (continued)

2. Each Member which avails itself of the provisions of paragraph 1 of this Article shall specify, in a declaration appended to its ratification, the branches of economic activity or types of undertakings to which it will apply the provisions of the Convention.

3. The provisions of the Convention shall be applicable as a minimum to the following: mining and quarrying; manufacturing; construction; electricity, gas and water; sanitary services; transport, storage and communication; and plantations and other agricultural undertakings mainly producing for commercial purposes, but excluding family and small-scale holdings producing for local consumption and not regularly employing hired workers.

4. Any Member which has limited the scope of application of this Convention in pursuance of this Article - (a) shall indicate in its reports under article 22 of the Constitution of the International Labour Organisation the general position as regards the employment or work of young persons and children in the branches of activity which are excluded from the scope of application of this Convention and any progress which may have been made towards wider application of the provisions of the Convention; (b) may at any time formally extend the scope of application by a declaration addressed to the Director-General of the International Labour Office.

Article 6. This Convention does not apply to work done by children and young persons in schools for general, vocational or technical education or in other training institutions, or to work done by persons at least 14 years of age in undertakings, where such work is carried out in accordance with conditions prescribed by the competent authority, after consultation with the organisations of employers and workers concerned, where such exist, and is an integral part of - (a) a course of education or training for which a school or training institution is primarily responsible; (b) a programme of training mainly or entirely in an undertaking, which programme has been approved by the competent authority; or (c) a programme of guidance or orientation designed to facilitate the choice of an occupation or of a line of training.

Article 7. 1. National laws or regulations may permit the employment or work of persons 13 to 15 years of age on light work which is - (a) not likely to be harmful to their health or development; and (b) not such as to prejudice their attendance at school, their participation in vocational orientation or training programmes approved by the competent authority or their capacity to benefit from the instruction received.

2. National laws or regulations may also permit the employment or work of persons who are at least 15 years of age but have not yet completed their compulsory schooling on work which meets the requirements set forth in sub-paragraphs (a) and (b) of paragraph 1 of this Article.

3. The competent authority shall determine the activities in which employment or work may be permitted under paragraphs 1 and 2 of this Article and shall prescribe the number of hours during which and the conditions in which such employment or work may be undertaken.

4. Notwithstanding the provisions of paragraphs 1 and 2 of this Article, a Member which has availed itself of the provisions of paragraph 4 of Article 2 may, for as long as it continues to do so, substitute the ages 12 and 14 for the ages 13 and 15 in paragraph 1 and the age 14 for the age 15 in paragraph 2 of this Article.

ILO (continued)

Convention No. 138 (continued)

Article 8. 1. After consultation with the organisations of employers and workers concerned, where such exist, the competent authority may, by permits granted in individual cases, allow exceptions to the prohibition of employment or work provided for in Article 2 of this Convention, for such purposes as participation in artistic performances.

2. Permits so granted shall limit the number of hours during which and prescribe the conditions in which employment or work is allowed.

Article 9. 1. All necessary measures, including the provision of appropriate penalties, shall be taken by the competent authority to ensure the effective enforcement of the provisions of this Convention.

2. National laws or regulations or the competent authority shall define the persons responsible for compliance with the provisions giving effect to the Convention.

3. National laws or regulations or the competent authority shall prescribe the registers or other documents which shall be kept and made available by the employer; such registers or documents shall contain the names and ages or dates of birth, duly certified wherever possible, of persons whom he employs or who work for him and who are less than 18 years of age."

Source. ILO: Official Bulletin, Volume LVI, Number 1, 1973, pages 21-27.

Minimum Age Recommendation, 1973 (No. 146)

This Recommendation, adopted by the General Conference of the ILO in 1973, supplements Convention No. 138. It expresses the desire of the Conference "to define further certain elements of policy which are the concern of the International Labour Organisation". These relate to national policy, minimum age, hazardous employment or work, conditions of employment, and enforcement. The text of the operative part of the Recommendation follows.

"I. National Policy. 1. To ensure the success of the national policy provided for in Article 1 of the Minimum Age Convention, 1973, high priority should be given to planning for and meeting the needs of children and youth in national development policies and programmes and to the progressive extension of the inter-related measures necessary to provide the best possible conditions of physical and mental growth for children and young persons.

2. In this connection special attention should be given to such areas of planning and policy as the following:

(a) firm national commitment to full employment, in accordance with the Employment Policy Convention and Recommendation, 1964, and the taking of measures designed to promote employment-oriented development in rural and urban areas;

(b) the progressive extension of other economic and social measures to alleviate poverty wherever it exists and to ensure family living standards and income which are such as to make it unnecessary to have recourse to the economic activity of children;

ILO (continued)

Recommendation No. 146 (continued)

(c) the development and progressive extension, without any discrimination, of social security and family welfare measures aimed at ensuring child maintenance, including children's allowances;

(d) the development and progressive extension of adequate facilities for education and vocational orientation and training appropriate in form and content to the needs of the children and young persons concerned;

(e) the development and progressive extension of appropriate facilities for the protection and welfare of children and young persons, including employed young persons, and for the promotion of their development.

3. Particular account should as necessary be taken of the needs of children and young persons who do not have families or do not live with their own families and of migrant children and young persons who live and travel with their families. Measures taken to that end should include the provision of fellowships and vocational training.

4. Full-time attendance at school or participation in approved vocational orientation or training programmes should be required and effectively ensured up to an age at least equal to that specified for admission to employment in accordance with Article 2 of the Minimum Age Convention, 1973.

5. (1) Consideration should be given to measures such as preparatory training, not involving hazards, for types of employment or work in respect of which the minimum age prescribed in accordance with Article 3 of the Minimum Age Convention, 1973, is higher than the age of completion of compulsory full-time schooling.

(2) Analogous measures should be envisaged where the professional exigencies of a particular occupation include a minimum age for admission which is higher than the age of completion of compulsory full-time schooling.

II. Minimum Age. 6. The minimum age should be fixed at the same level for all sectors of economic activity.

7. (1) Members should take as their objective the progressive raising to 16 years of the minimum age for admission to employment or work specified in pursuance of Article 2 of the Minimum Age Convention, 1973.

(2) Where the minimum age for employment or work covered by Article 2 of the Minimum Age Convention, 1973, is still below 15 years, urgent steps should be taken to raise it to that level.

8. Where it is not immediately feasible to fix a minimum age for all employment in agriculture and in related activities in rural areas, a minimum age should be fixed at least for employment on plantations and in the other agricultural undertakings referred to in Article 5, paragraph 3, of the Minimum Age Convention, 1973.

III. Hazardous Employment or Work. 9. Where the minimum age for admission to types of employment or work which are likely to jeopardise the health, safety or morals of young persons is still below 18 years, immediate steps should be taken to raise it to that level.

ILO (continued)

Recommendation No. 146 (continued)

10. (1) In determining the types of employment or work to which Article 3 of the Minimum Age Convention, 1973, applies, full account should be taken of relevant international labour standards, such as those concerning dangerous substances, agents or processes (including ionising radiations), the lifting of heavy weights and underground work.

(2) The list of the types of employment or work in question should be re-examined periodically and revised as necessary, particularly in the light of advancing scientific and technological knowledge.

11. Where, by reference to Article 5 of the Minimum Age Convention, 1973, a minimum age is not immediately fixed for certain branches of economic activity or types of undertakings, appropriate minimum age provisions should be made applicable therein to types of employment or work presenting hazards for young persons.

IV. Conditions of Employment. 12. (1) Measures should be taken to ensure that the conditions in which children and young persons under the age of 18 years are employed or work reach and are maintained at a satisfactory standard. These conditions should be supervised closely.

(2) Measures should likewise be taken to safeguard and supervise the conditions in which children and young persons undergo vocational orientation and training within undertakings, training institutions and schools for vocational or technical education and to formulate standards for their protection and development.

13. (1) In connection with the application of the preceding Paragraph, as well as in giving effect to Article 7, paragraph 3, of the Minimum Age Convention, 1973, special attention should be given to -

(a) the provision of fair remuneration and its protection, bearing in mind the principle of equal pay for equal work;

(b) the strict limitation of the hours spent at work in a day and in a week, and the prohibition of overtime, so as to allow enough time for education and training (including the time needed for homework related thereto), for rest during the day and for leisure activities;

(c) the granting, without possibility of exception save in genuine emergency, of a minimum consecutive period of 12 hours' night rest, and of customary weekly rest days;

(d) the granting of an annual holiday with pay of at least four weeks and, in any case, not shorter than that granted to adults;

(e) coverage by social security schemes, including employment injury, medical care and sickness benefit schemes, whatever the conditions of employment or work may be;

(f) the maintenance of satisfactory standards of safety and health and appropriate instruction and supervision.

(2) Sub-paragraph (1) of this Paragraph applies to young seafarers in so far as they are not covered in respect of the matters dealt with therein by international labour Conventions or Recommendations specifically concerned with maritime employment.

ILO (continued)

Recommendation No. 146 (continued)

V. Enforcement. 14. (1) Measures to ensure the effective application of the Minimum Age Convention, 1973, and of this Recommendation should include -

(a) the strengthening as necessary of labour inspection and related services, for instance by the special training of inspectors to detect abuses in the employment or work of children and young persons and to correct such abuses; and

(b) the strengthening of services for the improvement and inspection of training in undertakings.

(2) Emphasis should be placed on the role which can be played by inspectors in supplying information and advice on effective means of complying with relevant provisions as well as in securing their enforcement.

(3) Labour inspection and inspection of training in undertakings should be closely co-ordinated to provide the greatest economic efficiency and, generally, the labour administration services should work in close co-operation with the services responsible for the education, training, welfare and guidance of children and young persons.

15. Special attention should be paid -

(a) to the enforcement of provisions concerning employment in hazardous types of employment or work; and

(b) in so far as education or training is compulsory, to the prevention of the employment or work of children and young persons during the hours when instruction is available.

16. The following measures should be taken to facilitate the verification of ages:

(a) the public authorities should maintain an effective system of birth registration, which should include the issue of birth certificates;

(b) employers should be required to keep and to make available to the competent authority registers or other documents indicating the names and ages or dates of birth, duly certified wherever possible, not only of children and young persons employed by them but also of those receiving vocational orientation or training in their undertakings;

(c) children and young persons working in the streets, in outside stalls, in public places, in itinerant occupations or in other circumstances which make the checking of employers' records impracticable should be issued licences or other documents indicating their eligibility for such work."

Source. ILO: Official Bulletin, Volume LVI, Number 1, 1973, pages 34-37.

ILO (continued)

Night work

Night Work of Children and Young Persons (Agriculture) Recommendation, 1921 (No. 14)

"The General Conference of the International Labour Organisations recommends:

I. That each Member of the International Labour Organisation take steps to regulate the employment of children under the age of fourteen years in agricultural undertakings during the night, in such a way as to ensure to them a period of rest compatible with their physical necessities and consisting of not less than ten consecutive hours.

II. That each Member of the International Labour Organisation take steps to regulate the employment of young persons between the ages of fourteen and eighteen years in agricultural undertakings during the night, in such a way as to ensure to them a period of rest compatible with their physical necessities and consisting of not less than nine consecutive hours."

Source. ILO: Official Bulletin, Volume IV, Number 22, 30 November 1921, pages 492-493.

Night Work of Young Persons (Non-Industrial Occupations) Convention, 1946 (No. 79)

Excerpts, Articles 1 to 6.

"Article 1. 1. This Convention applies to children and young persons employed for wages, or working directly or indirectly for gain, in non-industrial occupations.

2. For the purpose of this Convention, the term "non-industrial occupation" includes all occupations other than those recognised by the competent authority as industrial, agricultural or maritime occupations.

3. The competent authority shall define the line of division which separates non-industrial occupations from industrial, agricultural and maritime occupations.

4. National laws or regulations may exempt from the application of this Convention - (a) domestic service in private households, and (b) employment on work which is not deemed to be harmful, prejudicial, or dangerous to children or young persons, in family undertakings in which only parents and their children or wards are employed.

Article 2. 1. Children under fourteen years of age who are admissible for full-time or part-time employment and children over fourteen years of age who are still subject to full-time compulsory school attendance shall not be employed nor work at night during a period of at least fourteen consecutive hours, including the interval between eight o'clock in the evening and eight o'clock in the morning.

2. Provided that national laws or regulations may, where local conditions so require, substitute another interval of twelve hours of which the beginning shall not be fixed later than eight thirty o'clock in the evening nor the termination earlier than six o'clock in the morning.

ILO (continued)

Convention No. 79 (continued)

Article 3. 1. Children over fourteen years of age who are no longer subject to full-time compulsory school attendance and young persons under eighteen years of age shall not be employed nor work at night during a period of at least twelve consecutive hours, including the interval between ten o'clock in the evening and six o'clock in the morning.

2. Provided that, where there are exceptional circumstances affecting a particular branch of activity or a particular area, the competent authority may, after consultation with the employers' and workers' organisations concerned, decide that in the case of children and young persons employed in that branch of activity or area, the interval between eleven o'clock in the evening and seven o'clock in the morning may be substituted for that between ten o'clock in the evening and six o'clock in the morning.

Article 4. 1. In countries where the climate renders work by day particularly trying, the night period may be shorter than that prescribed in the above articles if compensatory rest is accorded during the day.

2. The prohibition of night work may be suspended by the Government for young persons of sixteen years of age and over when in case of serious emergency the national interest demands it.

3. National laws or regulations may empower an appropriate authority to grant temporary individual licences in order to enable young persons of sixteen years of age and over to work at night when the special needs of vocational training so require, subject to the period of rest being not less than eleven consecutive hours in every period of twenty-four hours.

Article 5. 1. National laws or regulations may empower an appropriate authority to grant individual licences in order to enable children or young persons under the age of eighteen years to appear at night as performers in public entertainments or to participate at night as performers in the making of cinematographic films.

2. The minimum age at which such a licence may be granted shall be prescribed by national laws or regulations.

3. No such licence may be granted when, because of the nature of the entertainment or the circumstances in which it is carried on, or the nature of the cinematographic film or the conditions under which it is made, participation in the entertainment or in the making of the film may be dangerous to the life, health, or morals of the child or young person.

4. The following conditions shall apply to the granting of licences:

(a) the period of employment shall not continue after midnight;

(b) strict safeguards shall be prescribed to protect the health and morals, and to ensure kind treatment of, the child or young person and to avoid interference with his education;

(c) the child or young person shall be allowed a consecutive rest period of at least fourteen hours.

ILO (continued)

Convention No. 79 (continued)

Article 6. 1. In order to ensure the due enforcement of the provisions of this Convention, national laws or regulations shall -

(a) provide for a system of public inspection and supervision adequate for the particular needs of the various branches of activity to which the Convention applies;

(b) require every employer to keep a register, or to keep available official records, showing the names and dates of birth of all persons under eighteen years of age employed by him and their hours of work; in the case of children and young persons working in the streets or in places to which the public have access, the register or records shall show the hours of service agreed upon in the contract of employment;

(c) provide suitable means for assuring identification and supervision of persons under eighteen years of age engaged, on account of an employer or on their own account, in employment or occupations carried on in the streets or in places to which the public have access;

(d) provide penalties applicable to employers or other responsible adults for breaches of such laws or regulations.

2. There shall be included in the annual reports to be submitted under Article 22 of the Constitution of the International Labour Organisation full information concerning all laws and regulations by which effect is given to the provisions of this Convention and, more particularly, concerning -

(a) any interval which may be substituted for the interval prescribed in paragraph 1 of Article 2 in virtue of the provisions of paragraph 2 of that Article;

(b) the extent to which advantage is taken of the provisions of paragraph 2 of Article 3;

(c) the authorities empowered to grant individual licences in virtue of the provisions of paragraph 1 of Article 5 and the minimum age prescribed for the granting of licences in accordance with the provisions of paragraph 2 of the said Article."

Source. ILO: Official Bulletin, Volume XXIX, Number 4, 15 November 1946, pages 274-280.

Night Work of Young Persons (Industry) Convention (Revised), 1948 (No. 90)

Excerpts, Articles 1 to 6.

"Article 1. 1. For the purpose of this Convention, the term "industrial undertaking" includes particularly -

(a) mines, quarries, and other works for the extraction of minerals from the earth;

ILO (continued)

Convention No. 90 (continued)

(b) undertakings in which articles are manufactured, altered, cleaned, repaired, ornamented, finished, adapted for sale, broken up or demolished, or in which materials are transformed, including undertakings engaged in shipbuilding or in the generation, transformation or transmission of electricity or motive power of any kind;

(c) undertakings engaged in building and civil engineering work, including constructional, repair, maintenance, alteration and demolition work;

(d) undertakings engaged in the transport of passengers or goods by road or rail, including the handling of goods at docks, quays, wharves, warehouses or airports.

2. The competent authority shall define the line of division which separates industry from agriculture, commerce and other non-industrial occupations.

3. National laws or regulations may exempt from the application of this Convention employment on work which is not deemed to be harmful, prejudicial, or dangerous to young persons in family undertakings in which only parents and their children or wards are employed.

Article 2. 1. For the purpose of this Convention the term "night" signifies a period of at least twelve consecutive hours.

2. In the case of young persons under sixteen years of age, this period shall include the interval between ten o'clock in the evening and six o'clock in the morning.

3. In the case of young persons who have attained the age of sixteen years but are under the age of eighteen years, this period shall include an interval prescribed by the competent authority of at least seven consecutive hours falling between ten o'clock in the evening and seven o'clock in the morning; the competent authority may prescribe different intervals for different areas, industries, undertakings or branches of industries or undertakings, but shall consult the employers' and workers' organisations concerned before prescribing an interval beginning after eleven o'clock in the evening.

Article 3. 1. Young persons under eighteen years of age shall not be employed or work during the night in any public or private industrial undertaking or in any branch thereof except as hereinafter provided for.

2. For purposes of apprenticeship or vocational training in specified industries or occupations which are required to be carried on continuously, the competent authority may, after consultation with the employers' and workers' organisations concerned, authorise the employment in night work of young persons who have attained the age of sixteen years but are under the age of eighteen years.

3. Young persons employed in night work in virtue of the preceding paragraph shall be granted a rest period of at least thirteen consecutive hours between two working periods.

4. Where night work in the baking industry is prohibited for all workers, the interval between nine o'clock in the evening and four o'clock in the morning may, for purposes of apprenticeship or vocational training of young persons who have attained the age of sixteen years, be substituted by the competent authority for the interval of at least seven consecutive hours falling between ten o'clock in the evening and seven o'clock in the morning prescribed by the authority in virtue of paragraph 3 of Article 2.

ILO (continued)

Convention No. 90 (continued)

Article 4. 1. In countries where the climate renders work by day particularly trying, the night period and barred interval may be shorter than that prescribed in the above articles if compensatory rest is accorded during the day.

2. The provisions of Articles 2 and 3 shall not apply to the night work of young persons between the ages of sixteen and eighteen years in case of emergencies which could not have been controlled or foreseen, which are not of a periodical character, and which interfere with the normal working of the industrial undertaking.

Article 5. The prohibition of night work may be suspended by the government, for young persons between the ages of sixteen and eighteen years, when in case of serious emergency the public interest demands it.

Article 6. 1. The laws or regulations giving effect to the provisions of this Convention shall -

(a) make appropriate provision for ensuring that they are known to the persons concerned;

(b) define the persons responsible for compliance therewith;

(c) prescribe adequate penalties for any violation thereof;

(d) provide for the maintenance of a system of inspection adequate to ensure effective enforcement; and

(e) require every employer in a public or private industrial undertaking to keep a register, or to keep available official records, showing the names and dates of birth of all persons under eighteen years of age employed by him and such other pertinent information as may be required by the competent authority.

2. The annual reports submitted by Members under Article 22 of the Constitution of the International Labour Organisation shall contain full information concerning such laws and regulations and a general survey of the results of the inspections made in accordance therewith."

Source. ILO: Official Bulletin, Volume XXXI, Number 1, 31 August 1948, pages 24-31.

Hazardous employment

Lead Poisoning (Women and Children) Recommendation, 1919 (No. 4)

Excerpts.

"1. The General Conference recommends to the Members of the International Labour Organisation that, in view of the danger involved to the function of maternity and to the physical development of children, women and young persons under the age of eighteen years be excluded from employment in the following processes:

ILO (continued)

Recommendation No. 4 (continued)

(a) in furnace work in the reduction of zinc or lead ores;

(b) in the manipulation, treatment, or reduction of ashes containing lead, and the desilvering of lead;

(c) in melting lead or old zinc on a large scale;

(d) in the manufacture of solder or alloys containing more than ten per cent of lead;

(e) in the manufacture of litharge, massicot, red lead, white lead, orange lead, or sulphate, chromate or silicate (frit) of lead;

(f) in mixing and pasting in the manufacture or repair of electric accumulators;

(g) in the cleaning of workrooms where the above processes are carried on.

2. It is further recommended that the employment of women and young persons under the age of eighteen years in processes involving the use of lead compounds be permitted only subject to the following conditions:

(a) locally applied exhaust ventilation, so as to remove dust and fumes at the point of origin;

(b) cleanliness of tools and workrooms;

(c) notification to Government authorities of all cases of lead poisoning, and compensation therefor;

(d) periodic medical examination of the persons employed in such processes;

(e) provision of sufficient and suitable cloak-room, washing, and mess-room accommodation, and of special protective clothing;

(f) prohibition of bringing food or drink into workrooms.

3. It is further recommended that in industries where soluble lead compounds can be replaced by non-toxic substances, the use of soluble lead compounds should be strictly regulated.

4. For the purpose of this Recommendation, a lead compound should be considered as soluble if it contains more than five per cent of its weight (estimated as metallic lead) soluble in a quarter of one per cent solution of hydrochloric acid."

Source. ILO: Official Bulletin, Volume I, April 1919-August 1920, pages 428-429.

ILO (continued)

White Lead (Painting) Convention, 1921 (No. 13)

Excerpt.

"Article 3. 1. The employment of males under eighteen years of age and of all females shall be prohibited in any painting work of an industrial character involving the use of white lead or sulphate of lead or other products containing these pigments."

Source. ILO: Official Bulletin, Supplement to Volume IV, Number 23, 7 December 1921, pages 13-16.

Radiation Protection Convention, 1960 (No. 115)

Excerpts.

"Article 6. 1. Maximum permissible doses of ionising radiations which may be received from sources external to or internal to the body and maximum permissible amounts of radioactive substances which can be taken into the body shall be fixed ... for various categories of workers.

2. Such maximum permissible doses and amounts shall be kept under constant review in the light of current knowledge.

Article 7. 1. Appropriate levels shall be fixed in accordance with Article 6 for workers who are directly engaged in radiation work and are - (a) aged 18 and over; (b) under the age of 18.

2. No worker under the age of 16 shall be engaged in work involving ionising radiations."

Source. ILO: Official Bulletin, Volume XLIII, Number 2, 1960, pages 41-46.

Benzene Convention, 1971 (No. 136)

Excerpt.

"Article 11. 1. ...

2. Young persons under 18 years of age shall not be employed in work processes involving exposure to benzene or products containing benzene: Provided that this prohibition need not apply to young persons undergoing education or training who are under adequate technical and medical supervision."

Source. ILO: Official Bulletin, Volume LIV, Number 3, 1971, pages 246-251.

Benzene Recommendation, 1971 (No. 144)

Benzene Recommendation, 1971 (No. 144)

Excerpt.

"20. Young persons under 18 years of age should not be employed in work processes involving exposure to benzene or products containing benzene, except where they are undergoing education or training and are under adequate technical and medical supervision."

Source. ILO: Official Bulletin, Volume LIV, Number 3, 1971, pages 255-259.

Occupational Safety and Health (Dock Work) Convention, 1979 (No. 152)

Excerpt.

"Article 38. 1. ...

2. A lifting appliance or other cargo-handling appliance shall be operated only by a person who is at least 18 years of age and who possesses the necessary aptitudes and experience or a person under training who is properly supervised."

Source. ILO: Official Bulletin, Volume LXII, Number 2, Series A, 1979, pages 70-76.

Maximum weight

Maximum Weight Convention, 1967 (No. 127)

Excerpts.

"Article 1. For the purpose of this Convention - ... the term "young worker" means a worker under 18 years of age.

...

"Article 7. 1. The assignment of women and young workers to manual transport of loads other than light loads shall be limited.

2. Where women and young workers are engaged in the manual transport of loads, the maximum weight of such loads shall be substantially less than that permitted for adult male workers."

Source. ILO: Official Bulletin, Volume L, Number 3, Series I, July 1967, pages 1-4.

ILO (continued)

Maximum Weight Recommendation, 1967 (No. 128)

Excerpts.

"1. For the purpose of this Recommendation ... the term "young worker" means a worker under 18 years of age.

...

"19. Where young workers are engaged in the manual transport of loads, the maximum weight of such loads should be substantially less than that permitted for adult workers of the same sex.

20. As far as possible, young workers should not be assigned to regular manual transport of loads.

21. Where the minimum age for assignment to manual transport of loads is less than 16 years, measures should be taken as speedily as possible to raise it to that level.

22. The minimum age for assignment to regular manual transport of loads should be raised, with a view to attaining a minimum age of 18 years.

23. Where young workers are assigned to regular manual transport of loads, provision should be made -

(a) as appropriate, to reduce the time spent on actual lifting, carrying and putting down of loads by such workers;

(b) to prohibit the assignment of such workers to certain specified jobs, comprised in manual transport of loads, which are especially arduous."

Source. ILO: Official Bulletin, Volume L, Number 3, Series I, July 1967, pages 25-29.

Medical examinations

Medical Examination of Young Persons (Sea) Convention, 1921 (No. 16)

Excerpts.

"Article 2. The employment of any child or young person under eighteen years of age on any vessel, other than vessels upon which only members of the same family are employed, shall be conditional on the production of a medical certificate attesting fitness for such work, signed by a doctor who shall be approved by the competent authority.

ILO (continued)

Convention No. 16 (continued)

Article 3. The continued employment at sea of any such child or young person shall be subject to the repetition of such medical examination at intervals of not more than one year, and the production, after each such examination, of a further medical certificate attesting fitness for such work. Should a medical certificate expire in the course of a voyage, it shall remain in force until the end of the said voyage."

Source. ILO: Official Bulletin, Supplement to Volume IV, Number 23, 7 December 1921, pages 24-25.

Medical Examination of Young Persons (Industry) Convention, 1946 (No. 77)

Excerpts.

"Article 2. 1. Children and young persons under eighteen years of age shall not be admitted to employment by an industrial undertaking unless they have been found fit for the work on which they are to be employed by a thorough medical examination.

...

Article 3. 1. The fitness of a child or young person for the employment in which he is engaged shall be subject to medical supervision until he has attained the age of eighteen years.

2. The continued employment of a child or young person under eighteen years of age shall be subject to the repetition of medical examinations at intervals of not more than one year.

3. National laws or regulations shall -

(a) make provision for the special circumstances in which a medical re-examination shall be required in addition to the annual examination or at more frequent intervals in order to ensure effective supervision in respect of the risks involved in the occupation and of the state of health of the child or young person as shown by previous examinations; or

(b) empower the competent authority to require medical re-examinations in exceptional cases.

Article 4. 1. In occupations which involve high health risks medical examination and re-examinations for fitness for employment shall be required until at least the age of twenty-one years.

2. National laws or regulations shall either specify, or empower an appropriate authority to specify, the occupations or categories of occupations in which medical examination and re-examinations for fitness for employment shall be required until at least the age of twenty-one years.

ILO (continued)

Convention No. 77 (continued)

Article 5. The medical examination required by the preceding Articles shall not involve the child or young person, or his parents, in any expense.

...

Article 7. 1. The employer shall be required to file and keep available to labour inspectors either the medical certificate for fitness for employment or the work permit or workbook showing that there are no medical objections to the employment as may be prescribed by national laws or regulations.

2. National laws or regulations shall determine the other methods of supervision to be adopted for ensuring the strict enforcement of this Convention."

Source. ILO: Official Bulletin, Volume XXIX, Number 4, 15 November 1946, pages 254-261.

Medical Examination of Young Persons (Non-Industrial Occupations) Convention, 1946 (No. 78)

Excerpts.

"Article 2. 1. Children and young persons under eighteen years of age shall not be admitted to employment or work in non-industrial occupations unless they have been found fit for the work in question by a thorough medical examination.

...

Article 3. 1. The fitness of a child or young person for the employment in which he is engaged shall be subject to medical supervision until he has attained the age of eighteen years.

2. The continued employment of a child or young person under eighteen years of age shall be subject to the repetition of medical examinations at intervals of not more than one year.

3. National laws or regulations shall -

(a) make provision for the special circumstances in which a medical re-examination shall be required in addition to the annual examination or at more frequent intervals in order to ensure effective supervision in respect of the risks involved in the occupation and of the state of health of the child or young person as shown by previous examinations; or

(b) empower the competent authority to require medical re-examinations in exceptional cases.

Article 4. 1. In occupations which involve high health risks medical examination and re-examinations for fitness for employment shall be required until at least the age of twenty-one years.

ILO (continued)

Convention No. 78 (continued)

2. National laws or regulations shall either specify, or empower an appropriate authority to specify, the occupations or categories of occupations in which medical examination and re-examination for fitness for employment shall be required until at least the age of twenty-one years.

Article 5. The medical examinations required by the preceding Articles shall not involve the child or young person, or his parents, in any expense.

...

Article 7. 1. The employer shall be required to file and keep available to labour inspectors either the medical certificate for fitness for employment or the work permit or workbook showing that there are no medical objections to the employment as may be prescribed by national laws or regulations.

2. National laws or regulations shall determine -

(a) the measures of identification to be adopted for ensuring the application of the system of medical examination for fitness for employment to children and young persons engaged either on their own account or on account of their parents in itinerant trading or in any other occupation carried on in the streets or in places to which the public have access; and

(b) the other methods of supervision to be adopted for ensuring the strict enforcement of the Convention."

Source. ILO: Official Bulletin, Volume XXIX, Number 4, 15 November 1946, pages 261-268.

United Nations

Convention on the Rights of the Child, 1989

Text adopted by the General Assembly of the United Nations on 20 November 1989. Excerpts (Part I).

"Preamble. The States Parties to the present Convention,

Considering that, in accordance with the principles proclaimed in the Charter of the United Nations, recognition of the inherent dignity and of the equal and inalienable rights of all members of the human family is the foundation of freedom, justice and peace in the world,

Bearing in mind that the peoples of the United Nations have, in the Charter, reaffirmed their faith in fundamental human rights and in the dignity and worth of the human person, and have determined to promote social progress and better standards of life in larger freedom,

Recognizing that the United Nations has, in the Universal Declaration of Human Rights and in the International Covenants on Human Rights, proclaimed and agreed that everyone is entitled to all the rights and freedoms set forth therein, without distinction of any kind, such as race, colour, sex, language, religion, political or other opinion, national or social origin, property, birth or other status,

Recalling that, in the Universal Declaration of Human Rights, the United Nations has proclaimed that childhood is entitled to special care and assistance,

Convinced that the family, as the fundamental group of society and the natural environment for the growth and well-being of all its members and particularly children, should be afforded the necessary protection and assistance so that it can fully assume its responsibilities within the community,

Recognizing that the child, for the full and harmonious development of his or her personality, should grow up in a family environment, in an atmosphere of happiness, love and understanding,

Considering that the child should be fully prepared to live an individual life in society, and brought up in the spirit of the ideals proclaimed in the Charter of the United Nations, and in particular in the spirit of peace, dignity, tolerance, freedom, equality and solidarity,

Bearing in mind that the need to extend particular care to the child has been stated in the Geneva Declaration of the Rights of the Child of 1924 and in the Declaration of the Rights of the Child adopted by the United Nations on 20 November 1959 and recognized in the Universal Declaration of Human Rights, in the International Covenant on Civil and Political Rights (in particular in articles 23 and 24), in the International Covenant on Economic, Social and Cultural Rights (in particular in article 10) and in the statutes and relevant instruments of specialized agencies and international organizations concerned with the welfare of children,

Bearing in mind that, as indicated in the Declaration of the Rights of the Child, 'the child, be reason of his physical and mental immaturity, needs special safeguards and care, including appropriate legal protection, before as well as after birth',

United Nations (continued)

Convention on the Rights of the Child (continued)

Recalling the provisions of the Declaration on Social and Legal Principles relating to the Protection and Welfare of Children, with Special Reference to Foster Placement and Adoption Nationally and Internationally; the United Nations Standard Minimum Rules for the Administration of Juvenile Justice ('The Beijing Rules'); and the Declaration on the Protection of Women and Children in Emergency and Armed Conflict,

Recognizing that, in all countries in the world, there are children living in exceptionally difficult conditions, and that such children need special consideration,

Taking due account of the importance of the traditions and cultural values of each people for the protection and harmonious development of the child,

Recognizing the importance of international co-operation for improving the living conditions of children in every country, in particular in the developing countries,

Have agreed as follows:

Part I

Article 1. For the purposes of the present Convention, a child means every human being below the age of 18 years unless, under the law applicable to the child, majority is attained earlier.

Article 2. 1. States Parties shall respect and ensure the rights set forth in the present Convention to each child within their jurisdiction without discrimination of any kind, irrespective of the child's or his or her parent's or legal guardian's race, colour, sex, language, religion, political or other opinion, national, ethnic or social origin, property, disability, birth or other status.

2. States Parties shall take all appropriate measures to ensure that the child is protected against all forms of discrimination or punishment on the basis of the status, activities, expressed opinions, or beliefs of the child's parents, legal guardians, or family members.

Article 3. 1. In all actions concerning children, whether undertaken by public or private social welfare institutions, courts of law, administrative authorities or legislative bodies, the best interests of the child shall be a primary consideration.

2. States Parties undertake to ensure the child such protection and care as is necessary for his or her well-being, taking into account the rights and duties of his or her parents, legal guardians, or other individuals legally responsible for him or her, and, to this end, shall take all appropriate legislative and administrative measures.

3. States Parties shall ensure that the institutions, services and facilities responsible for the care or protection of children shall conform with the standards established by competent authorities, particularly in the areas of safety, health, in the number and suitability of their staff, as well as competent supervision.

United Nations (continued)

Convention on the Rights of the Child (continued)

Article 4. States Parties shall undertake all appropriate legislative, administrative, and other measures for the implementation of the rights recognized in the present Convention. With regard to economic, social and cultural rights, States Parties shall undertake such measures to the maximum extent of their available resources and, where needed, within the framework of international co-operation.

Article 5. States Parties shall respect responsibilities, rights and duties of parents or, where applicable, the members of the extended family or community as provided for by local custom, legal guardians or other persons legally responsible for the child, to provide, in a manner consistent with the evolving capacities of the child, appropriate direction and guidance in the exercise by the child of the rights recognized in the present Convention.

Article 6. 1. States Parties recognize that every child has the inherent right to life.

2. States Parties shall ensure to the maximum extent possible the survival and development of the child.

Article 7. 1. The child shall be registered immediately after birth and shall have the right from birth to a name, the right to acquire a nationality and, as far as possible, the right to know and be cared for by his or her parents.

2. States Parties shall ensure the implementation of these rights in accordance with their national law and their obligations under the relevant international instruments in this field, in particular where the child would otherwise be stateless.

Article 8. 1. States Parties undertake to respect the right of the child to preserve his or her identity, including nationality, name and family relations as recognized by law without unlawful interference.

2. Where a child is illegally deprived of some or all of the elements of his or her identify, States Parties shall provide appropriate assistance and protection, with a view to speedily re-establishing his or her identity.

Article 9. 1. States Parties shall ensure that a child shall not be separated from his or her parents against their will, except when competent authorities subject to judicial review determine, in accordance with applicable law and procedures, that such separation is necessary for the best interests of the child. Such determination may be necessary in a particular case such as one involving abuse or neglect of the child by the parents, or one where the parents are living separately and a decision must be made as to the child's place of residence.

2. In any proceedings pursuant to paragraph 1 of the present article, all interested parties shall be given an opportunity to participate in the proceedings and make their views known.

3. States Parties shall respect the right of the child who is separated from one or both parents to maintain personal relations and direct contact with both parents on a regular basis, except if it is contrary to the child's best interests.

United Nations (continued)

Convention on the Rights of the Child (continued)

4. Where such separation results from any action initiated by a State Party, such as the detention, imprisonment, exile, deportation or death (including death arising from any cause while the person is in the custody of the State) of one or both parents or of the child, that State Party shall, upon request, provide the parents, the child or, if appropriate, another member of the family with the essential information concerning the whereabouts of the absent member(s) of the family unless the provision of the information would be detrimental to the well-being of the child. States Parties shall further ensure that the submission of such a request shall of itself entail no adverse consequences for the person(s) concerned.

Article 10. 1. In accordance with the obligation of States Parties under article 9, paragraph 1, applications by a child or his or her parents to enter or leave a State Party for the purpose of family reunification shall be dealt with by States Parties in a positive, humane and expeditious manner. States Parties shall further ensure that the submission of such a request shall entail no adverse consequences for the applicants and for the members of their family.

2. A child whose parents reside in different States shall have the right to maintain on a regular basis, save in exceptional circumstances personal relations and direct contacts with both parents. Towards that end and in accordance with the obligation of States Parties under article 9, paragraph 1, States Parties shall respect the right of the child and his or her parents to leave any country, including their own, and to enter their own country. The right to leave any country shall be subject only to such restrictions as are prescribed by law and which are necessary to protect the national security, public order (ordre public), public health or morals or the rights and freedoms of others and are consistent with the other rights recognized in the present Convention.

Article 11. 1. States Parties shall take measures to combat the illicit transfer and non-return of children abroad.

2. To this end, States Parties shall promote the conclusion of bilateral or multilateral agreements or accession to existing agreements.

Article 12. 1. States Parties shall assure to the child who is capable of forming his or her own views the right to express those views freely in all matters affecting the child, the views of the child being given due weight in accordance with the age and maturity of the child.

2. For this purpose, the child shall in particular be provided the opportunity to be heard in any judicial and administrative proceedings affecting the child, either directly, or through a representative or an appropriate body, in a manner consistent with the procedural rules of national law.

Article 13. 1. The child shall have the right to freedom of expression; this right shall include freedom to seek, receive and impart information and ideas of all kinds, regardless of frontiers, either orally, in writing or in print, in the form of art, or through any other media of the child's choice.

2. The exercise of this right may be subject to certain restrictions, but these shall only be such as are provided by law and are necessary:

United Nations (continued)

Convention on the Rights of the Child (continued)

(a) For respect of the rights or reputations of others; or

(b) For the protection of national security or of public order (ordre public), or of public health or morals.

Article 14. 1. States Parties shall respect the right of the child to freedom of thought, conscience and religion.

2. States Parties shall respect the rights and duties of the parents and, when applicable, legal guardians, to provide direction to the child in the exercise of his or her right in a manner consistent with the evolving capacities of the child.

3. Freedom to manifest one's religion or beliefs may be subject only to such limitations as are prescribed by law and are necessary to protect public safety, order, health or morals, or the fundamental rights and freedoms of others.

Article 15. 1. States Parties recognize the rights of the child to freedom of association and to freedom of peaceful assembly.

2. No restrictions may be placed on the exercise of these rights other than those imposed in conformity with the law and which are necessary in a democratic society in the interests of national security or public safety, public order (ordre public), the protection of public health or morals or the protection of the rights and freedoms of others.

Article 16. 1. No child shall be subjected to arbitrary or unlawful interference with his or her privacy, family, home or correspondence, nor to unlawful attacks on his or her honour and reputation.

2. The child has the right to the protection of the law against such interference or attacks.

Article 17. States Parties recognize the important function performed by the mass media and shall ensure that the child has access to information and material from a diversity of national and international sources, especially those aimed at the promotion of his or her social, spiritual and moral well-being and physical and mental health. To this end, States Parties shall:

(a) Encourage the mass media to disseminate information and material of social and cultural benefit to the child and in accordance with the spirit of article 29;

(b) Encourage international co-operation in the production, exchange and dissemination of such information and material from a diversity of cultural, national and international sources;

(c) Encourage the production and dissemination of children's books;

(d) Encourage the mass media to have particular regard to the linguistic needs of the child who belongs to a minority group or who is indigenous;

(e) Encourage the development of appropriate guidelines for the protection of the child from information and material injurious to his or her well-being, bearing in mind the provisions of articles 13 and 18.

United Nations (continued)

Convention on the Rights of the Child (continued)

Article 18. 1. States Parties shall use their best efforts to ensure recognition of the principle that both parents have common responsibilities for the upbringing and development of the child. Parents or, as the case may be, legal guardians, have the primary responsibility for the upbringing and development of the child. The best interests of the child will be their basic concern.

2. For the purpose of guaranteeing and promoting the rights set forth in the present Convention, States Parties shall render appropriate assistance to parents and legal guardians in the performance of their child-rearing responsibilities and shall ensure the development of institutions, facilities and services for the care of children.

3. States Parties shall take all appropriate measures to ensure that children of working parents have the right to benefit from child-care services and facilities for which they are eligible.

Article 19. 1. States Parties shall take all appropriate legislative, administrative, social and educational measures to protect the child from all forms of physical or mental violence, injury or abuse, neglect or negligent treatment, maltreatment or exploitation, including sexual abuse, while in the care of parent(s), legal guardian(s) or any other person who has the care of the child.

2. Such protective measures should, as appropriate, include effective procedures for the establishment of social programmes to provide necessary support for the child and for those who have the care of the child, as well as for other forms of prevention and for identification, reporting, referral, investigation, treatment and follow-up of instances of child maltreatment described heretofore, and, as appropriate, for judicial involvement.

Article 20. 1. A child temporarily or permanently deprived of his or her family environment, or in whose own best interests cannot be allowed to remain in that environment, shall be entitled to special protection and assistance provided by the State.

2. States Parties shall in accordance with their national laws ensure alternative care for such a child.

3. Such care could include, inter alia, foster placement, Kafala of Islamic law, adoption, or if necessary placement in suitable institutions for the care of children. When considering solutions, due regard shall be paid to the desirability of continuity in a child's upbringing and to the child's ethnic, religious, cultural and linguistic background.

Article 21. States Parties that recognize and/or permit the system of adoption shall ensure that the best interests of the child shall be the paramount consideration and they shall:

(a) Ensure that the adoption of a child is authorized only by competent authorities who determine, in accordance with applicable law and procedures and on the basis of all pertinent and reliable information, that the adoption is permissible in view of the child's status concerning parents, relatives and legal guardians and that, if required, the persons concerned have given their informed consent to the adoption on the basis of such counselling as may be necessary;

United Nations (continued)

Convention on the Rights of the Child (continued)

(b) Recognize that inter-country adoption may be considered as an alternative means of child's care, if the child cannot be placed in a foster or an adoptive family or cannot in any suitable manner be cared for in the child's country of origin;

(c) Ensure that the child concerned by inter-country adoption enjoys safeguards and standards equivalent to those existing in the case of national adoption;

(d) Take all appropriate measures to ensure that, in inter-country adoption, the placement does not result in improper financial gain for those involved in it;

(e) Promote, where appropriate, the objectives of the present article by concluding bilateral or multilateral arrangements or agreements, and endeavour, within this framework, to ensure that the placement of the child in another country is carried out by competent authorities or organs.

Article 22. 1. States Parties shall take appropriate measures to ensure that a child who is seeking refugee status or who is considered a refugee in accordance with applicable international or domestic law and procedures shall, whether incompliancies or accompanied by his or her parents or by any other person, receive appropriate protection and humanitarian assistance in the enjoyment of applicable rights set forth in the present Convention and in other international human rights or humanitarian instruments to which the said States are Parties.

2. For this purpose, States Parties shall provide, as they consider appropriate, co-operation in any efforts by the United Nations and other competent inter-governmental organizations or non-government organizations co-operating with the United Nations to protect and assist such a child and to trace the parents or other members of the family of any refugee child in order to obtain information necessary for reunification with his or her family. In cases where no parents or other members of the family can be found, the child shall be accorded the same protection as any other child permanently or temporarily deprived of his or her environment for any reason, as set forth in the present Convention.

Article 23. 1. States Parties recognize that a mentally or physically disabled child should enjoy a full and decent life, in conditions which ensure dignity, promote self-reliance, and facilitate the child's active participation in the community.

2. States Parties recognize the right of the disabled child to special care and shall encourage and ensure the extension, subject to available resources, to the eligible child and those responsible for his or her care, or assistance for which application is made and which is appropriate to the child's condition and to the circumstances of the parents or others caring for the child.

3. Recognizing the special needs of a disabled child, assistance extended in accordance with paragraph 2 of the present article shall be provided free of charge, whenever possible, taking into account the financial resources of the parents or others caring for the child, and shall be designed to ensure that the disabled child has effective access to and receives education, training, health care services, rehabilitation services, preparation for employment and recreation opportunities in a manner conducive to the child's achieving the fullest possible social integration and individual development, including his or her cultural and spiritual development.

United Nations (continued)

Convention on the Rights of the Child (continued)

4. States Parties shall promote, in the spirit of international co-operation, the exchange of appropriate information in the field of preventive health care and of medical, psychological and functional treatment of disabled children, including dissemination of and access to information concerning methods of rehabilitation, education and vocational services, with the aim of enabling States Parties to improve their capabilities and skills and to widen their experience in these areas. In this regard, particular account shall be taken of the needs of developing countries.

Article 24. 1. States Parties recognize the right of the child to the enjoyment of the highest attainable standard of health and to facilities for the treatment of illness and rehabilitation of health. States Parties shall strive to ensure that no child is deprived of his or her right of access to such health care services.

2. States Parties shall pursue full implementation of this right and, in particular, shall take appropriate measures:

(a) To diminish infant and child mortality;

(b) To ensure the provision of necessary medical assistance and health care to all children with emphasis on the development of primary health care;

(c) To combat disease and malnutrition including within the framework of primary health care, through inter alia the application of readily available technology and through the provision of adequate nutritious foods and clean drinking water, taking into consideration the dangers and risks of environmental pollution;

(d) To ensure appropriate pre-natal and post-natal health care for mothers;

(e) To ensure that all segments of society, in particular parents and children, are informed, have access to education and are supported in the use of basic knowledge of child health and nutrition, the advantages of breast-feeding, hygiene and environmental sanitation and the prevention of accidents;

(f) To develop preventive health care, guidance for parents and family planning education and services.

3. States Parties shall take all effective and appropriate measures with a view to abolishing traditional practices prejudicial to the health of children.

4. States Parties undertake to promote and encourage international co-operation with a view to achieving progressively the full realization of the right recognized in the present article. In this regard, particular account shall be taken of the needs of developing countries.

Article 25. States Parties recognize the right of a child who has been placed by the competent authorities for the purposes of care, protection or treatment of his or her physical or mental health, to a periodic review of the treatment provided to the child and all other circumstances relevant to his or her placement.

United Nations (continued)

Convention on the Rights of the Child (continued)

Article 26. 1. States Parties shall recognize for every child the right to benefit from social security, including social insurance, and shall take the necessary measures to achieve the full realization of this right in accordance with their national law.

2. The benefits should, where appropriate, be granted, taking into account the resources and the circumstances of the child and persons having responsibility for the maintenance of the child, as well as any other consideration relevant to an application for benefits made by or on behalf of the child.

Article 27. 1. States Parties recognize the right of every child to a standard of living adequate for the child's physical, mental, spiritual, moral and social development.

2. The parent(s) or others responsible for the child have the primary responsibility to secure, within their abilities and financial capacities, the conditions of living necessary for the child's development.

3. States Parties, in accordance with national conditions and within their means, shall take appropriate measures to assist parents and others responsible for the child to implement this right and shall in case of need provide material assistance and support programmes, particularly with regard to nutrition, clothing and housing.

4. States Parties shall take all appropriate measures to secure the recovery of maintenance for the child from the parents or other persons having financial responsibility for the child, both within the State Party and from abroad. In particular, where the person having financial responsibility for the child lives in a State different from that of the child, States Parties shall promote the accession to international agreements or the conclusion of such agreements, as well as the making of other appropriate agreements.

Article 28. 1. States Parties recognize the right of the child to education, and with a view to achieving this right progressively and on the basis of equal opportunity, they shall, in particular:

(a) Make primary education compulsory and available free to all;

(b) Encourage the development of different forms of secondary education, including general and vocational education, make them available and accessible to every child, and take appropriate measures such as the introduction of free education and offering financial assistance in case of need;

(c) Make higher education accessible to all on the basis of capacity by every appropriate means;

(d) Make educational and vocational information and guidance available and accessible to all children;

(e) Take measures to encourage regular attendance at schools and the reduction of drop-out rates.

2. States Parties shall take all appropriate measures to ensure that school discipline is administered in a manner consistent with the child's human dignity and in conformity with the present Convention.

United Nations (continued)

Convention on the Rights of the Child (continued)

3. States Parties shall promote and encourage international co-operation in matters relating to education, in particular with a view to contributing to the elimination of ignorance and illiteracy throughout the world and facilitating access to scientific and technical knowledge and modern teaching methods. In this regard, particular account shall be taken of the needs of developing countries.

Article 29. 1. States Parties agree that the education of the child shall be directed to:

(a) The development of the child's personality, talents and mental and physical abilities to their fullest potential;

(b) The development of respect for human rights and fundamental freedoms, and for the principles enshrined in the Charter of the United Nations;

(c) The development of respect for the child's parents, his or her own cultural identity, language and values, for the national values of the country in which the child is living, the country from which he or she may originate, and for civilizations different from his or her own;

(d) The preparation of the child for responsible life in a free society, in the spirit of understanding, peace, tolerance, equality of sexes, and friendship among all peoples, ethnic, national and religious groups and persons of indigenous origin;

(e) The development of respect for the natural environment.

2. No part of the present article or article 28 shall be construed so as to interfere with the liberty of individuals and bodies to establish and direct educational institutions, subject always to the observance of the principles set forth in paragraph 1 of the present article and to the requirements that the education given in such institutions shall conform to such minimum standards as may be laid down by the State.

Article 30. In those States in which ethnic, religious or linguistic minorities or persons of indigenous origin exist, a child belonging to such a minority or who is indigenous shall not be denied the right, in community with other members of his or her group, to enjoy his or her own culture, to profess and practise his or her own religion, or to use his or her own language.

Article 31. 1. States Parties recognize the right of the child to rest and leisure, to engage in play and recreational activities appropriate to the age of the child and to participate freely in cultural life and the arts.

2. States Parties shall respect and promote the right of the child to participate fully in cultural and artistic life and shall encourage the provision of appropriate and equal opportunities for cultural, artistic, recreational and leisure activity.

Article 32. 1. States Parties recognize the right of the child to be protected from economic exploitation and from performing any work that is likely to be hazardous or to interfere with the child's education, or to be harmful to the child's health or physical, mental, spiritual, moral or social development.

United Nations (continued)

Convention on the Rights of the Child (continued)

2. States Parties shall take legislative, administrative, social and educational measures to ensure the implementation of the present article. To this end, and having regard to the relevant provisions of other international instruments, States Parties shall in particular:

(a) Provide for a minimum age or minimum ages for admissions to employment;

(b) Provide for appropriate regulation of the hours and conditions of employment;

(c) Provide for appropriate penalties or other sanctions to ensure the effective enforcement of the present article.

Article 33. States Parties shall take all appropriate measures, including legislative, administrative, social and educational measures, to protect children from the illicit use of narcotic drugs and psychotropic substances as defined in the relevant international treaties, and to prevent the use of children in the illicit production and trafficking of such substances.

Article 34. States Parties undertake to protect the child from all forms of sexual exploitation and sexual abuse. For these purposes, States Parties shall in particular take all appropriate national, bilateral and multilateral measures to prevent:

(a) The inducement or coercion of a child to engage in any unlawful sexual activity;

(b) The exploitative use of children in prostitution or other unlawful sexual practices;

(c) The exploitative use of children in pornographic performances and materials.

Article 35. States Parties shall take all appropriate national, bilateral and multilateral measures to prevent the abduction of, the sale of or traffic in children for any purpose or in any form.

Article 36. States Parties shall protect the child against all other forms of exploitation prejudicial to any aspects of the child's welfare.

Article 37. States Parties shall ensure that:

(a) No child shall be subjected to torture or other cruel, inhuman or degrading treatment or punishment. Neither capital punishment nor life imprisonment without possibility of release shall be imposed for offences committed by persons below 18 years of age;

(b) No child shall be deprived of his or her liberty unlawfully or arbitrarily. The arrest, detention or imprisonment of a child shall be in conformity with the law and shall be used only as a measure of last resort and for the shortest appropriate period of time;

(c) Every child deprived of liberty shall be treated with humanity and respect for the inherent dignity of the human person, and in a manner which takes into account the needs of persons of his or her age. In particular every child deprived of liberty shall be separated from adults unless it is considered in the child's best interest not to do so and shall have the right to maintain contact with his or her family through correspondence and visits, save in exceptional circumstances.

United Nations (continued)

Convention on the Rights of the Child (continued)

(d) Every child deprived of his or her liberty shall have the right to prompt access to legal and other appropriate assistance, as well as the right to challenge the legality of the deprivation of his or her liberty before a court or other competent, independent and impartial authority, and to a prompt decision on any such action.

Article 38. 1. States Parties undertake to respect and to ensure respect for rules of international humanitarian law applicable to them in armed conflicts which are relevant to the child.

2. States Parties shall take all feasible measures to ensure that persons who have not attained the age of 15 years do not take a direct part in hostilities.

3. States Parties shall refrain from recruiting any person who has not attained the age of 15 years into their armed forces. In recruiting among those persons who have attained the age of 15 years but who have not attained the age of 18 years, States Parties shall endeavour to give priority to those who are oldest.

4. In accordance with their obligations under international humanitarian law to protect the civilian population in armed conflicts, States Parties shall take all feasible measures to ensure protection and care of children who are affected by an armed conflict.

Article 39. States Parties shall take all appropriate measures to promote physical and psychological recovery and social reintegration of a child victim of: any form of neglect, exploitation, or abuse; torture or any other form of cruel, inhuman or degrading treatment or punishment; or armed conflicts. Such recovery and reintegration shall take place in an environment which fosters the health, self-respect and dignity of the child.

Article 40. 1. States Parties recognize the right of every child alleged as, accused of, or recognized as having infringed the penal law to be treated in a manner consistent with the promotion of the child's sense of dignity and worth, which reinforces the child's respect for the human rights and fundamental freedoms of others and which takes into account the child's age and the desirability of promoting the child's reintegration and the child's assuming a constructive role in society.

2. To this end, and having regard to the relevant provisions of international instruments, States Parties shall, in particular, ensure that:

(a) No child shall be alleged as, be accused of, or recognized as having infringed the penal law by reason of acts or omissions that were not prohibited by national or international law at the time they were committed;

(b) Every child alleged as or accused of having infringed the penal law has at least the following guarantees:

(i) To be presumed innocent until proven guilty according to law;

(ii) To be informed promptly and directly of the charges against him or her, and, if appropriate, through his or her parents or legal guardians, and to have legal or other appropriate assistance in the preparation and presentation of his or her defence;

United Nations (continued)

Convention on the Rights of the Child (continued)

(iii) To have the matter determined without delay by a competent, independent and impartial authority or judicial body in a fair hearing according to law, in the presence of legal or other appropriate assistance and, unless it is considered not to be in the best interest of the child, in particular, taking into account his or her age or situation, his or her parents or legal guardians;

(iv) Not to be compelled to give testimony or to confess guild; to examine or have examined adverse witnesses and to obtain the participation and examination of witnesses on his or her behalf under conditions of equality;

(v) If considered to have infringed the penal law, to have this decision and any measures imposed in consequence thereof reviewed by a higher competent, independent and impartial authority or judicial body according to law;

(vi) To have the free assistance of an interpreter if the child cannot understand or speak the language used;

(vii) To have his or her privacy fully respected at all stages of the proceedings.

3. States Parties shall seek to promote the establishment of laws, procedures, authorities and institutions specifically applicable to children alleged as, accused of, or recognized as having infringed the penal law, and, in particular:

(a) The establishment of a minimum age below which children shall be presumed not to have the capacity to infringe the penal law;

(b) Whenever appropriate and desirable, measures for dealing with such children without resorting to judicial proceedings, providing that human rights and legal safeguards are fully respected.

4. A variety of dispositions, such as care, guidance and supervision orders; counselling; probation; foster care; education and vocational training programmes and other alternatives to institutional care shall be available to ensure that children are dealt with in a manner appropriate to their well-being and proportionate both to their circumstances and the offence.

Article 41. Nothing in the present Convention shall affect any provisions which are more conducive to the realization of the rights of the child and which may be contained in:

(a) The law of a State Party; or

(b) International law in force for that State."

Source. Text of the Convention on the Rights of the Child, adopted by the General Assembly of the United Nations on 20 November 1989 (printed separately).

United Nations (continued)

World Declaration on the Survival, Protection and Development of Children, 1990

The World Summit for Children, held in New York, adopted on 30 September 1990 a declaration and a plan of action on the survival, protection and development of children. The Declaration is reproduced in full; exerpts of the Plan of Action follow.

"1. We have gathered at the World Summit for Children to undertake a joint commitment and to make an urgent universal appeal -- to give every child a better future.

2. The children of the world are innocent, vulnerable and dependent. They are also curious, active and full of hope. Their time should be one of joy and peace, of playing, learning and growing. Their future should be shaped in harmony and co-operation. Their lives should mature, as they broaden their perspectives and gain new experiences.

3. But for many children, the reality of childhood is altogether different.

The challenge

4. Each day, countless children around the world are exposed to dangers that hamper their growth and development. They suffer immensely as casualties of war and violence; as victims of racial discrimination, apartheid, aggression, foreign occupation and annexation; as refugees and displaced children, forced to abandon their homes and their roots; as disabled; or as victims of neglect, cruelty and exploitation.

5. Each day, millions of children suffer from the scourges of poverty and economic crisis -- from hunger and homelessness, from epidemics and illiteracy, from degradation of the environment. They suffer from the grave effects of the problems of external indebtedness and also from the lack of sustained and sustainable growth in many developing countries, particularly the least developed ones.

6. Each day, 40,000 children die from malnutrition and disease, including acquired immunodeficiency syndrome (AIDS), from the lack of clean water and inadequate sanitation and from the effects of the drug problem.

7. These are challenges that we, as political leaders, must meet.

The opportunity

8. Together, our nations have the means and the knowledge to protect the lives and to diminish enormously the suffering of children, to promote the full development of their human potential and to make them aware of their needs, rights and opportunities. The Convention on the Rights of the Child provides a new opportunity to make respect for children's rights and welfare truly universal.

United Nations (continued)

World Declaration on the Survival, Protection and Development of Children (continued)

9. Recent improvements in the international political climate can facilitate this task. Through international co-operation and solidarity it should not be possible to achieve concrete results in many fields -- to revitalize economic growth and development, to protect the environment, to prevent the spread of fatal and crippling diseases and to achieve greater social and economic justice. The current moves towards disarmament also mean that significant resources could be released for purposes other than military ones. Improving the well-being of children must be a very high priority when these resources are reallocated.

The task

10. Enhancement of children's health and nutrition is a first duty, and also a task for which solutions are now within reach. The lives of tens of thousands of boys and girls can be saved each day, because the causes of their death are readily preventable. Child and infant mortality is unacceptably high in many parts of the world, but can be lowered dramatically with means that are already known and easily accessible.

11. Further attention, care and support should be accorded to disabled children, as well as to other children in very difficult circumstances.

12. Strengthening the role of women in general and ensuring their equal rights will be to the advantage of the world's children. Girls must be given equal treatment and opportunities from the very beginning.

13. At present, over 100 million children are without basic schooling, and two-thirds of them are girls. The provision of basic education and literacy for all are among the most important contributions that can be made to the development of the world's children.

14. Half a million mothers die each year from causes related to childbirth. Safe motherhood must be promoted in all possible ways. Emphasis must be placed on responsible planning of family size and on child spacing. The family, as a fundamental group and natural environment for the growth and well-being of children, should be given all necessary protection and assistance.

15. All children must be given the chance to find their identity and realize their worth in a safe and supportive environment, through families and other care-givers committed to their welfare. They must be prepared for responsible life in a free society. They should, from their early years, be encouraged to participate in the cultural life of their societies.

16. Economic conditions will continue to influence greatly the fate of children, especially in developing nations. For the sake of the future of all children, it is urgently necessary to ensure or reactivate sustained and sustainable economic growth and development in all countries and also to continue to give urgent attention to an early, broad and durable solution to the external debt problems facing developing debtor countries.

17. These tasks require a continued and concerted effort by all nations, through national action and international co-operation.

United Nations (continued)

World Declaration on the Survival, Protection and Development of Children (continued)

The commitment

18. The well-being of children requires political action at the highest level. We are determined to take that action.

19. We ourselves hereby make a solemn commitment to give high priority to the rights of children, to their survival and to their protection and development. This will also ensure the well-being of all societies.

20. We have agreed that we will act together, in international co-operation, as well as in our respective countries. We now commit ourselves to the following 10-point programme to protect the rights of children and to improve their lives:

(1) We will work to promote earliest possible ratification and implementation of the Convention on the Rights of the Child. Programmes to encourage information about children's rights should be launched world-wide, taking into account the distinct cultural and social values in different countries.

(2) We will work for a solid effect of national and international action to enhance children's health, to promote pre-natal care and to lower infant and child mortality in all countries and among all peoples. We will promote the provision of clean water in all communities for all their children, as well as universal access to sanitation.

(3) We will work for optimal growth and development in childhood, through measures to eradicate hunger, malnutrition and famine, and thus to relieve millions of children of tragic sufferings in a world that has the means to feed all its citizens.

(4) We will work to strengthen the role and status of women. We will promote responsible planning of family size, child spacing, breastfeeding and safe motherhood.

(5) We will work for respect for the role of the family in providing for children and will support the efforts of parents, other care-givers and communities to nurture and care for children, from the earliest stages of childhood through adolescence. We also recognize the special needs of children who are separated from their families.

(6) We will work for programmes that reduce illiteracy and provide educational opportunities for all children, irrespective of their background and gender; that prepare children for productive employment and lifelong learning opportunities, i.e. through vocational training; and that enable children to grow to adulthood within a supportive and nurturing cultural and social context.

(7) We will work to ameliorate the plight of millions of children who live under especially difficult circumstances -- as victims of apartheid and foreign occupation; orphans and street children and children of migrant workers; the displaced children and victims of natural and man-made disasters; the disabled and the abused, the socially disadvantaged and the exploited. Refugee children must be helped to find new roots in life. We will work for special protection of the working child and for the abolition of illegal child labour. We will do our best to ensure that children are not drawn into becoming victims of the scourge of illicit drugs.

United Nations (continued)

World Declaration on the Survival, Protection and Development of Children (continued)

(8) We will work carefully to protect children from the scourge of war and to take measures to prevent further armed conflicts, in order to give children everywhere a peaceful and secure future. We will promote the values of peace, understanding and dialogue in the education of children. The essential needs of children and families must be protected even in times of war and in violence-ridden areas. We ask that periods of tranquillity and special relief corridors be observed for the benefit of children, where war and violence are still taking place.

(9) We will work for common measures for the protection of the environment, at all levels, so that all children can enjoy a safer and healthier future.

(10) We will work for a global attack on poverty, which would have immediate benefits for children's welfare. The vulnerability and special needs of the children of the developing countries, and in particular the least developed ones, deserve priority. But growth and development need promotion in all States, through national action and international co-operation. That calls for transfers of appropriate additional resources to developing countries as well as improved terms of trade, further trade liberalization and measures for debt relief. It also implies structural adjustments that promote world economic growth, particularly in developing countries, while ensuring the well-being of the most vulnerable sectors of the populations, in particular the children.

The next steps

21. The World Summit for Children has presented us with a challenge to take action. We have agreed to take up that challenge.

22. Among the partnerships we seek, we turn especially to children themselves. We appeal to them to participate in this effort.

23. We also seek the support of the United Nations system, as well as other international and regional organizations, in the universal effort to promote the well-being of children. We ask for greater involvement on the part of non-governmental organizations, in complementing national efforts and joint international action in this field.

24. We have decided to adopt and implement a Plan of Action, as a framework for more specific national and international undertakings. We appeal to all our colleagues to endorse that Plan. We are prepared to make available the resources to meet these commitments, as part of the priorities of our national plans.

25. We do this not only for the present generation, but for all generations to come. There can be no task nobler than given every child a better future."

Source. World Summit for Children: World Declaration on the Survival, Protection and Development of Children and Plan of Action for implementing the World Declaration on the Survival, Protection and Development of Children in the 1990s (United Nations, New York, September 1990).

United Nations (continued)

Plan of Action for Implementing the World Declaration on the Survival, Protection and Development of Children in the 1990s, 1990

"I. Introduction

1. This Plan of Action is intended as a guide for national Governments, international organizations, bilateral aid agencies, non-governmental organizations (NGOs) and all other sectors of society in formulating their own programmes of action for ensuring the implementation of the Declaration of the World Summit for Children.

2. The needs and problems of children vary from country to country, and indeed from community to community. Individual countries and groups of countries, as well as international, regional, national and local organizations, may use this Plan of Action to develop their own specific programmes in line with their needs, capacity and mandates. However, parents, elders and leaders at all levels throughout the world have certain common aspirations for the well-being of their children. This Plan of Action deals with these common aspirations, suggesting a set of goals and targets for children in the 1990s, strategies for reaching those goals and commitments for action and follow-up measures at various levels.

3. Progress for children should be a key goal of overall national development. It should also form an integral part of the broader international development strategy for the Fourth United Nations Development Decade. As today's children are the citizens of tomorrow's world, their survival, protection and development is the prerequisite for the future development of humanity. Empowerment of the younger generation with knowledge and resources to meet their basic human needs and to grow to their full potential should be a primary goal of national development. As their individual development and social contribution will shape the future of the world, investment in children's health, nutrition and education is the foundation for national development.

4. The aspirations of the international community for the well-being of children are best reflected in the Convention on the Rights of the Child unanimously adopted by the General Assembly of the United Nations in 1989. This Convention sets universal legal standards for the protection of children against neglect, abuse and exploitation, as well as guaranteeing to them their basic human rights, including survival, development and full participation in social, cultural, educational and other endeavours necessary for their individual growth and well-being. The Declaration of the World Summit calls on all Governments to promote earliest possible ratification and implementation of the Convention.

5. In the past two years, a set of goals for children and development in the 1990s has been formulated in several international forums attended by virtually all Governments, relevant United Nations agencies and major NGOs. In support of these goals and in line with the growing international consensus in favour of greater attention to the human dimension of development in the 1990s, this Plan of Action calls for concerted national action and international co-operation to strive for the achievement, in all countries, of the following major goals for the survival, protection and development of children by the year 2000.

(a) Reduction of 1990 under-5 child mortality rates by one third or to a level of 70 per 1,000 live births, whichever is the greater reduction;

United Nations (continued)

Plan of Action (continued)

(b) Reduction of maternal mortality rates by half of 1990 levels;

(c) Reduction of severe and moderate malnutrition among under-5 children by one half of 1990 levels;

(d) Universal access to safe drinking water and to sanitary means of excreta disposal;

(e) Universal access to basic education and completion of primary education by at least 80 per cent of primary school age children;

(f) Reduction of the adult illiteracy rate to at least half its 1990 level (the appropriate age group to be determined in each country), with emphasis on female literacy;

(g) Protection of children in especially difficult circumstances, particularly in situations of armed conflicts.

.....

II. Specific actions for child survival, protection and development

.....

The Convention on the Rights of the Child

8. The Convention on the Rights of the Child, unanimously adopted by the United Nations General Assembly, contains a comprehensive set of international legal norms for the protection and well-being of children. All Governments are urged to promote earliest possible ratification of the Convention, where it has not already been ratified. Every possible effort should be made in all countries to disseminate the Convention and, wherever it has already been ratified, to promote its implementation and monitoring.

.....

Role of women, maternal health and family planning

15. Women in their various roles play a critical part in the well-being of children. The enhancement of the status of women and their equal access to education, training, credit and other extension services constitute a valuable contribution to a nation's social and economic development. Efforts for the enhancement of women's status and their role in development must begin with the girl child. Equal opportunity should be provided for the girl child to benefit from the health, nutrition, education and other basic services to enable her to grow to her full potential.

.....

United Nations (continued)

Plan of Action (continued)

Role of the family

18. The family has the primary responsibility for the nurturing and protection of children from infancy to adolescence. Introduction of children to the culture, values and norms of their society begins in the family. For the full and harmonious development of their personality, children should grow up in a family environment, in an atmosphere of happiness, love and understanding. Accordingly, all institutions of society should respect and support the efforts of parents and other care-givers to nurture and care for children in a family environment.

19. Every effort should be made to prevent the separation of children from their families. Whenever children are separated from their family owing to force majeur [sic] or in their own best interest, arrangements should be made for appropriate alternative family care or institutional placement, due regard being paid to the desirability of continuity in a child's upbringing in his or her own cultural milieu. Extended families, relatives and community institutions should be given support to help to meet the special needs of orphaned, displaced and abandoned children. Efforts must be made to ensure that no child is treated as an outcast from society.

Basic education and literacy

20. The international community, including virtually all the Governments of the world, have undertaken a commitment at the World Conference on Education for All at Jomtien, Thailand, to increase significantly educational opportunity for over 100 million children and nearly 1 billion adults, two thirds of them girls and women, who at present have no access to basic education and literacy. In fulfilment of that commitment, specific measures must be adopted for (a) the expansion of early childhood development activities, (b) universal access to basic education, including completion of primary education or equivalent learning achievement by at least 80 per cent of the relevant school-age children with emphasis on reducing the current disparities between boys and girls, (c) the reduction of adult illiteracy by half, with emphasis on female literacy, (d) vocational training and preparation for employment and (e) increased acquisition of knowledge, skills and values through all educational channels, including modern and traditional communication media, to improve the quality of life of children and families.

21. Besides its intrinsic value for human development and improving the quality of life, progress in education and literacy can contribute significantly to improvement in maternal and child health, in protection of the environment and in sustainable development. As such, investment in basic education must be accorded a high priority in national action as well as international co-operation.

Children in especially difficult circumstances

22. Millions of children around the world live under especially difficult circumstances -- as orphans and street children, as refugees or displaced persons, as victims of war and natural and man-made disasters, including such perils as exposure to radiation and dangerous chemicals, as children of migrant workers and other socially disadvantaged groups, as child workers or youth trapped in the bondage of prostitution, sexual abuse and other forms of exploitation, as disabled children and juvenile delinquents and as victims of apartheid and foreign occupation. Such children deserve special attention, protection and assistance from their families and communities and as part of national efforts and international co-operation.

United Nations (continued)

Plan of Action (continued)

23. More than 100 million children are engaged in employment, often heavy and hazardous and in contravention of international conventions which provide for their protection from economic exploitation and from performing work that interferes with their education and is harmful to their health and full development. With this in mind, all States should work to end such child-labour practices and see how the conditions and circumstances of children in legitimate employment can be protected to provide adequate opportunity for their healthy upbringing and development.

24. Drug abuse has emerged as a global menace to very large numbers of young people and, increasingly, children - including permanent damage incurred in the pre-natal stages of life. Concerted action is needed by Governments and intergovernmental agencies to combat illicit production, supply, demand, trafficking and distribution of narcotic drugs and psychotropic substances to counter this tragedy. Equally important is community action and education, which are vitally needed to curb both the supply of and the demand for illicit drugs. Tobacco and alcohol abuse are also problems requiring action, especially preventive measures and education among young people.

.....

Alleviation of poverty and revitalization of economic growth

28. Achievement of child related goals in the areas of health, nutrition, education, etc., will contribute much to alleviating the worst manifestations of poverty. But much more will need to be done to ensure that a solid economic base is established to meet and sustain the goals for long-term child survival, protection and development.

29. As affirmed by the international community at the eighteenth special session of the United Nations General Assembly (April 1990), a most important challenge for the 1990s is the need for revitalization of economic growth and social development in the developing countries and to address together the problems of abject poverty and hunger that continue to afflict far too many people in the world. As the most vulnerable segment of human society, children have a particular stake in sustained economic growth and alleviation of poverty, without which their well-being cannot be secured.

30. To foster a favourable international economic environment, it is essential to continue to give urgent attention to an early, broad and durable solution to the external debt problems facing developing debtor countries; to mobilize external and domestic resources to meet the increasing needs for development finance of developing countries; to take steps to ensure that the problems of the net transfer of resources from developing to developed countries does not continue in the 1990s and that its impact is effectively addressed; to create a more open and equitable trading system to facilitate the diversification and modernization of the economies of developing countries, particularly those that are commodity-dependent; and to make available substantial concessional resources, particularly for the least developed countries.

31. In all of these efforts the fulfilment of the basic needs of children must receive a high priority. Every possible opportunity should be explored to ensure that programmes benefiting children, women and other vulnerable groups are protected in times of structural adjustments and other economic restructuring. For example, as countries reduce military expenditures, part of the resources released should be channelled to programmes for social and economic development, including those benefiting children. Debt-relief schemes could be formulated in ways that the budget reallocations and renewed economic growth made possible through such schemes would benefit

United Nations (continued)

Plan of Action (continued)

programmes for children. Debt relief for children, including debt swaps for investment in social development programmes, should be considered by debtors and creditors. The international community, including private-sector creditors, are urged to work with developing countries and relevant agencies to support debt relief for children. To match increased efforts by developing countries themselves, the donor countries and international institutions should consider targetting more development assistance to primary health care, basic education, low-cost water and sanitation programmes and other interventions specifically endorsed in the Summit Declaration and this Plan of Action.

.....

Appendix: Goals for children and development in the 1990s

The following goals have been formulated through extensive consultation in various international forums attended by virtually all Governments, the relevant United Nations agencies including the World Health Organization (WHO), UNICEF, the United Nations Population Fund (UNFPA), the United Nations Educational, Scientific and Cultural Organization (UNESCO), the United Nations Development Programme (UNDP) and the International Bank for Reconstruction and Development (IBRD) and a large number of NGOs. These goals are recommended for implementation by all countries where they are applicable, with appropriate adaptation to the specific situation of each country in terms of phasing, standards, priorities and availability of resources, with respect for cultural, religious and social traditions. Additional goals that are particularly relevant to a country's specific situation should be added in its national plan of action.

I. Major goals for child survival, development and protection

(a) Between 1990 and the year 2000, reduction of infant and under-5 child mortality rate by one third or to 50 and 70 per 1,000 live births respectively, whichever is less;

(b) Between 1990 and the year 2000, reduction of maternal mortality rate by half;

(c) Between 1990 and the year 2000, reduction of severe and moderate malnutrition among under-5 children by half;

(d) Universal access to safe drinking water and to sanitary means of excreta disposal;

(e) By the year 2000, universal access to basic education and completion of primary education by at least 80 per cent of primary school-age children;

(f) Reduction of the adult illiteracy rate (the appropriate age group to be determined in each country) to at least half its 1990 level with emphasis on female literacy;

(g) Improved protection of children in especially difficult circumstances.

United Nations (continued)

Plan of Action (continued)

II. Supporting/sectoral goals

A. Women's health and education

(i) Special attention to the health and nutrition of the female child and to pregnant and lactating women;

(ii) Access by all couples to information and services to prevent pregnancies that are too early, too closely spaced, too late or too many;

(iii) Access by all pregnant women to pre-natal care, trained attendants during childbirth and referral facilities for high-risk pregnancies and obstetric emergencies;

(iv) Universal access to primary education with special emphasis for girls and accelerated literacy programmes for women.

B. Nutrition

(i) Reduction in severe, as well as moderate malnutrition among under-5 children by half of 1990 levels;

(ii) Reduction of the rate of low birth weight (2.5 kg or less) to less than 10 per cent;

(iii) Reduction of iron deficiency anaemia in women by one third of the 1990 levels;

(iv) Virtual elimination of iodine deficiency disorders;

(v) Virtual elimination of vitamin A deficiency and its consequences, including blindness;

(vi) Empowerment of all women to breast-feed their children exclusively for four to six months and to continue breast-feeding, with complementary food, well into the second year;

(vii) Growth promotion and its regular monitoring to be institutionalized in all countries by the end of the 1990s;

(viii) Dissemination of knowledge and supporting services to increase food production to ensure household food security.

C. Child health

(i) Global eradication of poliomyelitis by the year 2000;

(ii) Elimination of neonatal tetanus by 1995;

(iii) Reduction by 95 per cent in measles deaths and reduction by 90 per cent of measles cases compared to pre-immunization levels by 1995, as a major step to the global eradication of measles in the longer run;

United Nations (continued)

Plan of Action (continued)

(iv) Maintenance of a high level of immunization coverage (at least 90 per cent of children under one year of age by the year 2000) against diphtheria, pertussis, tetanus, measles, poliomyelitis, tuberculosis and against tetanus for women of child-bearing age;

(v) Reduction by 50 per cent in the deaths due to diarrhoea in children under the age of five years and 25 per cent reduction in the diarrhoea incidence rate;

(vi) Reduction by one third in the deaths due to acute respiratory infections in children under five years.

D. Water and sanitation

(i) Universal access to safe drinking water;

(ii) Universal access to sanitary means of excreta disposal;

(iii) Elimination of guinea-worm disease (dracunculiasis) by the year 2000.

E. Basic education

(i) Expansion of early childhood development activities, including appropriate low-cost family- and community-based interventions;

(ii) Universal access to basic education, and achievement of primary education by at least 80 per cent of primary school-age children through formal schooling or non-formal education of comparable learning standard, with emphasis on reducing the current disparities between boys and girls;

(iii) Reduction of the adult illiteracy rate (the appropriate age group to be determined in each country) to at least half its 1990 level, with emphasis on female literacy;

(iv) Increased acquisition by individuals and families of the knowledge, skills and values required for better living, made available through all educational channels, including the mass media, other forms of modern and traditional communication and social action, with effectiveness measured in terms of behavioural change.

F. Children in difficult circumstances

Provide improved protection of children in especially difficult circumstances and tackle the root causes leading to such situations."

Source. World Summit for Children: World Declaration on the Survival, Protection and Development of Children and Plan of Action for implementing the World Declaration on the Survival, Protection and Development of Children in the 1990s (United Nations, New York, September 1990).

Council of Europe

The European Social Charter

The Charter sets out rights and principles, including the rights of children to special protection against physical and moral hazards and to appropriate social and economic protection, which are elaborated in Article 7 as follows:

"Article 7. The right of children and young persons to protection. With a view to ensuring the effective exercise of the right of children and young persons to protection, the Contracting Parties undertake:

(1) to provide that the minimum age of admission to employment shall be 15 years, subject to exceptions for children employed in prescribed light work without harm to their health, morals or education;

(2) to provide that a higher minimum age of admission to employment shall be fixed with respect to prescribed occupations regarded as dangerous or unhealthy;

(3) to provide that persons who are still subject to compulsory education shall not be employed in such work as would deprive them of the full benefit of their education;

(4) to provide that the working hours of persons under 16 years of age shall be limited in accordance with the needs of their development, and particularly with their need for vocational training;

(5) to recognise the right of young workers and apprentices to a fair wage or other appropriate allowances;

(6) to provide that the time spent by young persons in vocational training during the normal working hours with the consent of the employer shall be treated as forming part of the working day;

(7) to provide that employed persons of under 18 years of age shall be entitled to not less than three weeks' annual holiday with pay;

(8) to provide that persons under 18 years of age shall not be employed in night work with the exception of certain occupations provided for by national laws or regulations;

(9) to provide that persons under 18 years of age employed in occupations prescribed by national laws or regulations shall be subject to regular medical control;

(10) to ensure special protection against physical and moral dangers to which children and young persons are exposed, and particularly against those resulting directly or indirectly from their work."

Source. The European Social Charter, European Treaty Series No. 35.

National Safety Council - India

Chairman of the National Organising Committee for the XIIIth World Congress on Occupational Safety and Health
National Safety Council - Post Box No 26754, C.L.I. Building - Sion, Bombay 400 022 - INDIA - Fax: + 91-22-525-657

CHANDRAKANT GARWARE

Président du Comité National d'Organisation du XIIIème Congrès Mondial sur la Sécurité et la Santé au Travail
National Safety Council - P.O.B. 26754, C.L.I. - Building - Sion. Bombay 400 022 - INDIA - Fax: + 91-22-525-657

Edition: CIS - CH 1211 - GENEVA 22

www.ingramcontent.com/pod-product-compliance
Lightning Source LLC
Chambersburg PA
CBHW081508290326
41932CB00050B/3084
* 9 7 8 9 2 2 1 0 7 7 5 1 0 *